ALSO BY CHRISTINE VACHON

Shooting to Kill (with David Edelstein)

A Killer Life

How an Independent Film Producer Survives
Deals and Disasters in Hollywood and Beyond

Christine Vachon

with Austin Bunn

Foreword by John Pierson

for Kent —

[signature]

Simon & Schuster

NEW YORK · LONDON · TORONTO · SYDNEY

SIMON & SCHUSTER
Rockefeller Center
1230 Avenue of the Americas
New York, NY 10020

For information about special discounts for bulk purchases,
please contact Simon & Schuster Special Sales at
1-800-456-6798 or business@simonandschuster.com.

DESIGNED BY PAUL DIPPOLITO

Manufactured in the United States of America

10   9   8   7   6   5   4   3   2   1

Library of Congress Cataloging-in-Publication Data

Vachon, Christine
    A killer life : how an independent film producer survives deals
and disasters in Hollywood and beyond / Christine Vachon, with
Austin Bunn ; foreword by John Pierson.
        p.   cm.
    Filmography: p.
    1. Vachon, Christine. 2. Motion picture producers and directors—
United States—Biography. 3. Independent filmmakers—United
States—Biography. I. Bunn, Austin. II. Title.

PN1998.3.V32A3 2006
791.4302'32092—dc22
    [B]   2006043722

ISBN-13: 978-0-7432-5630-8
ISBN-10:   0-7432-5630-1

For
Marlene and Guthrie

Enjoy the process.

But get out of the way.

Money costs money.

Push for the pragmatic.

It's always your fault.

Money has a personality.

Read *Variety* stories backwards.

The budget is not the aesthetic.

Never put in your own money.

OK, Sometimes it has to be your money.

(Money is overrated.)

Did they pass the director's quiz?

Identify talent and stick to it like glue.

Every little picture needs a big picture.

In the big picture, we need little pictures.

Fight the obvious: if it's on the nose, it goes.

Keep this triangle: talent, producer, money.

Never ask a question you don't know the answer to.

Less money = more control; more money = less control.

The deal is not the thing. It's just a big part of the thing.

Find the intersection of an investor's courage and cash.

Do what you love; do it consistently. Everything else will follow.

Every story behind a movie that gets made is a success story.

This is the best job in the world.

Contents

Cast of Characters

Killer Films

Pam Koffler, business partner, producer
Katie Roumel, business partner, producer
Jocelyn Hayes, producer, head of development
Charles Pugliese, production and development/my former assistant
Michael Wiggins ("Wigs"), accountant/business affairs

My Family

John Vachon, my father
Marie Vachon, my mother
Marlene McCarty, my partner
Guthrie McCarty-Vachon, my daughter
Michael Vachon, my brother
Brian Vachon, my brother
Ann Vachon, my sister
Gail Vachon, my sister

Writers and Directors

Robert Altman, director (*The Company*)
Fenton Bailey, writer/director (*The Eyes of Tammy Faye, Inside Deep Throat, Party Monster*)
Randy Barbato, writer/director (*The Eyes of Tammy Faye, Inside Deep Throat, Party Monster*)

Keith Bunin, screenwriter (*The Extra Man, A Home at the End of the World*)

Larry Clark, director (*Kids, Bully, Ken Park*)

Michael Cunningham, author/screenwriter (*A Home at the End of the World*)

Scott Elliott, writer/director (*The Good Life, A Map of the World*)

David Gordon Green, writer/director (*George Washington, All The Real Girls, Undertow, Goat*)

Mary Harron, writer/director (*I Shot Andy Warhol, American Psycho, The Notorious Bettie Page*)

Todd Haynes, writer/director (*Poison, Safe, Velvet Goldmine, Far from Heaven, I'm Not There*)

Tom Kalin, writer/director (*Swoon, Savage Grace*)

Michael Mayer, director (*A Home at the End of the World*)

Doug McGrath, writer/director (*Emma, Nicholas Nickleby, Infamous*)

Dan Minahan, writer/director (*Series 7, Simply Halston*)

John Cameron Mitchell, actor/writer/director (*Hedwig and the Angry Inch*)

Isaac Mizrahi, director (*The Extra Man*)

Phyllis Nagy, writer/director (*Mrs. Harris*)

Kim Peirce, writer/director (*Boys Don't Cry*)

John Ridley, writer/director (*Three Kings, Undercover Brother, Positively Fifth Street*)

Mark Romanek, writer/director (*One Hour Photo*)

Todd Solondz, writer/director (*Welcome to the Dollhouse, Happiness, Storytelling, Palindromes*)

Rose Troche, writer/director (*Go Fish, The Safety of Objects*)

John Waters, writer/director (*Hairspray, Pink Flamingos, A Dirty Shame*)

Agents, Producers, Lawyers, Executives, and Everybody Else

Rowena Arguelles, agent, CAA

Bob Berney, head of Picturehouse Films, former head of Newmarket Films

Craig Gering, agent, CAA

Mark Gill, former head of Warner Independent Pictures

Scott Greenstein, former head of USA Films

Jeff Hill, our publicist

Ted Hope, producer, This is that Productions (*American Splendor, The Door in the Floor*)

Alan Horn, head of Warner Bros.

Tom Hulce, producer (*A Home at the End of the World*)

Kevin Huvane, partner, CAA

David Linde, head of Focus Features (*The Pianist, Far From Heaven, The Door in the Floor*)

Jody Patton, younger sister of Paul Allen and head of Vulcan

Ed Pressman, film producer and co-CEO of Content Film

Peter Rice, head of Fox Searchlight (*Garden State, Napoleon Dynamite, Boys Don't Cry, One Hour Photo*)

Jeff Rosen, Bob Dylan's business manager and my co-producer on *I'm Not There*

James Schamus, head of Focus Features (*The Pianist, Far From Heaven, The Door in the Floor*)

John Schmidt, co-founder of October Films, co-CEO of film production and distribution at Content Film

Brad Simpson, president of Appian Way, producer (and Jocelyn's husband)

John Sloss, Killer's lawyer and head of Sloss Law and Cinetic Media

Vulcan Productions (formerly Clear Blue Sky Productions), Paul Allen's film financing company

Harvey Weinstein, former head of Miramax, head of Weinstein Co.

John Wells, film and television producer, head of John Wells Productions (*E.R., Third Watch, The West Wing*)

Foreword

by John Pierson

Frumpy. Blunt. Doesn't suffer fools gladly. Unrepentant. Ruthless. A killer even.

Hey, that's fun, picking out a few choice descriptions for Christine Vachon after she's done the same to you in this very book. She calls 'em how she sees 'em. And you better take a closer look at yourself, your values, and your work after she's through with you because there's undoubtedly some unvarnished truth in her no-bullshit gaze.

Elongated geek. Heavy glasses. Opportunistic investor. Burned out. No, no, not me. Well, maybe.

In the end there's only one thing that really seems to matter to her and that's a passion for movies that are worthwhile. Movies that stick to your ribs or, in one infamous case at the outset of her career, spit in your face. If you've got that passion, she's your fellow traveler. But on most days, it's likely that her flame will burn the brightest of all. Did I mention she's not in it for the perks? And that she's still convinced that *Far from Heaven* is a better film than *The Pianist* and that Focus Features should have seen that?

When last we left the published record of Christine's pilgrim's progress as one of the most forceful film producers in New York, the 1990s, her first decade, were coming to an end. The indie avalanche was picking up speed from Tarantino's *Pulp Fiction* to Van Sant's

Good Will Hunting. Since Vachon herself would later make a film with Robin Williams, one can only hope her critique of the Boston weepie wasn't too merciless.

She was just beginning the long march on Kimberly Peirce's somewhat edgier *Boys Don't Cry.* It would become the Academy Award–winning *Boys Don't Cry* when Hilary Swank won Best Actress at the turn of the millennium. As you'll read, it was a difficult production (hardly unusual when there's too little time and money) and a marathon postproduction (also par for the course). But the filmmaking team, reflective of the Vachon modus operandi, got it right with a tremendous end result.

Like I said, independent film had become a big fucking career-catapulting deal. For some people who are in it for the wrong reasons, this might have been a huge turning point—entrée to Tinseltown. Yet somehow many people who know Christine best would be hard-pressed to describe how she's any different seven years later. Still lives and works in Manhattan's East Village, still doesn't drive. Her profile is higher, but her ambition is to leave a mark, not to top the *Entertainment Weekly* Power List.

The volume of her Killer Films production shingle has increased by leaps and bounds. Gone are the days when scraping together the money for Todd Haynes's *Poison,* selling it, then scraping together the money for Tom Kalin's *Swoon* and selling it was the only possible one-step-at-a-time alternative. But apparently the scraping part is alive and well. It just involves millions of dollars not thousands, so it requires more than a few recognizable names on the marquee, which leads to her juggling as many as half a dozen features at once. And still she finds time to tell her story.

At Sundance 2006 Vachon joked, with her trademark bite, that many people have the mistaken impression that funding production is now easy for her, after nearly forty features. These things are all relative. She writes herein that the third film she ever produced—back in 1994, Rose Troche's *Go Fish*—was the easiest to finance. I put up a grand total of $53,000 after one Chicago hotel room tryst where I didn't even remove my socks. We've had a healthy debate about the money trail ever since.

John Waters, John Cameron Mitchell, Mark Romanek, Larry Clark, Robert Altman, Julian Schnabel, David Gordon Green, Doug McGrath, Kim Peirce, Mary Harron (twice), Todd Solondz (twice), Rose Troche (twice), Todd Haynes (five times!) are just some of the directors with whom she's collaborated. They've been gay or straight—or bi or undeclared. They've been young and old. There's been a notable willingness to work with numerous first-time filmmakers, but there's also a place for a thirtieth-timer like Robert Altman. In one of the richest ongoing producer/director relationships in contemporary film, Christine is to American independent film's greatest visual stylist, Todd Haynes, as Ross Hunter was to Douglas Sirk.

A Killer Life is really a book about process, day-to-day and film-to-film, and it builds on Vachon's earlier book, *Shooting to Kill.* That how-to book is the best text by a working producer that you could ever assign to a producing class in film school. I know because I assign it every semester at the University of Texas at Austin. After they read it, I have the students write a hypothetical pitch letter to Vachon seeking her backing for one of the many unique titles in her filmography as if it didn't already exist. Students love this assignment and choose a very wide array of her films. As I read their impassioned and calculated pitches, I always wonder: if Christine hadn't produced these films, would anyone else have been able to make them happen? The concept, the screenplay, the director, the money, the production—and sometimes that's only the half of it.

The more commercially minded future producers in film school tend to gravitate toward *One Hour Photo*—number one on the Vachon box office chart. Perhaps they also have a tendency to package their pitch a bit too cleverly (and predictably) in a photo drop envelope. But even that's a pretty messed-up, dark film. And despite the discouraging news in this book that Killer Films has never ever seen any net profits, we certainly hope that Robin Williams is enjoying his back end.

The question at the heart of Christine Vachon's life as a film producer, and in her writing about it, is not so much "how to" as "why bother." Her passion for filmmaking is the lesson most essential to convey to the next generation to keep our film culture alive and well. And that's why I'll be assigning both her books in class from here on out. In the UK during the peak punk era there was a great independent record label called Stiff Records, whose motto was "If it ain't stiff, it ain't worth a damn."

If it ain't Killer, why bother?

Introduction
"Do You Want to Be in Our Gang?"

I'm standing with my longtime friend and director Todd Haynes in Yonkers, New York, and looking into a camera monitor. I do this a lot. We're in the middle of filming the opening shot of *Far from Heaven*, Todd's Sirkian melodrama about a housewife struggling to deal with her husband's homosexuality. Every time I hire crews to work on one of Todd's films, I warn them that we have more ambition than money and that they will be working harder than they have ever worked. But, I say, working on a movie with Todd will be one of the most creatively satisfying experiences of their lives.

Far from Heaven will go on to garner four Oscar nominations, but at the moment you would never predict it. We're working with a massive, troublesome crane, whose movements are infuriating to coordinate. Todd wants a swooping establishing shot; the camera needs to glide through trees and descend into the town square, setting up the 1950s period of the film. All the actors—the guy feeding the pigeons, the women walking in their pillbox hats, Julianne Moore driving a vintage Chrysler—have to hit their marks just so. The afternoon sun is sinking way too fast. We've already tried the shot several times. The crew grumbles. This is what every producer dreads: you're running out of time and you don't have the shot.

These days, it's getting harder to remember that film is an art form. Movies get treated like a commodity business, some abstract uptick or spiral down on the Hollywood stock exchange. Small-town newspapers print box office returns in the Arts pages so even your parents can know that *Anacondas: The Hunt for the Blood Orchid* opened big. I'm not sure when this happened, or why, but I'll tell you this: it misses the point. For me, film isn't about the margins, boffo weekend numbers, or the back end. (Well, back end would be nice . . .) Film is about the *process*—a long, complicated, passionate process toward something larger than the sum of its parts. In production every film is different and most are accidents waiting to happen. Amid all the chaos and cold coffee of production, the art of film can be hard to keep in mind. But it's what I live for—the flash of magic that eclipses everything.

We try for the shot one last time. Todd calls, "Action!" Up on the crane, the camera pushes through brilliant red and gold leaves and floats across the immaculate town square. Elmer Bernstein's heart-breaking piano theme and Marlene McCarty's period titles are already mapped onto my memory of this, even though they are months away from being realized. But watching the monitor, I can see Todd's entire film writ small—a ravishing, manicured world on the verge of massive change.

We nail it.

It's just as Todd wanted, just as I imagined it when I read his script. For a brief moment, I step away from the problems of the day and see that we are making something beautiful.

It's been almost ten years since I wrote my last book, *Shooting to Kill*, a nuts-and-bolts guide for first-time producers. And while the world of independent film was never manicured nor ravishing, some serious changes have taken place, for the industry, for me personally, and for my company. Independently financed and produced films, from *Blair Witch* to *The Passion of the Christ*, have become an undeniable part of the industry's profit margin, so much so that each studio now operates its own "classics" division to develop (and acquire) the darlings of Sundance and beyond. Since the mid-1990s, the first generation of scrappy, mostly male writer-directors (like Steven Soderbergh, Quentin Tarantino, Robert Rodriguez, and Richard Linklater) have flourished in studio gigs (like *Erin Brockovich*, *Spy Kids*, and *School of Rock*). They've proven that an outsider sensibility can be turned to a studio's advantage.

As the head of Killer Films, an independent film production company based in New York, I've managed to endure longer than many colleagues and friends. This book is an attempt to explain why. In the past twelve years, Killer has managed to produce over thirty films, including *Far from Heaven*, *One Hour Photo*, *Boys Don't Cry*, and *Happiness*, and I'll admit, the odds were against us. In the time since *Shooting to Kill*, other indie production companies, like the Shooting Gallery and Good Machine, have disappeared or been bought, merged, and radically changed. Some producers, like Good Machine's James Schamus and David Linde, have graduated upward and been absorbed into the studio system to run the "classics" divisions. Others, like Cary Woods, the producer on *Kids* and *Citizen Ruth*, or Scott Greenstein, who ran USA Films (*Traffic*), have gone into completely different media. Even Miramax, New York's minimajor studio and the company that altered the scale of independent film, hasn't been able to stay Miramax.

For sure, Killer has changed too. We now have an "overhead" deal with television producer John Wells, the executive producer of *E.R.*, *The West Wing*, and *Third Watch*. In the world of television, you don't get more successful than John Wells, unless you're Aaron Spelling and you make shows about teenage witches and sex-deprived nurses. Wells pays all our salaries and office costs and underwrites our development costs, like buying options for books and having scripts rewritten. In return, Wells gets an executive producer credit on all our films. It's a great arrangement. He likes and understands Killer's films and doesn't interfere.

On the personal level, I'm a mother now of a six-year-old girl named Guthrie. My business partner Pam Koffler is a mother too. Our offices in downtown New York finally have windows that actually face the street, not an airshaft like before. I don't take material through the transom anymore. And one of these days Killer Films will make a kids' movie. Yes, we'll change our name for it.

And yet some things never change; interns *still* answer the phone when you call us. We *still* don't have any walls in our office because I don't like them; visit Killer and you'll hear us calling over the five-foot walls to each other. And for every meeting I might have with Julia or conference call with Jude's representation, I still pound the streets of Cannes each May, as I've done for a decade, trying to drum up the financing for the movies that speak to me. But *how* do you stay relevant in an industry that is constantly changing? It's a question people ask me all the time. I built my company on a rebellion against conventional taste, against the no-rough-edges, film-by-consensus style, until that rebellion itself (christened "independent film") became part of Hollywood.

My strategy is to stay a moving target. I've got a reputation for "edgy," "dark" material—the kind of movie where you're maybe rooting for the bad guy. I'm also frequently accused of operating with a political agenda. A gay agenda. An aggressive–New Yorker agenda. When I go to L.A. for meetings, sometimes I feel like I have to put on my "uniform"—black pants, black T-shirt, combat boots—so that nobody gets confused and thinks I've come over to the bright side. Yes, I go for the kind of stories that challenge viewers, and I like to approach a story from an unexpected place. But my films aren't all about gay people, they aren't necessarily dark, and I'm not trying to peddle an ideology. I think that in order to realize the artistic possibilities of film, you've got to be in tune with the social and political realities of the times: the ravages of AIDS, or the complexity of gender, or social anomie, American-style. This is why I'm attracted to scripts inspired by true stories. When you stop retreading the conventional fairy tales—when you quit with the fairy tales entirely—you make better art. You also make people a little nervous.

Independent film has changed considerably in ten years. Killer Films has changed and will keep changing. But what is changing the most is the way people think about movies. For one, audiences are smarter, savvier. Digital video has lowered the threshold for potential filmmakers, and the advent of DVDs, with extensive director's commentaries, has given amateurs a taste of how the elements come and don't come together. Magazines like *US Weekly* and *In Touch*—the one with the section that has Cameron Diaz taking out the trash and Lara Flynn Boyle racing to stop a meter maid from ticketing her SUV—convince us that were it not for the ten-thousand-square-foot manse in the Hollywood Hills and that little bit o' Botox, the A list is no different from us.

But to fall for these publicity snapshots and director's cuts and "bonus material" is to mistake the ends for the means. The whole reason we know these films and recognize these stars is that some producer brought together the talent, the financing, and the studio to deliver it to you. A *producer*. Now, there are thousands of producers out there and they're all different. Take *Variety*. You can read heaps about the deals, points, and back ends without any sense of why any of it matters. That's because for some producers, the money is *all* that matters. Studios have a yearly slate to fill and somebody—hey, why not you?—has got to go and make those movies.

As independent film keeps getting bigger, I want to make it small again. I want people to get out of the way, so that risky, bold movies can get made. The success of independent film has raised wild expectations. Now everybody wants a home run, a *Napoleon Dynamite*, bought for $5 million at Sundance (and made by Brigham Young University film grads for a fraction of that), that makes $40 million. The unconventional singles and doubles, the movies that make film dynamic and diverse, have become increasingly hard to make. So far, Killer has endured on a principle I call "big picture, little picture." After "big picture" paydays, many actors seek out career-making parts in "little pictures," the ones too offbeat or unconventional for studios to make. It's a complementary relationship.

But without a fertile landscape for little pictures, I'm beginning to feel that film itself, in the era of tent poles and trilogies, has lost sight of the Big Picture: movies as an art form, as an opportunity to ask questions and challenge assumptions. Let the studios plaster their posters everywhere and merchandise their movies to within an inch of their lives. Independent film needs to remind people what movies can be.

I don't blame the studios. Their primary interest is to make money. But ten years later, I feel that independent film itself has lost its intimacy and sense of community. Pam and I have this anecdote from the *Velvet Goldmine* production that always makes us laugh, but I keep going back to it. When the $9 million budget had to take a *million-dollar* haircut right before production started, I didn't know what to do. It was like trying to fit a rock star into children's clothing. Department budgets were going to get slaughtered. People were going to have to take pay cuts. I thought, "How am I going to tell everybody?" Just then, my co-producer on the film, Scott Meek, came up to me. In his thick Scottish brogue, he said, "Christine, just tell them, 'Do you want to be in our gang? If you do, then great. We're making the movie with you. If you don't, then good-bye.'" In a funny way, it's true. Do you want to be in our gang? Do you want to make movies or do you want to talk about them?

At this point, I want to reclaim the business for myself. I want to say producers are the ones who find the material, make the challenges for actors, create career pinnacles and opportunities to do meaningful work. Why are *we* always at the mercy of this star system? Why can't the stars be at ours? The way I know how to bring back the independent film that I know and love is to tell just one story—mine—and tell it to scale. I've made thirty-three films in thirteen years, many of them by first-time directors that you'll read about here, telling stories some studios wouldn't touch: a pregnant serial killer goes on a spree; a check-forging transsexual gets murdered; sex addicts overtake suburbia.

This book is my attempt to help a next generation of young producers find a way in. I've tried to outline the process, but I also want you to meet some of the people. I've threaded through this book the voices of my colleagues, directors, and friends—people who can give you a sense of how this industry works. You'll also see "producer's diaries," unvarnished dispatches from my daily to-do lists. I hope they will help train a next generation of producers to bring back the kind of filmmaking I love.

People have asked me why I haven't "sold out." My first, and somewhat disingenuous, answer is that nobody's ever asked me. But as I get older, my autonomy means more and more to me. Outside is a good place for artists, and it's where I feel comfortable. Lots of writing about the film industry promises to take you "inside" Hollywood. Even *in* Hollywood, most people are obsessed with being even further "inside," on getting a first-look, the right of first refusal, the hottest invitations. It's a culture that thrives on exclusion.

In *How to Lose Friends and Alienate People*, Toby Young's riotous memoir about his time "working" for *Vanity Fair*, Editor in Chief Graydon Carter says to him on his first day, "You think you've arrived? You're only in the *first room.*" He goes on to tell Young, "There are plenty of people in this town who got to the first room and then didn't get any further. After a year or so, maybe longer, you'll discover a secret doorway at the back of the first room that leads to the second room. In time, if you're lucky, you'll discover a doorway in the back of the second room that leads to a third. There are seven rooms in total and you're in the first. Doncha forget it." The seventh room, I imagine, is total access. Journalistic nirvana. To be "first room" is to be late and last on the list, if you're even on it.

Hollywood works the same way. Actors, directors, and agents are always concerned with Where is the VIP room? And when you're in the VIP room, the question becomes Where's the next one, the VVIP room? And who's in it? And so on. It's hard not to get sucked in. But if I've learned anything in the past seven years, working with studios and stars, unknowns and first-timers, it's that the only way inside is by doing the real work *outside:* do what you love, do it consistently, and everything will follow.

Two Definitions

What does a producer do exactly?

Let's look at the application. Yes, there is an application. To join the Academy of Motion Picture Arts and Sciences—the only way to vote for the Oscars and get free screeners—you've got to fill out an eight-page form describing the work you've done on notable films. I've worked with every studio out there, and yet completing this form, I felt like I was a teenager trying to get into college. The story of a producer's life.

The AMPAS application shows you how difficult it can be to quantify the producer's job. First off, to qualify as a producer with the AMPAS, you've got to have at least two sole producer screen credits—not executive producer, not co-producer or associate producer. Just producer.

"Executive producer" sounds higher than "producer," and in television, it is. But in film, the credit "executive producer" can be a symbolic gesture, a title doled out as a favor or used to lend a project credibility. It can mean lots of things, but usually it goes to someone who was critical in getting the financing secured for the movie. For example, on the credits for Bob Altman's *The Company*, there are two German guys listed as executive producers whom I've never met, but they controlled access to some tax fund that was helping finance the picture. On the other hand, the executive producer line can be used to generate publicity. George Clooney came aboard *Far from Heaven* because he believed in Todd. He wasn't on the set, but his lending his name as an executive producer was a handy publicity tool. (He did cohost a splendid Oscar party for us.) And if his name got two people to see the movie, great.

On one of the first movies I worked on, I watched this guy pull out his hair trying to get everything to the set, keep the director focused, and supply the actors with everything they needed. I thought, "Who wants to be a producer? That job is *insane*." But then I got the crew sheet and saw that the guy I'd been watching was listed as the "line producer." Four people I'd never even heard of were listed as "producers." I thought, "Oh, so that's how this works." The classic producer is the one who finds the material, then marries it to a director and writer and actor. Who works on the highest level. Now, every producer has a different style and some producers love to be on set all the time. I know my friend Ted Hope loves to write the memo to the crew about where they should park.

Producers are the ones who get movies made, from the concept to the contracts to bankrolling the folks at the craft services table. This is why producers are the only ones who go up to accept the Best Picture Oscar: they got the film in the can. For their work, producers get paid a fee, typically a percentage of the budget or a "quote" based on the scale of the movie. Depending on his or her track record, a producer's quote might fall between 0 (it happens) and $400,000 for a film budgeted between $1.5 and $3 million. For a film budgeted between $3 and $5 million, it could go as high as $600,000. Past $5 million, it might even reach $800,000, and so on. That may seem like a lot of money, but then lawyers and agents take their cut, you've got to pump money into your business overhead, and maybe you split your fee with a producing partner. Soon $600,000 is closer to $150,000, and that's assuming you haven't deferred your salary into limbo. Many producers angle to drive budgets upward to trigger bigger fees. I have a different way of measuring success: I count up the number of my creations. Maybe it's a more feminine way of thinking. I don't have a country house, and each year it's an open question whether I can afford to send my daughter, Guthrie, to a private elementary school in New York. But when I look at the dozens of film posters that ring the walls of my office, I'm incredibly proud. Because I've believed in every film.

Of course, an unmitigated hit would be nice. And I'd like to never have to defer my salary again. Because I know how to get every cent of a film's budget on screen, it often feels like financiers and distributors are underbidding me. When you can make an Oscar contender like *Boys Don't Cry* for $1.7 million (chump change to Hollywood), they want you to keep doing it, over and over. Once, on the way to a birthday party for one of her friends, I asked Guthrie what we should get as a gift. She answered, straight-faced, "How about nothing?" I laughed because I hear that all the time, from across the million conference tables I've sat at, in answer to the question, "What will you give me to make this movie?" How about nothing? Hollywood is all about the *opposite* of nothing. For producers with blockbuster track records, studios will offer bits of "gross participation"; Brian Grazer might make somewhere around $12 million a film in producer fees, plus 7 to 10 percent of the film's profits. Killer operates fine at a fraction of that.

With every other credit in a film, you know exactly what it means; the production designer on *Camp* did exactly the same job as the production designer on *Cold Mountain*. But "producer" is a catchall. In the morning, I could be talking to David Schwimmer about potential parts in our movies, because he got into the business to be De Niro, not "Ross" from *Friends*. By the afternoon, I might be negotiating with a big composer's agent to do the score for *One Hour Photo* (and when he laughs at what we can afford to pay, we spin the Rolodex and go elsewhere). By the afternoon, I could be on a plane up to Toronto to support Glenn Close on set, who is having a hard time with her character and is nervous about working with a whip-smart but slightly overwhelmed director.

If it's hard to understand just what a producer does, that's because producers tend to do a little of everything, and what they don't do, they have opinions about. David Mamet, in a recent piece for *The Guardian* in London, lambasted producers as the guys who "sell all parts of the pig but the squeal. And then they sell the squeal." He talks about the secretaries getting an "associate producer" credit on *State and Main* instead of a raise. "A few [producers] are entrepreneurs, raising money for a project under their control; a few are what the old Jewish village knew as 'schtadlans,' that is, intermediaries between the powerless (in this case, the filmmaker) and the State (or Studio); the rest are clerks or clerk-sycophants." He's right in one way: it takes about ten cents to print up a business card that says "producer." I think producing is about being fearless but also about being lucky. When you find people who are really talented, you stick to them like glue and you try to make a project work for them. If you're lucky, your persistence pays off.

In the Academy rules, if you share producer credit with someone, you only get half credit for the film. Now, movies with a *single* producer credit on them are as rare as movies with a single screenwriter. Certain producers, like Brain Grazer (*Apollo 13*, *A Beautiful Mind*) and Jerry Bruckheimer (*Pearl Harbor, Pirates of the Caribbean*) take sole producer credit on their films (or share with the director). But if you've had to go find the money for your movie—as I often do—you're going to have to share producer credit. Scott Rudin (*The Hours, The Village, The Manchurian Candidate*) shares credit a lot, because the fact is even the biggest names can't muscle sole credit. The more money you have to go looking for, the more crowded the credit will get. Sometimes co-producing is a tight partnership, as with me and Pam, my diplomatic, unflappable partner at Killer Films, on *Hedwig and the Angry Inch*. Or with fellow veteran indie producer Ted Hope on *Happiness* and *A Dirty Shame*. Sometimes not; Jody Patton shares a producer credit with me on *Far from Heaven;* after she wrote the initial check, I never spoke to her again. I'm generous when I have to be. Unfortunately credit is often the only bargaining chip we have. Sometimes you have to give it to the hairdresser because that's how you got the actor.

Usually though, the producer slot is a mash of partners, money people, no shows, and jerks. It got so crowded that in 1997 the Academy had to step in. After *Shakespeare in Love* doled out five Oscars to its five producers, the Academy capped the number of possible producer-awardees at three. These days some producers get it written into the contract that they will be the ones to go up and accept the statue. As far as I'm concerned, my job is to get the movie made. What's on the poster is low on my list. With a name that starts with a *V,* I'm always at the end anyway.

For my application, I list five movies: *Far From Heaven* (2002), *One Hour Photo* (2002), *Hedwig and the Angry Inch* (2001), *Happiness* (1998), *Velvet Goldmine* (1998). For each, I need to describe its development, production, and release—and how I was instrumental in making them happen. As I write, I flash back to the barely controlled chaos that is an independent film production: "Universal forced October to abandon the film . . ." "At the eleventh hour, the financiers demanded we cut our budget by $1 million . . ." "Todd and I met with Harvey Weinstein and helped secure a sale to Miramax two days before shooting began . . ." "The editing process ended up taking almost a year . . ." These were some of the hardest, most maddening productions I've ever gone through, to make the films I'm most proud of. Of course, the biggest lie of this entire application is how much "I" and "me" I'm required to claim. Beyond the fact that I run Killer with Pam Koffler, and that many of these films wouldn't have been pulled off without the energy and focus of Killer producers (and the occasional former intern!) Katie Roumel, Jocelyn Hayes, Brad Simpson, and Charles Pugliese, there's the unavoidable truth that these movies are not mine. They are the products of the imaginations of Todd Haynes, Todd Solondz, Kim Peirce, Mark Romanek, and others.

Killer is the catalyst. Directors come to us because Killer has the reputation of defending their vision—which often means having to make films for less, so that the risks are lower but control is higher. Other producers glom on to "properties" and actors and scout for franchises. They look to see how to match their taste with the studio's needs; *somebody's* got to produce movies based on amusement park rides (*Pirates of the Caribbean*). At Killer the director and the script are the starting point. We don't mind working with first-timers, because their first projects tend to be their passion projects. They have something to say and the steam pressure to say it. We go for true stories, dark ones, and have no problem with unlikely protagonists. This beat doesn't come from nihilism. At Killer we don't believe people make the right choice, then the wrong choice, then fix everything with minutes to spare. People make choices but they rarely change. The reason so many American mainstream movies feature characters with a "secret dream" is that most movies are wish fulfillment. These films certainly don't challenge audiences.

I've worked outside the AMPAS for so long, why join it now? Becoming a member of the Academy is good for three things: free screener DVDs, the chance to nominate films and vote for the Oscars, and a potential ticket to the show at the Kodak (it's a lottery). The year *Far from Heaven* was nominated, I couldn't even vote for it. That'll be the last time that happens!

Does independent film exist anymore?

In 2002 *Variety* made a chart of the "Best-Performing Independent Films" of the year. At the top was *My Big Fat Greek Wedding* followed by Killer's *One Hour Photo*. I was a little taken aback. *One Hour Photo* was fully financed by Fox Searchlight, a wholly owned subsidiary of Twentieth Century-Fox. How is this movie on a list of "independent films"?

Traditionally, an independent film is a movie shot and finished with private money that a producer takes to a marketplace—say, Sundance or the Independent Film Project, the yearly market of low-budget movies—to sell to a distributor. The distributor pays for the right to show the movie in a certain market, say the United States. But this process happens rarely now. Most of Killer's films are presold to distributors long before we're finished with them. By that definition, *One Hour Photo* is not even close to an independent film. *My Big Fat Greek Wedding*, on the other hand, fits the definition fine. It also shows how the old definition is pretty much meaningless.

Let's look at *Greek Wedding* more specifically. At some point in the late 1990s, the actress Rita Wilson saw a one-woman show at the Acme Theater in L.A. The show, written and acted by Nia Vardalos, was about her crazy Greek family. Rita loved the show, she's half-Greek, and Nia had the screenplay version of her play in her bag. Rita took it home to her husband, Tom Hanks.

After *Band of Brothers*, Tom Hanks made a deal with HBO to develop film projects. So Wilson and Hanks used that HBO money, via their production company Playtone, to co-finance Vardalos's movie at $5 million with another company, called Gold Circle, run by Norm Waitt, the guy who founded Gateway Computers. But Playtone and Gold Circle don't release movies. They just pull together the money to make them. At the time they shot it, they thought *My Big Fat Greek Wedding* would be distributed by Lionsgate, the company that distributed *Monster's Ball* and Rob Zombie's *House of 1,000 Corpses*. (Hey, it made money.) Lionsgate recognizes the potential of darker material. They don't have a corporate parent. They do what they want. But when Lionsgate saw *Greek Wedding*, they had no idea what to do with a superficial mainstream romantic comedy. It didn't seem bold or risky enough. They passed on distributing it.

As we now know, a $350 million mistake.

Why didn't Wilson and Hanks just mosey over to Dreamworks or Paramount and get them to make it? They'd say that they wanted to make the movie with an unknown, thirty eight-year-old voice-over actress as the lead. It was her story, her perspective, her authenticity that made the story. Studios, on the other hand, understand the mar-

ket force of star power. It's never been any other way, and it's as true
for audiences as the industry. If you're reading this book, you're
probably the kind of person who walks out of a film and says, "Wow,
that was really well shot" or "That script was terrible." But no matter
what you think, it's performances that make or break movies. Most
people—and when you're talking about studio films, you're talking
about *millions of people*—walk into a theater wanting to see a
"Julia Roberts" or a "Robin Williams" movie. It's what's driving them
to go and pay the ten dollars instead of staying home and watching
reruns of *Will and Grace*. Wilson and Hanks knew this. Because
they were starting from the assumption that Nia Vardalos was the
star in her own film, they knew that they couldn't work with a studio. So they went ahead and made their movie, and after Lionsgate
bailed, they sold it to the Independent Film Channel.

My Big Fat Greek Wedding was directed by the television director Joel Zwick, the guy who hired Tom Hanks for *Bosom Buddies*
back in 1980 and went on to do *Webster* and *Love Boat: The Next
Wave*. His movie was as surefire and safe as anything he did for television. *Greek Wedding* might be an "independent film" in terms of
its financing, although at some level, Hanks's dollars were HBO dollars which are Time Warner dollars. They say the worst kind of independent film is the one that copies the Hollywood formula or its
slavishness to star appeal. But shouldn't an independent *vision* at
least count for something?

Here's my counterexample and an argument for a new definition
of the term "independent." Bearded and intense, Mark Romanek
directed music videos for over a decade. You could tell from his
videos that he thinks with his eyes. He'd made videos for Madonna
("Bedtime Story"), Nine Inch Nails ("Closer"), Beck ("Devil's Haircut"), even Michael Jackson ("Scream"). Two of his videos are in the
permanent collection of the Museum of Modern Art. In 2002 he was
so moved by a Johnny Cash cover of Trent Reznor's song "Hurt" that
he shot the video for free.

He came to us with the script for *One Hour Photo*, something
he'd written in three weeks on spec. But with *One Hour Photo*, we
had the opposite problem of *Greek Wedding:* Mark's lead character
was a middle-aged, sexually deprived stalker. Studio executives

believe people don't want to spend two hours in the company of a character like that. Peter Rice, the head of Fox Searchlight, was interested, but we had to come up with a budget and find a name to make Searchlight green-light it. We needed a star. We went first to Philip Seymour Hoffman, one of Mark's favorite actors. In fact, he had written the script with Hoffman in mind. But Philip turned us down, perhaps feeling he'd played his fair share of sad loners recently.

Tired from all the *Patch Adams* nice-guy parts, Robin Williams loved the script and signed on. Casting Robin was a far less obvious choice, and it "raised the bar" for the film on several levels, both conceptually and commercially. Then, finally, with a complete package—a script, a star, a director—all Peter Rice had to say was yes.

The whole setup of the studio versus the rugged, loner artist is, like most dualistic constructs, a false one. Look to autodidact Paul Thomas Anderson (*Magnolia, Punch Drunk Love*), skateboard video auteur Spike Jonze (*Adaptation*), and midwestern ironist Alexander Payne (*About Schmidt*), and you'll see directors who have made their strongest work within the studio system, with Hollywood casts. The *Nation* film critic Stuart Klawans has argued that "independent film" is another kind of branding, a marketing ploy. "What the [independent] movement is about is a commercial reconsolidation of the film industry," he told the *L.A. Times* in 2004. Where studios used to hedge their bets with two product lines—top-shelf "A pictures" and low-budget "B pictures"—now "the A-sized budgets come out on Warner Bros. while B pictures come out on Fine Line, a Time Warner Company."

In this formulation, B pictures are the ones independent producers like me care most about, and this hedged bet works in our favor: fewer executives are meddling because the studio's risk is lower. Which allows me to push for the kind of independence in the filmmaking process that is crucial for our writer-directors. "Independent film" as a media brand never interested me. And trust me, "independently financing" a film only makes my job harder. But guarding a filmmaker's autonomy and agency—to tell unconventional stories, to cast the right actress not the star, to reject studio notes, to cut a third out of the movie right before the delivery date—

is everything, since those values are what make film an art form and not just entertainment.

Audiences respond to that singularity of vision. Every now and then, people will recognize me on the street, and they'll say, "You made one of my favorite movies ever," and I never know which movie they're going to say: *Safe, Happiness, One Hour Photo, Velvet Goldmine, Go Fish, Hedwig and the Angry Inch.* I love that. A lot of the movies Killer makes aren't loved by everybody—not even *mostly* everybody. But each one can be *somebody's* favorite movie because of its clarity of vision, because of the distinctiveness of what it's saying. It's that distinctiveness that allows somebody to say, Yes, this is singular and it relates to my life in this particular way.

No one else but Mark Romanek could have made *One Hour Photo.* No one but Todd Haynes could have made *Far from Heaven,* or Todd Solondz *Happiness,* or Larry Clark *Kids.* If a real creativity is allowed to get what it wants, *that* is independent film: the freedom of the vision behind it.

Chapter 1
Getting Used to the Dark

My father, the documentarian—An Upper West Side
childhood—My family's resident bohemian—Life at
LaGuardia High—Parting Glances opens doors—
Apparatus opens even more—Superstar

LESSON: MAKE YOURSELF NECESSARY.

My father took pictures. He lived by them, through them. His life is almost a portfolio to me now, the sum of things that he saw: factory workers swimming in soot, the gutted ruins of Poland after World War II, starlets riding their fame. I grew up in New York City, but I met tragedy, resilience, and celebrity first in his photographs. John Vachon taught me that understanding the world is really a question of where you lay the frame.

Mostly, my father was gone. Later there came to be a lot of missing people in my life, but John Vachon was the first. From the time he was twenty-two until he was twenty-nine (still in his first marriage and long before me), John Vachon crisscrossed the country for the Farm Security Administration, vanishing into America. In 1935 the FSA program hired fifteen photographers, Dorothea Lange and *Fortune* magazine staffer Walker Evans among them, to fan out across the United States and document the effects of government relief efforts during the Depression, to prove that their federal cash loans were actually doing something. For photographers in the 1930s, a time when New York City had almost 50 percent unemployment, you couldn't find a better job. (Maybe you still can't. Roy Stryker, the Columbia economics graduate who ran the division that hired my father, said, "The FSA was one of those freak organizations, and it can't happen again.")

You've seen these shots even if you can't place them—sharecroppers in front of their corrugated shacks, Dust Bowl Okies in California's Imperial Valley scraping together a last dime. It is fierce, dark stuff. "You could look at the people and see fear and sadness and desperation, but you saw something else, too: a determination that not even the Depression could kill," Stryker said. "The photographers saw it—and documented it." By 1943, when the FSA closed shop, made irrelevant by the war, the photography program had become a free ride for photographers to travel and look around. At that point, my father had been on the road for four years and taken countless photos, increasingly outside the mandate of the FSA. He shot work horses in Kansas, black kids in porkpie hats and suspenders, even a slice of an 864-year-old redwood tree.

Then he got drafted. But for his tour of duty, he managed to land an official assignment to go to Poland with the United Relief and Rehabilitation Agency, a precursor to the United Nations, to shoot the devastation there. His portraits and letters home are incredibly depressing: the southern sections of Poland had been bulldozed flat by the Germans trying to deal with the "Ukrainian problem." After the war, his work became softer, less documentary and more concerned with portraiture. My first encounters with political art came through his FSA and UN prints; my first exposure to celebrities came through this later work. As a staff photographer for *Look* magazine—the *People* of its day—he juggled politics and glamour. He trailed the Kennedy campaign, took the cover shots of Judy Garland and Marilyn Monroe, then shuttled back to the riots in Selma. At some point, he fell in love with the young French au pair Marie Francoise, who was helping care for his youngest daughter while he was away. She was twenty years younger than he was. This was my mother.

Some people see a dot to connect here. My father's strongest work—and I'm not talking about the glamour shots—has an anthropological, unflinching quality that they say threads through the films that I've made. I won't argue. But it's not just noble or courageous to look at the overlooked. It's more *interesting*. When I heard that theater director Moises Kaufman was making his film *The Laramie Project*, a quasi documentary about the murder of gay Wyoming college student Matthew Shepard, I thought that's a movie Killer would never make. I told Kaufman, when he came to feel me out about it, that I'd rather make the film about the *killers*—Aaron McKinney and Russell Henderson—their reported meth addictions, and the speculation that they had known (and maybe even slept with) Shepard.

Look magazine folded in 1971, when I was nine, and my father passed away four years later. Those final years, the main period of our relationship, were bad years for him. A magazine would send him out on the road and he wouldn't come back or he'd return empty-handed. My mother was a graduate student in French literature at Columbia and unable to do more than be a full-time student, mother, and rescuer. My early childhood was very chaotic. You never knew what was going to happen when my father opened the door of our apartment at 119th Street and Riverside: charm or catastrophe. (Dealing with that chaos was definitely training for the job I do now.) When he passed away from cancer, a certain instability went with him. I read a study recently that said that something like 75 percent of successful women lost their fathers at an early age. I was really struck by that. I'm sure 75 percent of *unsuccessful* people have also lost people, but in my case, the statistic makes sense. Drive has to come from somewhere.

Maybe it's just survival instinct. When he died, my mom was poor and finishing her PhD. To make ends meet, she began translating travel guides to Florida, doing typing at night, anything to pay the rent. It also meant that her two teenagers—I and my younger brother, Michael—needed to become less like baggage and more like peers. She was our model for resilience: when I was about fifteen, she got hired at the UN in some small capacity. By the time I was in college, she was running their French language translation program.

Usually I hate exposition. The "let's see the main character at home, in her room, doing homework" scene is the first thing I'm going to want to cut. But I need you to picture New York in the 1970s and '80s, because so much spins out from there. New York at that time was actually gritty, when the squatters overran Tompkins Square Park, city services were spotty, the parks were dilapidated, and the subway cars exploded with graffiti. In the 1990s everything got polished and cleaned. Now Hollywood movies shot in New York need to cart in their own trash. Then, in the seventies, we lived through the garbage strike and the transit strike, when my neighborhood at 119th Street and Riverside was just a working and middle-class neighborhood, a mix of Irish and Puerto Rican families, for whom Columbia University (which was around the corner) barely registered. Now those blocks have become an annex of Columbia dorms. It's almost a little college town. My brother and I went to the local public school on 125th until it got too rough and I transferred to a private Episcopal school, Saint Hilda and Saint Hughes, and Michael went to Corpus Christi. Even though my mother was a French Catholic—meaning, extremely not religious—my father, as an old-school Catholic, made us go to church. I went to Sunday school and got confirmed. When my father died, Monsignor Burke from Corpus Christi said the last rites over him.

As kids, we were hopelessly naïve. We didn't have the money to buy the designer drugs that were becoming fashionable. We were rarely alone and the streets were never empty. The park and Grant's Tomb were right there, but it was the seventies, so the instant the sun descended, you stayed out of the park. No one had a car, which is probably where most suburban kids had their drug experiences and their sex experiences. Larry Clark's *Kids* this was not. We hung in three cliques: the jocks, the parkies (the kids who played Frisbee in the park and smoked pot), and the vast, unwashed rest of us who stayed to the side and thought, I hope I don't do anything too uncool. I enrolled at Music and Art, aka LaGuardia, on 135th Street. This is the public high school that was featured in *Fame*, then called *Hot Lunch*. I was a visual arts student, so we weren't featured in the movie. (They did use some of the gospel chorus, the senior orchestra, and some acting students as extras, but even then, I didn't understand the "fun" of standing around in the background.)

It wasn't hard for me to shine at Music and Art. Not many kids cared about doing well academically. I got so bored that I would do things for fun, like not study for a test until ten minutes before. My only pleasure was seeing how little I could get away with and still get terrific grades. (Producing movies is the exact opposite: how hard can you work and still *not* get credit?) I didn't enjoy high school— having to be in the same place every day for eight hours, knowing that you're going to have French at 1:30 today, 1:30 tomorrow, 1:30 the next day. Sometimes I would feel an intense wave of despair. I don't know how anybody does it.

I did, however, love going to the movies, and I think for anybody who ends up working in the business, adolescence is when the real romance starts. This was back when there were no DVDs or video-tapes. I grew up near the Olympia Theater, a legendary New York cinema where your feet stuck to the floor, where Saturday after-noons you could get in for a dollar. On the weekend, we would go and see whatever was playing. My parents took me to see *Patton*, which I loved (so did Nixon), probably because it had such a vivid and intense point of view—still a criterion for me of what makes a movie strong. I saw *The Poseidon Adventure* at the Olympia five times; it continues to be one of my favorite film-watching experi-ences of all time. The shot of the luxury liner going belly up was mind-blowing in 1976. It was our *Titanic*, plus Shelley Winters. The Olympia went through a million incarnations; at some point they divided it into four theaters so that you could see one movie while listening to the movie next door.

My best friend Paul Selig and I would venture down to Times Square together; sometimes we'd check out the repertory theaters, the art houses that were scattered throughout the city. When you said you were going to an art-house cinema, everybody assumed the movie would have subtitles: most "real" art films came from else-where. The Times Square theaters were run-down and filled with bums, whom we managed to ignore. We watched *Cousin Cousine*, *The Bicycle Thief, The Lacemaker*; stories about big issues told in colloquial, small ways. It's an aesthetic that I've never outgrown, even while "independent films" have pretty much pushed foreign films out of American cinemas.

But my real introduction to risky cinema came via my older sister Gail, our family's reigning bohemian. She was my half sister, the daughter of my father's first wife, twelve years older than me and a graduate of Bard and the Massachusetts School of Art. She would cart me off to obscure film screenings at a rambunctious downtown theater called the Collective for Living Cinema on White Street. It was small and cramped with terrible seats. Afterward, bewildered, I would say, "I'm not sure what that was all about." And Gail would say, "Why do you think it needs to be 'about' anything?"

The Collective quickly became the epicenter for experimental filmmaking in a city that was already wild for European auteurs like Bergman, Truffaut, and Fellini. The Collective showcased short, daring work, building an entire evening's slate around a single filmmaker. On Friday and Sunday nights you could catch, say, a handful of shorts by Stan Brakhage, the avant-garde filmmaker who made nearly four hundred films and whose aesthetic montage techniques were ripped off in the credit sequence in *Seven*. Then, on Saturday night, the Collective would screen a classic revival picture to cover rent. A number of filmmakers debuted their early work there, from Jim Jarmusch (*Stranger Than Paradise*) to fringier folk like Amos Poe (*Alphabet City, Frogs for Snakes*), Kenneth Anger (*Scorpio Rising*), and Bette Gordon (*Variety*).

Gail lived with us for a period, moonlighting in a punk band called Y Pants and making her own quirky Super 8 shorts that put the Vachons in the foreground. Every time one of Gail's films would screen at the Collective, my mom, my brother, and I would trek down to see it. Her films were very personal. One, titled *Jealousy*, begins with a photograph of our father and Gail's older sister in a living room together. It's just a still image, for two minutes. The next shot is the same photograph, but this time with the word "Jealousy" scratched into the film.

Gail proved to me that movies were possible, within reach. Watching her make her films showed me that movies weren't complex feats engineered only in Hollywood or Cinecittà. They could be done, and done well, and done differently from anything you'd seen before. Short film was the stepping stone. It's one of the larger tragedies of contemporary film that places like the Collective have died out. Places like the Anthology Film Archives and the Millennium Theater in New York continue to try to program short film. But it's not just a matter of screenings. Experimental film was supported by a network of grant-giving arts organizations that allowed visual artists to migrate into the medium and take narrative risks. At the same time, audiences saw shorts as an end not a means. Now if you're going to make a short film, it's a "calling card" for studio work. It's a placeholder until your first deal.

Soon enough, because my family was broke, I became aware that I would be far more likely to be able to afford college if I went to an expensive one. My mother made about $20,000 a year and tuition alone was $10,000. Expensive private schools were the only ones that could afford me. At LaGuardia, there was one guidance counselor for a graduating class of 350. I decided I wanted to go to Brown. The school was the height of hipness. Grades were optional. The semiotics department was taking apart everything from film to novels to ads. And there were no required classes.

Still, I really had no way to distinguish myself. My grades at a large New York high school and my semi-quasi paintings of brown paper bags wouldn't be enough. So I enrolled in a college-level poetry class, with students from the really prestigious public schools like Stuyvesant and Brooklyn Tech. I hadn't written poetry before and haven't since, but I spent the semester tooling around with free verse.

Every year, in the New York City schools, there is a poetry contest to choose the best poems by teenagers. Alice Walker and Grace Schulman were the judges that year. Winners got published in the *New York Times*, received a whopping one hundred dollars, and got the chance to pad their résumés knowing that they beat out hundreds of other kids. The new poem I wrote, "I Rode His Shoulders," about the strangeness of becoming the parent to my dad as he was dying, ended up taking second place in the contest. It's unsettling to look back on it now, since mine was by far the most intimate of the prize-winning entries. (The others had titles like "The Blues," "Convalescence in Jazz," and my least favorite, "The Water Rat.") And because the poem is so raw. My first recognized work of art, and it's all about loss. Maybe art always is.

Parting Glances

I can't really recall Bill Sherwood's funeral because I attended so many around the same time. It reminds me of an observation in John Weir's book *The Irreversible Decline of Eddie Socket*, set in the mid to late 1980s, about how all the memorial services became indistinct because all these gay men were kind of the same: they all liked show tunes, they all liked going to brunch, they all liked to talk on the phone. Since few of them were from New York, you'd attend a memorial service in the Village someplace—where the family didn't show—and you'd be like, Is this Larry's, or is this Robert's? Or Bill's?

During the mid to late 1980s, I went to a memorial service almost every week. If you didn't live through it, you really can't imagine it. You would see somebody, occasionally a junkie girl but far more likely a young man, and then suddenly you'd say, Hey, where is he? "Oh, he died." It was unreal. Sixteen thousand people died of AIDS in New York City between 1986 and 1989. People don't talk about the AIDS epidemic in the United States anymore; it's like it never happened, or it's happening elsewhere. But for about three years there, people would get diagnosed and be dead six weeks later.

Bill Sherwood was an acerbic but incredibly generous guy in his early thirties who gave me my first break. Cultivate your exposure to generous people. You always get paid back. Bill had a beard, wire-rimmed glasses, and he was big, but he was from Battle Creek, Michigan, the land of the big people. He stayed big until he got sick. He had gone to Interlochen, the music school, and was very into music. (Case in point: the soundtrack to his first—and only—feature used Bach and Bronksi Beat for the soundtrack.) Like the characters in his film, he could be vicious and then tender an instant later.

The way I met Bill was the way I met all my contacts then: I worked for somebody for free. I had gone to the Young Filmmakers office on Rivington Street on the Lower East Side scouting for work. I was just starting to think about film as an industry and not just an art form, and Young Filmmakers was a nonprofit community center for film aficionados. (It still exists but is now called Film/Video Arts.) I was very new to it. At Brown, my senior year, I took my first film class, and as we made our short films, people had started saying confidently, "I'm going to New York or L.A. and I'm going to work in film." And I said, "Yeah, me too!" but I didn't really know what that meant. I was ambitious but I didn't have any specific ideas. And when you don't have any specific ideas, you waitress.

I lived in a cavernous but terrible apartment pretty much right where the Manhattan Bridge dumps into Brooklyn. The only place worse would have been at the mouth of the Holland Tunnel. The Lower East Side wasn't much better. Visiting the Young Filmmakers office meant stepping over three bums just to get in and out of the subway.

Inside the office, I saw a flyer seeking help on a feature film. I took the number and called. A documentary filmmaker named Jill Godmillow answered. She was doing a docudrama about Solidarity called *Far from Poland*. She said, "I put that sign up ages ago." My heart sank. But then she explained that while she was done, she now needed help editing the film. Not production, fine, but a job. I went in and first she showed me her clips of *Far from Poland*, about how Americans were fascinated with the Polish revolution mainly because it was staged by white people wearing Western clothes. It was a provocative little movie.

Then she introduced me to the enormous, pale green editing console called a Steenbeck, and taught me how to sync dailies. Soon enough, I knew something. I had a skill. "Syncing dailies" used to be a traditional entrée into filmmaking—the front door for eager, clueless twentysomethings like me. Now it's a little like learning how to run an eight-track, since digital editing has replaced everything. My job was to match the visuals with the sound recording. On two giant reels, I would scan for the single frame of the slate (or "clapper") smacking together to mark the start of the scene. On another pair of reels, I would roll through the sound tape over the sound drum to find the moment of the *clap!* I'd take these two pieces, match them up exactly, and send them to a service to be "coded" so that they'd have the same number on them.

At Brown I had worked as a short-order cook so I was good at multitasking. I could hold fifteen orders in my head at a time. More important, I've found that, as a process, syncing dailies is tremendously educational because you see what a film boils down to. During the shoot, there's the chaos of production and the actors and dollies and lighting. But ultimately what it comes down to is a little strip of celluloid, where you see the consequences of choices that were made on set months before. For example, if you decide when you're shooting, Well, we're running out of time so instead of shooting a scene in one master shot and two close-ups, we're just going to do the one master shot. You think at the time, That's okay, it will play fine. Three months later the scene seems incredibly boring to you, but you've got nothing to cut to.

It's very hard, in the throes of production, to imagine yourself in that quiet room months later. But great filmmakers actually can. Hitchcock supposedly could see his entire film edited in his mind. Todd Haynes, the director of *Far from Heaven,* can too. If you were to ask him (and I have), "Todd, since we're heading into overtime, I think that maybe instead of doing this shot and this shot, you should do this one and this one," Todd will stop and think for a second. He's reeling film back in his head and watching the shots. Then he'll say, "We don't really need the shot of her at the window, but I really have to have the shot of her at the phone."

When I was done, it turned out Jill had a friend—her ex-assistant—who was shooting *his* first film and needed someone to sync *his* dailies. This was Bill Sherwood.

In December 1983, Bill had written a script called *Parting Glances,* about the last twenty-four hours in the life of a gay couple, right before one of them leaves for a year in Africa. The concept grew from his annoyance at the typical style of gay-themed movies (say the middlebrow *Personal Best*) that congratulated its characters for being gay or you, the audience, for tolerating them. In *Parting Glances,* the protagonists are a clever, frustrated book editor of sci-fi gay porn, his restless, more conservative boyfriend, and a pop-punk rock singer who is HIV positive but scoffs at the attempts to rescue him with a "macro-psychotic" diet. They were recognizable people—not simply gay men—and their sexuality was assumed. AIDS was never mentioned because Bill didn't want to date the film—and he was right. There still is a kind of timelessness about it. For me, at that time, movies were either pure Hollywood or grossly experimental or endurance tests to sit through. *Parting Glances* shattered that. It was heartfelt and small.

In the spring of 1984, Bill raised $40,000 from friends, angling to start production in June. SAG did away with the low-budget pay scale right before they started, which meant that pay rates shot up. Bill had to scrap his initial cast six weeks before they began filming. Kathy Kinney, a struggling theater actress, played the part of the best friend. (Years later, she became Drew Carey's foil on his sit-com.) Steve Buscemi swept in and got the part of the punk rocker. At the time, he was a New York City firefighter and did East Village performances with an actor named Mark Boone Jr., comedy routines that weren't funny but weren't supposed to be. The film turned out to be the turning point in his career. Most of the other actors were, like Bill himself, recent grads of NYU and Juilliard who were brave enough to put a "gay film" on their résumé. It could have been a pox on future work. Bill didn't care. Straight guys played gay and vice versa.

I had keys to Bill's apartment on the Upper West Side, and every day after work at about 10 p.m., I would let myself in, sit at the Steenbeck, and sync up the film that he had shot the day before. He would come home at midnight—they shot most of *Parting Glances* after hours to save money on locations—and he'd show me scenes from the film. Bill was the director and editor, so I was really in the center of the creative direction of the movie. But I can't say I had much affinity for the film. I thought it was bourgeois. I thought a lot of things were bourgeois. I was twenty-three and this film was about men who were thirty and concerned with apartments, nice restaurants, and good clothes. My concerns were exactly right for my age. Partying. Sex. Drugs. But I did learn one lesson working with him, and it was the most important. You don't need a giant infrastructure or budget to make your movie. Everyone needs this kind of person in their life at some point—the person who asks you, by the very fact of their ambition, What are you waiting for?

In 1985 the waiting had stopped. Jim Jarmusch's *Stranger Than Paradise* had gone to Cannes that year and taken the Caméra d'Or for first film. Spike Lee was scrambling around Fort Greene to finish *She's Gotta Have It*. Now when people reminisce about the "independent film" scene in the 1980s, they're dreaming. There was no scene. It was the movies themselves that brought people together. You would go work on a low-budget indie, like *Parting Glances*, and other people who were there would have worked on something small with Jarmusch. The collective consciousness came from the work, not the bars or screenings or festivals. It came from sitting in Bill Sherwood's apartment and hearing about his day.

Not surprisingly, even with all the donated locations and freebies, Bill ran out of money to complete his film. This was pretty common with independent movies back then: you would make half of it, make a reel of the good stuff, and try to raise money for the rest. By the spring of 1985, all the scenes in "Nick's Apartment"— Nick being the punk rocker played by Buscemi—remained to be shot. So Bill screened what he did have to potential backers, mostly gay men eager to see a vision of their life on screen. It helped that he spoke to a population that hadn't seen itself up there. In May, Paul Kaplan—the guy who brought the play *As is* to Broadway—stepped forward and plunked down the money for Bill to finish it. Bill did, and then he found out he was positive.

So the film comes out, to a great critical reception and real distribution. A lot of kids who saw it when they were seventeen or eighteen years old in the heartland thought, "That's it, that's it, that's the life I want to lead." In the middle of the epidemic, it was a life-affirming drama. And even though he was sick and getting sicker, Bill started getting lots of scripts sent to him. He began to pay me to read them. I was poor, but I wasn't out of work. My big gig was working for a cable television magazine proofreading the grid of TV listings for ten dollars an hour. I got all my friends hired there, including Todd Haynes. The perk was getting to do the one-line synopses of movies, and we'd have fun. We'd put the title of the movie and then the names of two or three actors you've never heard of—the extras or something—as the "stars." It was our way of subverting the system.

In 1987 posters appeared around the city—a stark black background with a pink triangle and the words "Silence Equals Death." Then posters of Reagan with the words "He Kills Me" emblazoned across were everywhere. Then "Time Isn't the Only Thing the FDA Is Killing." In March protesters stormed Wall Street to demonstrate against the profiteering of pharmaceutical companies like Burroughs Wellcome, the company that made AZT, the drug that was killing as many people as it was helping. The Gay Men's Health Crisis had just been christened, but Larry Kramer threw a hissy fit because the GMHC was basically toothless politically. ACT UP was born. Suddenly, the sick people were fighting back.

In 1987 airlines could refuse to fly HIV-positive people (then called PWA, "persons with AIDS"). The police wore rubber gloves when they corralled protesters. But ACT UP was working. Shortly after the mobilization on Wall Street, the FDA shortened its drug-approval process by two years.

ACT UP meetings, held at the Gay and Lesbian Center downtown, were our only way to make sense of a senseless time. You could go and feel righteously angry with a bunch of other people. Everybody was "queer"—even though there were plenty of straight girls and a few straight boys. One of the secrets of ACT UP was that lesbians and straight women came in and organized it because they'd been politically active for years. The guys weren't. They'd been going to Fire Island, doing crystal, and having sex for hours on the beach. By my late twenties, I wasn't really political or particularly straight. I dated men and women and I was fairly cavalier about it. I went to the Clit Club. I went to Boy Bar. I didn't feel like I needed to decide.

Going to ACT UP meant you saw the face of the crisis: a lot of people there were really sick, and many of them didn't make it. Imagine: you're in your twenties, so you're glorifying risk and death anyway. You're indestructible. But here death is real, tangible. You can't romanticize it; death isn't just a moment or a mood for your little film. It means cleaning up somebody's shit. It means watching a twenty-five-year-old die. So you start going to actions and getting arrested because it's the only thing you can do. I got arrested a lot.

My life wasn't just politics and police. I met people, like Tom Kalin, an articulate, aesthetically gifted installation artist from Chicago. He helped to start the art collective called Gran Fury (named after the car that undercover cops drove). They were responsible for the posters I kept seeing. (Tom would go on to direct *Swoon* for Killer.) Todd Haynes showed up at meetings. Even Marlene, my partner, was a member of Gran Fury, though I didn't know her then. AIDS and ACT UP were intense driving forces culturally.

A couple of years after *Parting Glances*, I got a call from a friend saying that I'd better go visit Bill Sherwood at Beth Israel because he was dying. It was only a matter of time. We had kept in touch a bit, but while Bill had become more reclusive, I had become the opposite. When he died in 1990, I flew to his funeral in Michigan. I met his family. People tell me that a whole bunch of us went. I wish I could remember.

Climbing the Ranks

During all this, I started to dabble in movies, my own movies. I wanted to see what I could do with a camera. At Brown, in my film and semiotics classes, the prevalent theory was that narrative was essentially evil because it subsumed the viewer in some way, made the viewer passive. Laura Mulvey's groundbreaking article "Visual Pleasure and Narrative Cinema" had radicalized the film department. She argued that women have to identify with men in order to enjoy a movie. When a movie objectifies a woman—shows her legs before her face, for example, as happens with Marilyn Monroe in *Some Like It Hot*—women watching it have to adopt the "male gaze" in order to get the pleasure from the story.

This was the continuation of what the Collective for Living Cinema had been trying to teach me. Suddenly there was a lot more at play when you went to the movies than just sticking popcorn in your mouth. Where was your source of identification in the film? How does a woman identify with the male protagonist? How does the filmmaker manipulate you into feeling X over Y? At the same time, the awakening was paralyzing. After you start thinking this way, there's no way you can go and simply tell a story. Or if you do, you'll be ridiculed in film class.

At Brown I made one short called *There's a Man in Your Room.* It was just a single scene of a man in a suit, sitting on the edge of a bed, with the words "There's a man in your room" intoned over the soundtrack. The camera jumped from angle to angle and you never quite saw his face. I wanted it to be eerie and unsettling, and people took notice.

After graduating, I kept making shorts: *The Way of the Wicked, Don't Look Up My Skirt Unless You Mean It, Days Are Numbered. The Way of the Wicked* went to Sundance. When I made it, I'd been going through a period of fascination with the literal mysticism of Catholicism; it's such an intense thing to grow up around that it's impossible not to react to it. I mined my earliest religious fears for the plot. In it, a woman shows up for a date at a chic restaurant. She goes to the bathroom and discovers a paper bag with a change of clothes. So she gets out of her outfit and transforms into a new person. But then there's a flashback to her as a little girl at communion. She's been told by the nuns—just as I was—that if you take the communion wafer out of your mouth, Jesus's blood will come out and the wafer will be a little patch of Christ's skin. Literal transubstantiation. So she wants to find out what happens. When she takes the wafer out, blood pours from her mouth, and people run screaming from the church. When you start to express yourself, all you have is your own experience to draw from. And I thought the most complicated, interesting thing that had happened to me was Catholicism.

Professionally, I spent most of my time on schlock. After *Parting Glances,* I had one credit to my name, but I couldn't find anything nearly as interesting or as independent-minded. So I ended up on low-budget commercial movies. I held back cars so that Scott Valentine—Justine Bateman's boyfriend on *Family Ties,* who was having his moment—could drive a limo backward up Third Avenue in *My Demon Lover.* Hey, it was 1987. I was responsible for the coffee for *Magic Sticks,* a film by a German director that was supposed to be a vehicle for one of those New York City street drum players. *The Golden Boat*, an arty, problem-plagued film made by the Chilean director Raul Ruiz, was released for two seconds but had the distinction of featuring the director Jim Jarmusch in a small role.

Soon I jumped up to "second assistant director." The first AD is in charge of the set and making sure everything comes off. "Second AD" sounds like the first AD's assistant, but in fact it's a completely different job. The second AD is the talent wrangler. You follow the stars around with your walkie-talkie so that you can report on their every move. If an actor says, "I want to walk down the block and get some air," you panic because you know the second he walks out, the first AD is going to say, "We need him on the set!" and you won't be able to find him. Remember: It's never the talent's fault. It's yours. So you're running up and down the street, trying to figure out where your actors went, with the first AD screaming at you. Those years, there was lots of screaming.

Building Apparatus

Barry Ellsworth was a very handsome, blond, blue-eyed film student who moved to New York with the rest of us and launched my career.

Barry sculpted, painted, did everything well except trust his own instincts. Though he came from money, he was very good at denying it. He was a Bingham of the Louisville Binghams, a family newspaper empire that crashed and burned. Still, he was a scion of the piles of money they had made. In the mid-1980s, when his mother offered to give him a lump sum of cash, Barry rounded up me and Todd Haynes and sat us down to figure out what we could do. We didn't really know each other or what we were doing. Todd thought I was a bossy short-order cook who dated the resident adviser in his dorm. Still, we sat around a table and decided that if we had this capital, we could form a kind of grant-giving organization for young filmmakers. But instead of just handing over $20,000 to the filmmakers, we would actually put ourselves to work for them. We would budget the film and produce it. We would be a little Killer before Killer. Or, in some ways, another Farm Security Administration, fifty years after the fact: giving artists the freedom to work but enough structure to guarantee a certain level of quality.

We called ourselves, in a moment of Soviet-style solidarity, Apparatus. The premise was that filmmakers received grants all the time and pissed away the money because, unlike a painter, a dancer, or a sculptor, filmmakers cannot exist in a vacuum. Film by nature is collaborative, so our organization made sense. We would all do something different and switch off: on one film, I would assistant-direct, Todd would edit, and Barry would cast and line-produce. Then we'd change it up. We each got $20,000 a year, which was a wild amount of money to us. Barry got us an office at 225 Lafayette Street in SoHo. We bought furniture at junk shops, borrowed some computers with WordPerfect (which really dates us), and we were off.

In two and a half years, we made seven short films, none of which you've ever heard of. We'd make them, and if we were lucky, they'd screen at Sundance, and then they'd vanish. *Oreos with Attitude*, our big project, a satire about buppies, never quite got the recognition we thought it deserved. Suzan-Lori Parks, the Pulitzer Prize–winning playwright, made a movie with us that disappeared from her résumé. Apparatus was intended to help launch these young filmmakers' careers. It actually launched *us*. It gave us the opportunity to understand filmmaking from every perspective, beginning to end, but on a small, safe scale.

Meanwhile, Todd had started stretching out on his own. He'd made a few out-of-pocket student films, *The Suicide, Sexshop*— both edited quasi-professionally via borrowed time in L.A. editing facilities—and an incredibly overreaching "period" film called *Assassins: A Film Concerning Rimbaud* that used intertitles. One afternoon, in 1986, he'd been sitting in Dante's, one of those run-down Italian cafés on MacDougal in the West Village, and they were playing a light FM station when he heard "Every sha-na-na, every wo-wo-wo," the refrain from the 1973 Karen Carpenter hit "Yesterday Once More." He had an intense reaction. It's a song about waiting for your favorite song to come on the radio. "I went through every emotion listening to it," Todd told me later. "I felt sentimental, then embarrassed because of the sentimentality of it, then angry at how it manipulated me, then laughing at it, then feeling saddened by knowing what Karen Carpenter had gone through, struggling with anorexia and eventually dying." He laid the tragedy of her life over the music and an authenticity emerged out of the plastic.

Suddenly he had the idea for a film about Carpenter that would deal, head on, with her anorexia. Except he wanted to make it with dolls. He had some history with this. As a kid, he and his sister used to go into her room, throw a blanket over her bedroom table, and dramatize stories for each other. They would take turns doing "shows" using her dolls and plastic horses. Even as a kid, Todd was really into the lighting; he set up complicated scenes with desk lamps and flashlights. And every story Todd "directed" with the dolls was about a little girl who would fall in love with her horse and the horse would run away or get shot. Of course, his sister would start crying. This was the genesis of his idea for *Superstar: The Karen Carpenter Story.*

He'd gone to Bard's summer MFA program and spent months, with his partner Cynthia Schneider, making the miniature bureaus and beds and recording studios for it. Almost as if in a demented children's show, the Karen and Richard dolls would move through these miniature sets. But dramatically, the film took itself seriously, with eerie intensity and intelligence. Throughout the film, Todd wanted to intercut images of Vietnam, antiwar protests, and even Nixon to clash against the detached wholesomeness of the Carpenters.

Barry had helped shoot the film. As he pulled together a rough edit, Todd brought me over to his apartment one night to show me what he had. It began in 1983, with a grainy, POV shot of Karen's mother searching desperately through her house for her daughter, who has overdosed. Then, using a voice-over, it flashes backward in time:

The year is 1970, and suddenly the nation finds itself asking the question, "What if, instead of the riots and assassinations, the protests and the drugs, instead of the angry words and hard-rock sounds, we were to hear something soft and smooth, and see something of wholesomeness and easy-handed faith?" This was the year that put the song onto the charts that made the Carpenters a household word . . .

I was astounded. *Superstar* was funny, creepy, and incredibly poignant. Over the course of the film, Todd literally scraped away the plastic "skin" of the Karen doll, so that by the end her disfigurement is utterly chilling. When the film stopped running and I heard the flapping of the last reel, I knew my days as a director were essentially over. Working for Apparatus, I could straddle the fence, playing both the artist and the producer.

Now I was choosing a side. I wanted to take Todd's ideas and make them happen, alone if I had to. People needed to see this, to see what he was capable of.

I said, "I want to produce your next movie."

Producer's Diary I

10 A.M. Dailies are in. Every morning, Killer gets a FedExed video dub of the previous day's shoot of *A Home at the End of the World*, our current film in production. I'm supposed to watch it. If people ever wonder what it is exactly that a producer produces, this is it: actors paid to show up on a rented set under borrowed lights captured on heaps and heaps of film.

I slide the tape into the VCR. I don't have to worry too much. Katie Roumel, my co-producer from Killer, is already stationed on set up in Toronto and I trust she's taken care of everything—like the director's worries about Colin Farrell's cute but recurrent Irish accent and Sissy Spacek's anxiety about SARS. Nothing gets past Katie. Down-to-earth and quick-witted, she's exactly the kind of person you want around when the shit hits the fan in multiple directions. She's done more outrageous gofer assignments for Killer (like tracking down amputee subway beggars) than anybody. Ever. She put the dialect coach on overtime and contracted with a doctor in Toronto to make a set call. Done.

In the movie, based on Michael Cunningham's second novel, Colin Farrell plays Bobby, a young man stuck in a love triangle with two best friends, Jonathan (played by Dallas Roberts) and Claire (played by Robin Wright Penn). As with all dailies, the intense material is mixed in with the interstitial establishing shots, reaction shots, etc., that make up a complete film. Everything is filmed based on convenience and economics, never chronology. So sometimes the dailies are riveting: the scene of the horrific accident that kick-starts the plot (the gash looks amazing), or Sissy spacing out to her first "joint." Other times, it's like watching someone scrape paint from a ceiling. Literally.

This morning, I've got five minutes of Colin Farrell attacking crumbling paint with a spackling knife in his right hand. It looks exhausting, shot after shot. Of course, the whole Killer office crowds in to watch the sometime Britney Spears boyfriend go at it. Then Colin turns to the camera and says, completely out of character, "I guess I'll be wanking with my left hand tonight." The crew, off screen, cracks up.

The next sequence is a medium shot of a very pregnant Robin Wright Penn, peering out the window of the farmhouse she's living in. Robin looks terrific in the ghostly winter light.

"Wow—is that real light?" someone in the office asks.

Must be an intern. On a film set, it's never "real" light.

11 A.M. Cannes is next week, and we're having a strategy meeting with our attorney/sales rep John Sloss and his company, Cinetic. Sloss has represented John Sayles, Richard Linklater, and Kevin Smith, and in our film deals at Cannes, he covers the financial details while I get to play the talent. I don't see a single movie at Cannes. I just shuttle from meeting to meeting, hyping our projects, convincing foreign movie sales companies to pony up cash.

Killer has two projects ready to sell: *Bettie Page,* a biopic about the saucy pinup, and *Mrs. Harris,* about the 1980 murder of the "Scarsdale Diet" creator Herman Tarnower by Jean Harris, his former mistress. Right now, *Mrs. Harris* is retaining water: we can't seem to get the budget under $9 million. With Annette Bening attached to star, it's too expensive to slim down any further. Foreign sales companies, the ones that pony up the money to help get it made, won't know what to make of it with that price tag. We'll send the script out and meet with whoever bites.

Mary Harron, the *Bettie Page* director, wants to make her movie in black and white, which sounds fine until you realize that *no one will pay to make a black-and-white movie,* even when you're only asking $3.5 million. This is despite the fact that Gretchen Mol (attached to play the lead) is half-naked for a good part of it. Over the phone, we spoke to one Japanese sales company who said, in their very sincere English-as-second-language tone, "The black and white is of concern."

In our pre-Cannes meeting, Sloss shakes his head. "This is a completely financeable project but for the fact that it's black and white," he says. "I don't know whether that makes it unfinanceable or just makes it more challenging." At this point it's Mary's call, and Mary is firm about the black and white. This is why directors come to Killer. We do it her way.

1 P.M. Now it's somebody else's turn to pass. The agent for Brittany Murphy (*8 Mile, Uptown Girls*) calls to tell me she doesn't want to play Liza Minnelli in *Simply Halston,* a biopic about the infamous fashion designer that Killer has had in development for ten years. She's "looking for bigger parts." Drew Barrymore told us the same.

It's actually nice when actors pass. At least you know. Since you can only send a script out to one actor at a time, Killer can spend weeks waiting to hear. I pull up our list for next in line: Parker Posey, Samantha Mathis, Selma Blair. They're all good actors, but Liza Minnelli is a tough nut to crack, so we'll ask them to audition on tape.

3 P.M. Killer gets a call from a record company, the one releasing the soundtrack to *Party Monster,* our club kid murder story. The record company is pulling out of releasing the soundtrack. They feel that the movie isn't going to make enough to drive the soundtrack off the shelves. But the company's advance for the soundtrack is paying for the rights to the music *that is already in the movie.* How did this happen?

Sometimes, no matter how much talent and energy you put into something, the money still gets scared. *Party Monster* was a really hard movie to get financed. It's the story of the rise and fall of downtown club kid Michael Alig. It took us five years to pull the financing together, and we finally shot it in 2002 with Macaulay Culkin and Seth Green. It's not an easy movie by any stretch: Alig was either hopped up on designer drugs or making out with boys (usually both at the same time) pretty much until the moment he murders his drug dealer. But it's directed with outrageous style by two fantastic documentarians, Fenton Bailey and Randy Barbato, who made *The Eyes of Tammy Faye* and *Inside Deep Throat.* You leave *Party Monster* either desperately wanting to snort some cocaine or never wanting to do it, ever.

We financed it by splitting the risk. We convinced ContentFilm, a young New York–based financing company, to pay $800,000 for the right to release it in America, and Fortissimo, a European sales company, to put up $1 million for the rights to the rest of the world. Content is run by Ed Pressman and John Schmidt and both are film veterans. Pressman has produced something like sixty films—from *Badlands* to *The Crow* to *Reversal of Fortune* to *Judge Dredd.* His partner Schmidt co-founded October Films, a former New York–based distribution company that launched Mike Leigh's and Lars von Trier's American reputations.

So I'm stunned at how shortsighted they're turning out to be. *Party Monster*—with a temp soundtrack—debuted at Sundance 2003, and the reviews were mixed at best. In my mind, it was review-proof because of the elements we had involved, especially Macaulay, who, no matter what you think of him, was once America's sweetheart kid and people are curious about the man he's turned out to be. We fielded two distribution offers: a modest one from Lionsgate, and a higher offer from DEJ Productions, a company you've never heard of because they are Blockbuster Video's acquisitions unit. They buy films to release them direct to video. Ever hear of *Boondock Saints?* DEJ bought it and released it straight to video and made almost $12 million off it.

Presented with these two offers, Content was determined to go with DEJ and get out their entire $800,000 to protect their investment. Even if it meant condemning the movie to a straight-to-video release. Even if it meant breaking the promise I thought we all made to Macaulay to give it a theatrical try. Right before we went into production, Ed Pressman and I had lunch with Mac's manager specifically so that she could hear Ed Pressman say, "We know what a big deal it is for Macaulay to do this movie" and "We will protect you" from a lame release.

But Content took the Blockbuster deal, and we're dealing with the consequences: the foreign buyers are furious. They invested in the film, thinking that it would have a domestic release here in the States, which would help build the international release. Seth and Macaulay feel stung and won't necessarily promote a video release, since standing on a red carpet in front of a Blockbuster is *not* what they thought they were getting into. And Randy and Fenton, the filmmakers, are shell-shocked and depressed, and we're all just trying to put a good face on it. And now, it turns out the record company is spooked. Who wants to release the soundtrack to a direct-to-video film?

All this is really hard to watch. If we had gone with Lionsgate and their smaller offer, at least they would have been willing to negotiate profit-sharing arrangements. We'd have had a domestic release and none of this would be happening. A single decision made in fear has screwed the fate of a small film.

Postscript: Strand Releasing eventually gave the film a small but decent domestic release.

4 P.M. Can someone explain this to me? *One Hour Photo,* produced for $13 million, made $33 million in theatrical release. I see in the trades that it made $72.6 million in DVD and videocassette. That's over $100 million. Doesn't Killer get *any* of that?

Robin Williams, who starred as your local psychotic photo development guy, had percentage points off the "first dollar" profits—meaning, Robin saw a slice of every single dollar you plunked down. No independent film company can promise that. Only studios, in this case Fox Searchlight, can do that since they control the financing *and release* of their films. It's how they get stars to work for less money up front.

But film accounting, particularly by studios, is a notoriously opaque business. Studios often assert that the marketing and advertising for a film cost more than the price of production, so big profits don't trickle down. I have Wigs, our accountant, take a closer look at the books to see if Killer is owed anything. Chances are slim. For anyone who thinks producers are powerful folk, this is the reality check.

5 P.M. A certified letter arrives from James Schamus at Focus, my oldest producing colleague in New York and the screenwriter of *The Hulk* and *The Ice Storm.* It's been months since the Oscars, but the drama over *Far from Heaven* isn't over yet.

As the head of Focus Features, James was responsible for distributing and promoting *Far from Heaven.* We opened the movie in the late fall of 2002, and by late winter—Oscar time—it had made $15 million. *The Pianist,* the other Oscar contender from Focus, opened a little later and made nearly double that. When our movie was overlooked at the Golden Globes and the Oscars—*The Pianist* took home multiple awards—as the producer, I wanted to blame Focus. Couldn't they have pushed it a little harder? Where were the big ads or the parties in "Julianne's honor"?

Now word has gotten back to James about my grousing. "Dear Christine," he writes, "Unfortunately, although you promised in an e-mail to me that you had 'moved on,' you continue to malign the people at Focus Features who put so much time, energy and ingenuity into promoting and distributing *Far from Heaven*." To prove his point, he's sent along a stack of revenue charts for *every film* Todd has ever made to show how little money they've made in comparison to *Far from Heaven*. A lot of work went into this analysis, and the point is well taken. *Far from Heaven* has outgrossed all the other Haynes films put together—by millions. At the end, I notice he cc'd this letter to George Clooney, Steven Soderbergh, John Wells—all the producers on the picture—and Todd himself. Thank you, James.

I'm not saying that I thought that *The Pianist* was getting full-page ads and we were getting postage stamps. Or that more promotion would have made a huge difference. I've never run a distribution company. What do I know? But I do feel that distributors can create an internal ceiling for how successful a film can be. Movies are somewhat a self-fulfilling prophecy: you predict how successful they are going to be and you spend accordingly. If I've maligned anyone or anything, it's not the people at Focus but the process. When Oscar time comes, distributors choose favorites—the films that will receive the lion's share of the advertisements, promotion, and hype. Look at Miramax, who bought full-page ads for *The Hours* and *Gangs of New York*. There's a reason why *40 Days and 40 Nights*, also a Miramax movie, didn't get the same treatment. In his letter, Schamus scoffs at a quote from *Variety* that he had to make a "Sophie's choice" between his two pictures.

I write back to James. "I will inevitably indulge in a degree of 20/20 hindsight on *Far from Heaven*. I can't help thinking, What if? and If only. I'm sure you've done the same when your films' performance did not match your expectations. . . . Good luck with all your upcoming films." I also cc'd George Clooney, who I'm sure really appreciates that we're keeping him abreast of all this.

Chapter 2
Target Practice

Superstar makes fans ... and enemies—*$250,000 to make*
Poison—*Our first Sundance*—*Too many funerals*—*Donald*
Wildmon hates us—*A "Fellini of fellatio" hits the talk show*
circuit—*Split Decision at Sundance*—*Twelve minutes of*
Go Fish—*Enter John Pierson*—*What trickles down*

LESSON: MAKE THE RIGHT ENEMIES.

Todd and I made an audacious, uncategorizable movie for
$250,000, and all anybody seemed to care about was the one scene
of prison sex and the tiniest wink of penis. And they hadn't even
seen the movie. I'd like to say that we planned it. That we knew
what we were doing. But we didn't. The controversy surrounding
Poison, my first producer credit and Todd's first feature, garnered
us headlines in all the major papers, coverage on the *CBS Evening
News, Entertainment Tonight,* and countless talk shows, and
nearly got the head of the NEA fired. By the time *Poison* opened at
the Angelika in New York on April 5, 1991, the line for tickets
stretched around the block. *Poison's* opening weekend broke
records. The joke is that we owe the furor surrounding the film to
the people who wanted to make sure nobody ever saw it.

Looking back, the biggest gift *Poison* (and *Swoon,* my second film) gave me was enemies. How do you get relevant and noticed in the film industry? You make adversaries. You figure out how to get on the right side of a controversy. (This works for Michael Moore, that's for sure.) I came of age when American culture was just starting to talk publicly about gay life, and the films we made helped spark that conversation, largely because we never approached the subject in conventional or moralistic ways. Even gay audiences were challenged. Two boyfriends commit the perfect murder? Gay desire in prison? I like to think these films would still feel offbeat and interesting if they were released today, in the era of *Will and Grace, Queer as Folk,* and *The L Word.* That offbeat quality came from their specific point of view, and it's still true in movies like *Hedwig and the Angry Inch* and *A Home at the End of the World.* If you're going to speak from a place, make sure you're not trying to speak *for* a place.

It didn't take long for me to get branded "a gay producer" by journalists. Two movies about gay men = a gay producer. But as much as I resisted the category—*any* category—the branding attracted other filmmakers to me, like Rose Troche with *Go Fish* and Nigel Finch with *Stonewall.* There's not a lot of ink in the world for producers, and the labeling gave the so-called New Queer Cinema a sense of an origin point. It also gave me a reason for being. I don't know how fledgling producers find their own reason except by seeking out talent where it lives. What I do know, what I learned firsthand, is that in the independent film business, it helps to become a target. Enemies can be your best asset.

It was Todd who first showed me that sometimes you have to deliberately draw the bull's-eye on yourself. In the most genuine, unaffected way, Todd made sure people noticed *Superstar.* Since he had worked in galleries and had fired off countless press releases for exhibitions, he had access to a list of all the names of the critics at the newspapers and magazines in New York. When he finished the edit and was ready to show it to audiences, he sent out a press release to all of them. He was his own best PR agent.

The only problem was he had no place to show it. Even though *Superstar* would later achieve outrageous "cult" status, the standard-bearer Collective for Living Cinema turned it down for a screening. The Millennium, the other showcase for art films, also rejected it. He showed it to the MOMA film department, who were enthusiastic, but they were scared by the illegal use of the music and the potential libel suits.

So Todd ended up renting the Millennium for a hundred bucks and screened the forty-three-minute *Superstar* on his own. At the same time, the Pyramid Club, a drag club on Avenue A, was willing to do a midnight screening as a kick start for their "Karen Carpenter" night. Now he had two venues. He sent off his press release and, because he'd just broken up with his boyfriend, he took an emergency trip around Cape Cod to clear his head before the screening. While he was gone, we got two urgent calls at the Apparatus office: one from J. Hoberman, the film critic at the *Village Voice*, and one from Barbara Kruger at *Art Forum*, both of whom received the press release and wanted to get copies of *Superstar*. This was a huge coup. At that time, the fall of 1986, the *Voice* was the arbiter of hipness and *Art Forum* of artistic credibility. If you got a positive review in either, every community center, museum, and gallery in the country would know about it. We made sure they got copies.

A week later, Hoberman's review came out and it was a rave. Suddenly, *Superstar* was a sensation. Everyone wanted to see and show it. After playing at Sundance in 1988, it toured the festival circuit for three years and even began to make some money. The commercial success of *Superstar* really astonished Todd. He thought it would be a little festival movie. But legit theaters were starting to book it. Even the Collective for Living Cinema came around and did a benefit screening of it at the Ziegfeld.

Then the Carpenters noticed. I think the estate believed if they ignored it, *Superstar* would just go away. They didn't want to draw more attention to it. But unlike what would come later with *Poison*, they didn't need to attack the content of the film to have a solid legal case: Todd had never bothered to try to get the rights to the Carpenter songs in part because he thought nobody would pay enough attention for him to need them and partly because he knew the estate would never give them to him. (Regardless, he wouldn't have been able to pay for them.) So two years after *Superstar*'s debut,

Todd got a cease and desist letter from Richard Carpenter's lawyer threatening to sue. Todd ingeniously proposed giving all the proceeds from the screenings to a foundation for anorexia research. The lawyer said no. And that was it. *Superstar* stopped screening and went underground.

Music rights are one of the trickiest issues for small films. The film business is only bested by the music business in difficult personalities. Often, songs have so many different people associated with the rights—songwriters, performers, managers, producers, labels—that it takes months to track down the right people to ask, "Can we use this?" Even then, they don't agree. For *I Shot Andy Warhol*, the director, Mary Harron, wanted to use Velvet Underground songs. Though John Cale would give us the rights, Lou Reed wouldn't. So we ended up not using any Velvet Underground songs at all; we had John Cale compose the score and we had Yo La Tengo play music that sounded very similar. (They'd be horrified to hear it described that way.) In some ways, it's liberating because period music can be so on the nose. People bring intense and personal reactions to a familiar song.

Then, there's just greed. When we made *Boys Don't Cry*, Kim Peirce had used Boston's "More Than a Feeling" as a temp score for the pivotal opening scene where Teena Brandon, the girl, passes as Brandon Teena, the boy, for the first time. The music plays over the opening credits, with Brandon taking his date to the skating rink. Kim thought the song perfectly captured the soaring feeling of Brandon's accomplishment—the kind of tune a kid in the heartland would listen to and be transported. But Boston would not license it—not for any amount of money. They were holding out in a bid to increase the song's value so that they could someday sell it for a million to a commercial. Kim was destroyed. Nothing would work as well as "More Than a Feeling." Normally, I'm wary of letting directors fall in love with their temp score. Many songs carry strong associations for audiences, so you're competing with all those private contexts. But in this case, we agreed that the movie needed a score from the first frame. So Kim stayed up all night with Randy Poster, the music supervisor, and Nathan Larsen, the composer, listening to virtually every piece of guitar rock from the seventies and eighties. And still nothing worked.

Then the day before we had to finalize the sound mix, Randy brought in "Just What I Needed" by the Cars. We laid it in with no edits, and as the first bold guitar licks played over the opening, we knew we had our song (and for a price we could afford).

On the other hand, sometimes you're lucky. When Todd Graff had one of his characters sing the Rolling Stones' "Wild Horses" in the original script for *Camp*, we knew it was a placeholder for something else. There was no way the Stones would let us license it for anything close to what we could pay. Microsoft had licensed "Start Me Up" for *$12 million*. But we'd negotiated $3,000 for the licensing rights to "The Ladies Who Lunch" with Stephen Sondheim and that was our linchpin. We proposed a most-favored nation treaty with every artist so that everybody got the same as Sondheim. The Stones read the *Camp* synopsis, thought it was genuine, and miraculously agreed. I guess when you're the Rolling Stones, $3,000 is pretty much toilet paper.

The underground life of *Superstar*, without question, helped launch Todd Haynes's career. The film squared off against the Carpenters' attempt to "own" a family tragedy that had, in fact, played out in the public eye. When I'm asked how to find new talent, I always answer that it's a question of gut, but it's also a matter of standing with those who are in the right fights for the right reasons.

By 1990 Todd had an idea for his first feature, *Poison*, the one that put us on the map. Very loosely based on writings by the late French author Jean Genet—one of Todd's college favorites—*Poison* would be split into three parts, "Hero," "Horror," and "Homo." If this design sounds deliberately arty, it was. Todd will tell you that he wanted to challenge the guilt foisted on gay people for their promiscuity and experimentation. *Poison*, then, became another kind of experimentation, this time aesthetic and narrative. It was a rejection of the sentimental grab for empathy that drove gay cinema then, in films like Norman René's elegiac *Longtime Companion*, which screened at Sundance in 1990 and became the touchstone gay film. Initially Todd wanted to make *Poison* an hourlong art film. But I argued, "If we're going to make it an hour, we might as well make it a feature so we can get it released and have a chance to make some money."

The first part, "Hero," was a documentary-style segment about a seven-year-old boy who murders his father (and flies out the window). It was, by far, the easiest to shoot. Set in blandest Levittown, the segment would be made up primarily of close-ups on the boy's mother, teachers, and classmates. In it, you would see Todd's interest in both celebrating and surgically dissecting the minutiae of suburbia, an interest that threads through his later films *Safe* and *Far from Heaven*. The second part, "Horror," was a "B-horror-ragamuffin" about a scientist who isolates the source of the human sex drive, represented by a bubbling black fluid. He drinks it, becomes horribly disfigured, and goes insane in his search for flesh. To Todd, this was a metaphor for the prurience projected by the mainstream media onto AIDS sufferers that supposedly justified their suffering.

The last section, "Homo," was to become the most controversial. A new inmate arrives in a male prison community and sparks new lust and jealousies among them. It was Todd's direct crib from Genet's *Our Lady of the Flowers*.

We pulled together every source of funding we learned about through Apparatus, like the Jerome Foundation for filmmakers in Minneapolis and the New York Foundation for the Arts. A handful of private investors filled in the rest of the budget, including *Gilligan's Island* and *Brady Bunch* creator Sherwood Schwartz, a friend of Todd's family in Los Angeles. By the end, we had raised $250,000. With inflation, that would probably be closer to $1 million today. A paltry figure, for sure, but if we were smart and resourceful—as we taught our Apparatus filmmakers to be—we could pull it off.

From a production standpoint, *Poison* was no different from any film Killer makes now. We hired real actors and paid a crew. It did take some imagination to stretch the budget. We shot one-third of the film for almost nothing on a soundstage at SUNY Purchase, with film student undergraduates running around as our (unpaid) production assistants. We budgeted a grand total of $1,000 on production design—looking back, a ridiculous number, but $250,000 is also pretty ridiculous.

If you're in the independent film world, you hear low budget numbers all the time. I read that twenty-seven-year-old David Gordon Green's first film, *George Washington*, was made for a staggering $50,000, shot on 35mm anamorphic widescreen in rural North Carolina. For $50,000 you can barely cover the cost of the film stock and processing. Before that, the low watermark was $7,000 for Robert Rodriguez's *El Mariachi*. (A number which a lot of people doubt.) Kevin Smith kept the credit card bills to show he made *Clerks* for $26,685, shooting nights in the same convenience store where he worked. I see these figures and it seems to me it's sort of a macho race to the bottom. How low can you go? People usually recount them proudly. I used to also. What is never accounted for is the sweat equity that goes into the films and the fact that people work for a fraction of their rate or for nothing at all. These days, when I read those numbers, I think, God, you're just telling people how cheap you'll work.

Digital video production companies, like InDigEnt, give directors $250,000 to make their films, but they have to convince a crew to work for free. This math can sometimes be worth it. Every member of the crew does, however, get a tiny percentage, say .5 percent of whatever the film is sold for. When the system works, it works well: Miramax bought Gary Winick's *Tadpole* for $5 million at Sundance in 2002 (though that movie tanked). For each gaffer and makeup person, that's $25,000 for a couple of months' work. Films that advertise their superlow budgets, that telegraph their seat-of-their-pants cred, are usually films in which the producers are making preemptive excuses for quality. In the early days, you could use the rough edges to your advantage, as we did with *Go Fish*, a movie that worked in part because of its funky, garage quality. Lesbians, it turned out, cared more about seeing themselves on screen than about production values. It was charming. It never worked against the movie. These days, though, crappy-looking, poorly lit and edited movies are exactly that.

Sundance News

The first time it mattered, I spent exactly twenty-four hours at the Sundance Film Festival. Todd and I had been once before, with

Superstar and my short *The Way of the Wicked*, respectively, when it was still called the U.S. Film Festival. In 1991, when Sundance became "Sundance," *Poison* was accepted into the competition. We were thrilled, and in January, Todd and I flew into Park City and crashed in the Deer Valley condo that the Sundance people reserved for us.

But as soon as we started to settle, I got an emergency call from my mother. Weeks before, her doctor had diagnosed her with ovarian cancer. At that point, they decided they had a small window of time before they'd operate, just enough time for me to go to Sundance with *Poison*. The timing was terrible but I *had* to. I was barely breaking even those days, and fortunately for me, my mother never questioned my commitment to my new film career. I was lucky that way. Very few of my friends got the support from their families I got from mine.

And as sustaining and encouraging as my mother was with me, she'd become mother to all my friends. We had a big apartment, and people crashed there all the time. I think if you were a young man or woman—particularly if you were gay—she conveyed a real warmth and acceptance. She also had an intellectual capability that a lot of the kids, on the run from asphyxiating middle-class homes elsewhere, saw romantically. She was French, smart, and willing to see anything. And she was not judgmental. Losing her would mean losing a refuge.

Before we even had a chance to get our boots wet in the snow, my mother said to me on the phone, "They say they have to operate tomorrow." Her condition was deteriorating. There was no more time to wait.

So I left Sundance. Two days later, I'm sitting in a hospital room in Mount Sinai, feeling torn between caring for my mother and wishing I were with Todd and *Poison*—feeling particularly awful for even thinking this way—when I get another call. This time it's James Schamus, calling from his hotel in Park City. (Need I remind you that we didn't have cell phones in those days? We relied on pay phones and calling cards or running back to our hotel in the middle of the day.)

He was beside himself. "I just heard a rumor that *Poison* is going to win the Grand Jury Prize. I'm going to go tell Todd."

"You can't tell Todd," I said.

"How can I not?" he asked.

I said, "If you tell him and it doesn't win, it's going to be a huge disappointment. You have to promise to keep your mouth shut."

I knew one thing, even from a distance: *Poison* had real competition. The sense of a burgeoning movement was undeniable. Richard Linklater's *Slacker*, Hal Hartley's *Trust*, and Matty Rich's *Straight Out of Brooklyn* were screening that year. *Slacker* was funny and structurally audacious, and Hal Hartley, whether you liked his movies or not (they always left me cold), was doing things with his films that people hadn't done before. He experimented, almost internally, with how you told a story and how you presented a character. His thing was to have his actors really act devoid of affect. For a while people found that intriguing. In the early nineties, if you asked somebody for the list of their favorite art-house, independent films, Hal Hartley's *The Unbelievable Truth* or *Trust* or *Simple Men* would have been on it. Now people are more likely to list *Shakespeare in Love* or *Frida* or *The English Patient* (and you have to start wondering if a list of "independent films" means anything anymore).

Like Sundance itself, Hal Hartley is a good marker for the larger transition in independent film, mostly because he *hasn't* made the transition. Not only is the line between studio and independent films completely blurred from a financing standpoint, but audiences have lost a certain appetite for filmmaking that is essentially experimental in nature, so that even independent films look, sound, and feel (in form and content) like commercial studio films. They've got their three-act structure, their likable characters, their polish. Hartley resisted the conventions and now seems almost archival.

On the phone, James was hesitant. He didn't think he could *physically* hold off telling Todd the news.

"Just go into your room," I told him, "and shut the door."

And he did. He didn't tell Todd. And we won. After Todd found out, he called me and he was over-the-moon jubilant. And I wanted to say, Exactly. All this from the bedside phone at Mount Sinai Hospital; I was hushed but ecstatic, my mother recuperating three feet away.

Even with a Grand Jury Prize, *Poison* only had distribution in

North America with Zeitgeist. "Going wide" with *Poison* meant six movie theaters. To sell it any further, James and I took it to the Berlin Film Festival, which comes in February, right after Sundance. I'd never tried to sell anything internationally before, but given *Poison*'s heady, experimental style, Berlin—the stomping ground of Fassbinder, Herzog, and Wenders—seemed like a good match.

We stayed in Berlin at the Arco—a prewar building that had been converted into a hotel, conveniently above a brothel. It was a very colorful place, right near the big Kempinski Hotel, where the fancy people stayed. It's gone now, torn down with the rest of the prewar buildings. At the festival, *Poison* garnered serious attention, with all of us fronting for an American gay avant-garde. Well, Todd and James for the most part. The Germans thought I was Schamus's secretary, since it was (and remains) rare to see female producers. They had no category for me.

We ended up with only one foreign distribution deal, to Mainline in England, and the film only played for two weeks there. But it was my first trip to sell a film, a forecast of the dozens of trips to come. The truth is that festivals can be lifelines. James Schamus knows this well. Back in 1993, with just $2,000 in the bank account to keep his company afloat, James and Ted Hope went to Berlin with Ang Lee's film *The Wedding Banquet*. It was an unlikely comedy about a green-card marriage between a gay Chinese American man and a Chinese woman looking to immigrate. They managed to do sales of $3 million on the picture and rescue their fledgling company. (According to *Variety, The Wedding Banquet* grossed $10 million and earned 4,000 percent more than it cost, becoming the most profitable film of 1993.)

As *Poison* was coming together, my life at home was falling apart. In the months after her surgery, my mother became miserable. Sure, she was mobile and living comfortably at home, but she was French and suddenly couldn't enjoy the pleasurable parts of life: eating and drinking and talking for hours.

She did a little bit of traveling that summer of 1991, but the last few months were pretty horrible. Are there any other kind? She died in June, right before she would have required full-time care. She got to see me win my first award and the launch of my film career, but I deeply regret that she hasn't seen everything since. I'd love for her to come to my office and see the thirty posters for the films I produced that line the wall. I know she'd be proud.

When Brian Greenbaum, one of my closest friends and my co-producer on *Poison*, died in February 1992 of AIDS-related complications, I'd come to the end of what I could handle. Brian willed me his apartment. Literally. All the physical stuff of his life packed into his one-bedroom in Chelsea. Cleaning it out was a pain in the ass. I felt like the production manager on the wrap of a set of somebody's life.

People wonder if I have a thick skin about death. By thirty, I'd seen both my parents and countless friends pass away. I wasn't alone. There are thousands of us who were witness to what HIV did, and I'm sure it changed my work. I guess you could say it only pushed me further into my days, to make something of them. I was on the jury for the Santa Monica Film Festival the day that Stanley Kubrick died. Julie Christie was on it with me, along with Larry Gross, the screenwriter of *48 Hrs.*, *Crime and Punishment in Suburbia*, and *Prozac Nation*. When we heard, Larry burst into tears.

Julie Christie looked at him: "What's the big deal? People die."

It's true. They do. Do something with your time.

Enter Reverend Wildmon

"Have you seen the *Washington Post*?" Jeff Hill asked over the phone, practically jumping out of his skin. Jeff was our publicist for *Poison*. He's a big, garrulous bolt of energy, and he's still Killer's publicist. You want someone as talkative as Jeff. Trolling the papers, he'd come across a story in that morning's *Post*—the lead story on page B1—titled, "NEA Plans Response to Latest Attack. Lawmakers Invited to See Film on Prison Life."

It was March 29, 1991, and I had never heard of Reverend Donald Wildmon; I doubt you had either. I was living at home on 119th Street with my mother, who was becoming increasingly weak. *Poi-*

son was about to open and my follow-up, the murder-romance *Swoon*, directed by my friend the artist and ACT UP activist Tom Kalin, was on the verge of production. Needless to say, I was distracted. The *Post* article described how Wildmon, the head of a non-profit called the American Family Association, had letter-bombed Congress the week before about *Poison*. On what basis, he wondered, did the National Endowment for the Arts finance a film that included "explicit porno scenes of homosexuals involved in anal sex"? In response, the chairman of the NEA, John Frohnmayer was calling for a press conference that day.

Wildmon was right about the NEA financing. The year before, we'd applied for $25,000 from the NEA to cover postproduction costs when the rest of our money ran out. We'd sent the NEA some footage, the script, and the grant application stating that the film would depict prison life "as both cruelly harsh and erotic," à la Genet. They'd come through with $25,000 to finish the film.

The NEA was no stranger to controversy. A year before, the endowment had been slapped with a suit by four performance artists—Holly Hughes, Tim Miller, Karen Finley, and John Fleck—who claimed their grant applications had been unconstitutionally denied because they were deemed "indecent" (read gay, lesbian, or in the case of Finley, out there). The case simmered until, six tangled years later, the artists won. But after that story had faded, *Poison* suddenly put the NEA back on the barbecue.

It turned out Wildmon was famous for letter-bombing Congress from his HQ in Tupelo, Mississippi, about whatever blasphemy bugged him that day. He'd once attacked a Mighty Mouse cartoon because, he said, it looked like Mighty was snorting coke. After a 1990 NEA-sponsored exhibit of David Wojnarowicz's *Sex Series* in Normal, Illinois, Wildmon cut and pasted pornographic details from Wojnarowicz images into a newsletter that he sent to church leaders, Christian radio stations, and every person in Congress. His flyer read, "Your Tax Dollars Helped Pay for These 'Works of Art.'" Wojnarowicz sued Wildmon for libel and copyright infringement and, surprisingly, won. (The judgment was for one dollar, but Wojnarowicz framed it.) In Wildmon's eyes, the culture war is still raging. "The American Family Association exists to motivate and equip citizens to change the culture to reflect Biblical truth," he writes on the website. "AFA is for people who are tired of cursing the darkness and who are ready to light a bonfire."

At some point in 1991, Wildmon must have gotten tired of cursing the darkness and picked up a copy of *Variety*, because that's where he read the Sundance review of *Poison* in January. It was a good review, as positive as we could have hoped for, deeming the film "conceptually bold" and a "compelling study of different forms of deviance." (It was published before we won the Grand Jury Prize.) Not surprisingly, it was the last segment of the film that got Wildmon's attention. *Variety* wrote, "'Homo' scrutinizes an obsessive relationship between a hardened criminal and a new arrival in a 1940s French prison. A mood of seething, violent homoeroticism permeates the proceedings, as one prisoner stalks another in an episode spiked with multiple glimpses of rear-entry intercourse and one of genital fondling." Rev. Wildmon stole the language straight from *Variety*.

I knew we had an ally in NEA chair John Frohnmayer. Since *Poison* had won the Grand Jury Prize at Sundance, Sundance head Robert Redford wrote Frohnmayer to personally thank him for the NEA's support of the film. And I knew that a letter from Robert Redford goes a long way. But as the *Washington Post* reported, Frohnmayer's press conference that afternoon got off to a creepy start. It was intended to rebut Wildmon, but it started as an overreaching confession of normalcy. Everybody in this debate over decency in the arts was taking it so personally.

"I grew up in a small town in southern Oregon, played football, sang in the church choir, was loved by my family, and learned what I believe are American values," Frohnmayer began. He went on to make sure to mention that he studied briefly for the ministry, "received a master's degree in Christian ethics," and fought in Vietnam with the U.S. Navy. I started to wonder just what he was doing working for the NEA, since it sounded like he preferred church and combat. But you have to remember: it'd been barely two months since the "liberation" of Kuwait. George Bush was in office. Progessive politics were under fire.

Once his red-blooded bona fides were in order, Frohnmayer went on to make one of his most impassioned defenses of publicly funded art before he was pushed out of office the following year. "We're not here to be censors, we are not here to create a blacklist, we are not here to tell what the subject matter should be," he said. "*Poison* is the work of a serious artist dealing with serious issues in our society. What I think is really objectionable . . . is for people who have not confronted the art to make statements about it, because art must be confronted."

So we took on Wildmon. We got Congress to confront the film. We sent a copy of *Poison* to Washington the following day, and virginal Republican congressional aides were sent over to the NEA to see it and report back. "NEA Screening More Boredom Than Sodom?" read the *Post* the next day. The worst that these aides could come up with was that it was "boring." One senator's wife said the movie made her want to "bathe in Clorox." Another called Todd "the Fellini of fellatio," which I considered a compliment.

But we couldn't just let that be the end of the argument. To win, we knew we needed to give the film a face. With Jeff's PR savvy, we booked Todd onto as many of the talk shows as we could. Wildmon wouldn't face us, but various members of Congress and religious figures would. So in a thin sweater, checkered thrift-store shirt, and jeans, Todd ran the talk show circuit, ably debating Texas Republican congressman Dick Armey on *Larry King Live* and Ralph Reed on *Good Morning America*. The joke was that neither of these two had actually seen the film, which Todd pointed out, so that made the debates comedic. The only person who had actually seen *Poison* and *still* wanted to argue with Todd was Samuel Lipman, the publisher of the art and culture journal *The New Criterion*.

That debate was the most disturbing to all of us because Lipman's point, as he said on television, was that "*Poison* was on the side of death and all great art is on the side of life." Todd had no idea how to respond to that. None of us did. Here was a man in his sixties who was condescendingly telling Todd that his film was on the side of death, as if many of Todd's friends weren't already dying. As if the movie weren't a testament to life.

Ultimately, audiences would decide. They always do. We were opening April 5; Wildmon's timing couldn't have been better. Nancy Gerstman and Emily Russo at Zeitgeist, a small distributor here in

New York with unshakable faith in us and impeccable taste (they released the early Peter Greenaway and Atom Egoyan films) were releasing *Poison.* We couldn't have had better people for the film. We loved and trusted them. And they got us a slot at the Angelika, downtown on Houston Street.

Frankly, I hate the Angelika. I won't see movies there. The seats are uncomfortable, the sound is crummy, you can hear the 4/5/6 train rumbling underneath you, and the film projectors are terrible. (Don't even get me started on how the Technicolor *Far from Heaven* looked on their screens. I couldn't watch.) But it's the kind of movie theater that other movie theaters play close attention to because it triggers tsunamis of word of mouth. The people who see movies at the Angelika like to *talk* about the movies they've seen at the Angelika. I remember when *The Crying Game* opened there in November of 1992, they had to put signs up telling people "Do Not Talk about the Movie" as people walked out, so as not to ruin the twist for all the hordes queued up outside. In the late 1980s and early 1990s, the Angelika was like a Grauman's Chinese Theatre of independent film—back when Grauman's actually meant something and wasn't just a placeholder between the David Hasselhoff beach towels and star maps on Hollywood Boulevard. Playing at the Angelika meant you had the best shot at entering the conversation. It was as close to the red carpet as you could get.

Poison stunned all of us. All that talk of rear-entry intercourse and genital fondling got people's attention. If conservatives hated it for the explicitness, the gay community's biggest beef was that there wasn't *enough* sex in it. But *Poison*'s returns weren't just impressive. They were unprecedented. The film did insane business. In movie accounting, you don't want to just look at gross box office numbers. A more revealing number is the per-screen average, since that tells you just how crowded the theaters are. Huge studio films can generate big grosses just by dumping their films on three thousand screens. Studios make money hand over fist by making their film impossible to *avoid.* Take a blockbuster: *The Matrix Reloaded* played on 3,600 screens its opening weekend, about as many as exhibitors will let you be on, and made an average of $33,000 per screen. After that, the per-screen averages dropped quickly, since word got out that the movie wasn't that hot. When *The Hulk* opened on 3,660 screens, it made a $22,335 per-screen average, and that number dropped 67 percent the next week to $7,360. Universal knew they had problems. By comparison, independent films are lucky if they hit 500 theaters, and you've got a huge hit if your film makes it to 1,000, as *Napoleon Dynamite* did, for just two weeks in a thirty-five-week run. With smaller-budget films, it's less a question of opening numbers and more about *legs*—seeing the per-screen average numbers stay steady or, better, *rise* over time.

In just one theater in New York, with no advertising budget to speak of, *Poison* earned just under $25,000 in three days—almost exactly the amount the NEA had given us—inching up past $41,000 for the week. It was a record that wouldn't get broken at the Angelika until the end of the decade, when a different kind of "independent film," made dirt cheap, outside the system, but politically brainless, cleared an average of $111,000 on each screen it played on. I still haven't seen *The Blair Witch Project*.

Spotlight: Tom Kalin

DIRECTOR *(SWOON)*

Developing *Swoon*

I came to New York in '87 as an installation artist with the Whitney Museum Independent Study Program. But that summer was when ACT UP started. And part of ACT UP was going to do a window installation called "Let the Record Show" at the New Museum, with photographic cutouts of people in the Reagan administration with their blatantly homophobic or racist quotes about HIV cut into slabs of concrete. I got involved pretty quickly, and from that group, I met Todd Haynes and Christine.

Todd encouraged me to submit a proposal to Apparatus, since I had started making experimental video art. I didn't. But I had taken on a job as a grant writer and had managed to raise $100,000 to make a film that I had been calling *Intolerance*, after D. W. Griffith's movie. It was a ridiculous epic idea about cultural resistance to homosexuality or whatever. And it was going to have three different sections of historical narrative—one about Teddy Roosevelt's using military men to entrap homosexuals, one about an explosion on a battleship that got blamed on a homosexual, and finally one about the Leopold and Loeb murder, where two men (who were lovers) murdered a boy. I'd grown up in Chicago, and my father worked in the prison system, specifically in the state penitentiary where Leopold and Loeb had been held after their trial. I wrote the script with Hilton Als, who now writes for the *New Yorker,* and he helped me pare it down to just the one story about Leopold and Loeb. Long development can be very good for a script.

So I had $100,000. I'd also gotten the American Film Institute Award and $25,000 from the NEA. I got pretty much every grant you could get at the time, in 1990. So I went to Christine with the script and the money and said, "Will you help me with your Rolodex?" And she said, "What if I produced the movie?"

We shot for ten days at first in the summer of 1990. We didn't have enough money to get through everything we needed to, so we had to stop about midway. And then I just edited for eight months. I think if I hadn't had those eight months, the movie would not have worked as well as it did. It gave me the time to figure out what I had and what I needed—where the gaps were. For example, I'd shot the murder of the boy in a very stylized, abstract way against a back-drop. Just a hand smashing down or over the kid's mouth. But when I saw it, the scene was just absurd and way too melodramatic. (When the movie came out, and I'd gotten enough positive reviews and could read the bad ones, I read Paul Rudnick's column in *Premiere* where he said *Swoon* was "a 90-minute Obsession ad. It's like reading a coffee-table book but not even as interesting." That murder scene, shot in my original way, would have just added more fuel to that fire.)

So I raised a bit more money through grants, and then we went back and shot for four more days. We redid the murder, shooting it from the car where they killed him. It was much more brutal.

Swoon went to Sundance in 1992, and I remember the awards ceremony was hosted by Alberto Garcia, who had hair to the middle of his back and wore a T-shirt during the ceremony. He said things like, "And uhm, I want to give . . . uhm, the award to . . ." Alexandre

Rockwell's *In the Soup* took top prize, beating out Tarantino's *Reservoir Dogs* and Allison Anders's *Gas, Food, Lodging*. I soon felt like I was watching through a window as this whole industry changed. By 1994, cell phones were swarming, and by 1996, the festival had transformed. You can tell by the numbers. The presale of *Swoon*, to Fine Line for distribution was a teeny, not-even-six-figure advance. It didn't even cover the budget. You could expect that an odd, indie movie might presell for $50,000. A year later, I got a call from a director whose film, just as off-kilter and dark as *Swoon*, presold to Fine Line for $125,000. And *Go Fish*, the movie I executive-produced with Christine, went for $400,000 two years later.

A Split Decision at Sundance

In 1993 Sundance asked me to come back as a judge on their jury. It felt like an enormous honor, a real marker of the fact that I'd arrived. I guess having enemies gets you noticed by the right people. I'd made two films that had played at Sundance, along with a handful of shorts. Suddenly I was jury material?

But that year, we broke the most basic rule of the gig: to pick a winner. That we couldn't agree tells you something about how the world of independent American films was splitting down the middle between quirky, regional films and more polished, commercial ventures, and how that fissure split audiences.

That year Sundance had four judges in the dramatic competition (and another four in documentaries): my fellow judges were Dave Kehr, the *New York Times* critic; Percy Adlon, who directed *Salmonberries*, with k.d. Lang, and *Bagdad Café;* and Charles Lane, the black filmmaker who did *Sidewalk Stories* and *True Identity*. That was the only year Sundance had four judges because, as it turned out, four was too divisive.

Now, as a judge of a film festival that prestigious, you're basically cordoned off. You are given passes that automatically open doors wherever you go. You're put up for the entire time. If you want to get treated like royalty, you have to go to Europe, to the A-list festivals like Berlin, Cannes, and Venice. They know how to treat their judges. (The B-list festivals are Locarno, San Sebastian, and Rotterdam, but they're really A-list because they're still spectacularly lush. Toronto is in a class by itself because there are no judges. It's a noncompetitive festival.)

Sundance is good, but Sundance is work. Your job is to see everything—seventeen movies in ten days. It's *agonizing* because a lot of the films at any given film festival aren't great. In 1993 there were bright spots, like Robert Rodriguez's *El Mariachi* and Leslie Harris's *Just Another Girl on the I.R.T.* X-Men director Bryan Singer's first film, *Public Access*—about a visitor to a small town who starts telling everybody's secrets over his public access show— screened that year. But mostly what Sundance is is *An Ambush of Ghosts* and *Fly by Night*—extremely personal movies that I couldn't tell you a thing about—and movies like *Boxing Helena* and Rob Weiss's *Amongst Friends* that everybody talks about for a year and then tries to forget. Movies that get a lot of buzz but were flops. The year I juried was the first Sundance where people started to say there's gold in them thar hills. It stopped being a celebration of regional filmmaking and turned into a feeding ground—a place to find the new stars, new acquisitions.

As jurors, we had one discussion at the midway point and another at the end. The problem was we split down the middle. There were members of the jury (out of respect for the process, I won't reveal names) who felt strongly that *Ruby in Paradise*, Victor Nuñez's very intimate regional film, should win the Grand Jury Prize. Nuñez had been working in film for years, making South Florida domestic epics about widowed women, landfills, and Ashley Judd in her first feature film role on a voyage of self-discovery. It took him six years to make a single film. In many ways, Nuñez deserved to win. There were others who thought *Public Access* was better: deeply flawed, completely unbuzzed about, but radiating an undeniable energy. You knew watching it that this was a young, fresh, new filmmaker with talent. Everyone looks for something different in their art, and having to decide between such different but equally deserving films proved impossible.

So we gave *two* Grand Jury Prizes.

That was the last time that happened at Sundance.

The Girls Are Out There

I had twelve minutes. Just twelve minutes of a very rough experiment called *Ely and Max*. It was a real garage production made by two twenty-eight-year-old gals in Chicago named Rose Troche and Guinevere Turner. They sent it to me blind. They'd seen Tom Kalin's *Swoon*, and he'd become a little celebrity in the film community in Chicago, where he was from. And Rose, who had an experimental film background, had fallen for *Poison* after seeing it play at a Human Rights Center benefit at the Music Box Theatre.

The movie was a mix of documentary, overreaching art film, and dramatic narrative about, as Rose called it, "what it's like trying to meet cute girls in Chicago." Rose and Guin, who were girlfriends at the time, burned through their life savings of $15,000, getting twelve minutes down. They cast it with friends, women they knew, and even one waitress they thought was hot, paid them nothing, and borrowed their apartments for locations. They shot it on a 16mm camera "borrowed" from the University of Illinois and shot everything night for night, after hours. They edited the film on a VHS assembly deck, equivalent to a crappy home four-track.

Then they got desperate and poor. Rose would go to delis and steal cans of soup. Fortunately, she came across an article by B. Ruby Rich in *Sight and Sound* called "New Queer Cinema," which featured black-and-white photos of Tom Kalin and Todd Haynes. She went through and highlighted all the production companies: Good Machine, Christine Vachon, etc. Ballsy, she called James and Ted at Good Machine first. Would they look at her film and consider helping finish it? They told her, "We don't really do that." So she called me and was amazed that I answered the phone.

"I have this film that I've been working on," Rose said. She was nervous.

"Just send me the script and a tape," I told her. At the time, all my work came through friends or the transom. It was a quick call. Rose seemed relieved to get off the phone. Days later, I got her package. Tom Kalin, my producing partner at the time, and I watched it. The dialogue was sharp and funny but the quality was pretty underwhelming. It would need serious work and, most of all, some guidance and support. I called Rose back. "OK, this is something we want to be involved with." She was thrilled. She told me later that she and Guin celebrated that night. They were like, "Christine Vachon is doing our film!" Little did they know that I didn't have any money either.

What I really had to do was to help them finish it without making it look too polished. That was part of Rose and Guin's movie's charm: its homemadeness. A lot of what made the film work was naïveté—all those spinning tops and tapping feet as segues. Not doing it the way it's been done. These days, I'm not sure I could step aside as easily as I did. And that footage never changed. If the movie had been too full of itself, you would have said, "Excuse me, your acting's bad and you're in black and white!" But as long as it had that sweetness to it, it was genuine. You started watching it and all that carping went out of your head.

I took it to every distributor I knew, trying to drum up the remaining funds, which we had calculated to be $53,000 for more shooting and editing. I showed it to Mark Tusk at Miramax, then their main acquisitions guy. I showed it to Jeff Lipsky at October. I showed it to New Line. And everyone told me, "I don't get what you like about this." At least Jeff Lipsky said, "If you are really talking about a movie that's the 'fun' lesbian movie that happens *after* everybody's come out, I want it." Which it was. But he didn't see it in the footage. I pounded the pavement for money and, for the first time in my career, I failed to find the money. It was a lesson I'd have to keep learning, and a good one to pick up early.

Skinny with heavy glasses, John Pierson looked like an elongated geek. Pierson programmed the Film Forum (and did the letters on marquees at movie theaters; he even announced his own wedding on one). Eventually he graduated to working for a German film distributor at the height of New German Cinema in the mid-1970s, when companies were actually fighting over Wim Wenders's *Kings of the Road* and Fassbinder. (One of his early career high points: driving Wenders across country on a college tour.) Pierson went on to work on one of the early independent film festivals, called American Mavericks, run out of a former Yiddish theater in the East Village. Pierson gradually came to know all the distributors of the small, quirky films that played there. By the mid-1980s, Pierson created Islet, a company designed to provide "finishing" or completion funds for small films and to help sell them to distribution companies for a fee. When directors and their producers ran out of options—people like Spike Lee, Richard Linklater, and Michael Moore—they called Pierson. Christened a "producer's rep," Pierson knew every possible door to open. At the beginning of the American independent wave, he had his fingers in *Parting Glances, She's Gotta Have It, Clerks, Slacker,* and *Roger and Me.*

With *Ely and Max* dangling in limbo, I called Pierson to see if he'd be interested in taking a look. He was heading into Chicago for the Independent Filmmakers Project (IFP) in Chicago and agreed to meet with Rose and Guinevere at his hotel. They showed up with the tape, and he put it on the VCR in his room. He lay down on his stomach, in his stocking feet, and watched the twelve minutes. We'd taken out the documentary elements, just left the dramatic scenes along with the tapping feet and the spinning top sequences. What we had in our favor was the track record of *Claire of the Moon,* a drama about a woman at a writers' retreat who has her first lesbian romance. Made on a shoestring, it had brought in almost $700,000. The movie had targeted a neglected audience; lesbians had flocked to it. Rose and Guin thought, "Is a straight guy going to get this extremely gay film? Can you laugh lying on your stomach?" At least he seemed to enjoy it.

"How much do you want?" Pierson asked.

"We need fifty-three thousand," they said.

"This title won't work. *Ely and Max?* No two-name titles."

Rose and Guin thought, Fuck you. It's a great title.

I heard from Pierson right after they left: yes. He'd pony up the money for his fee, paid when the film sold to a distributor. I called the filmmakers and they were thrilled. Having made two more films and episodes of *The L Word* for Showtime, Rose tells me that the response she got from Pierson is still the fastest that she's ever heard back from anyone, ever.

Pierson didn't give a lot of notes or edits, but he still hated the title. Rose and Guin now had the money to finish the shoot and edit it. They went out to a bar in Chicago, drank three beers apiece, and came up with some new names: *Watch That Girl, Leave It to Beaver, The Girl Is Out There* (which became the tagline), and finally *Go Fish*. This was the title. They loved its three references: the children's game to make pairs, the idea of fishing in a pond, and the naughty one I think you can imagine. The movie still dragged in places, but Tom Kalin helped them come up with a workable cut.

Then Pierson set up a screening for Geoff Gilmore, the programmer at the Sundance Film Festival, at the Sony Screening Room at Forty-ninth and Broadway. *Go Fish* got invited to the competition. Great news. Pierson, as I came to learn, had high expectations. He wanted to sell the film to a distributor *during* Sundance, unprecedented in 1994. In those days, there were no bidding wars, no negotiations over pizza and ribs, no contracts on napkins. You screened your film, hoped for some recognition and bites of interest you could follow up on. (*Poison* and *Swoon* were in the privileged positions of already having a distributor, Zeitgeist and Fine Line, by the time they went.) Acquisitions had always been a gentleman's business, slow and diplomatic with low stakes. Pierson was partly responsible for changing all that.

Pierson managed to whip the distributors up into a frenzy around *Go Fish* by not prescreening it before Sundance; he had one more stipulation: that they had to attend the Friday night show at the Egyptian Theater in Park City and have a deal ready. He'd hyped it as a "lesbian's *She's Gotta Have It*." It was a bold maneuver, since it meant *Go Fish* needed to get snapped up quickly or it might not get bought at all. That night Miramax, Sony Pictures Classics, and Fine Line all proved interested, but Pierson ended up selling the film to Tom Rothman of the Samuel Goldwyn company at a pizzeria for $400,000. (His book includes the deal memo, without the dinner stains.) By using Gay Pride month and the San Francisco Gay and

Lesbian Film Festival as the launching points, *Go Fish* made $800,000 in its first weekend wide on fifty-nine screens. It ended up making $3 million theatrically that summer, more than Tarantino's *Reservoir Dogs* did on its first release. Our intuition about *Go Fish's* potential audience had been right on. The bull's-eye worked. As Pierson quotes Tom Rothman, "There are lesbians everywhere."

What ended up trickling down to the filmmakers was not enormous. The $400,000 Rose and Guinevere got for their movie was split countless ways—to pay Pierson's fee, to cover outstanding debts, to deliver the film to Goldwyn. Rose still jokes that she had to beg for each $1,000. I don't think any of us were prepared for the costs of more shoots, reediting the film, music clearance issues. I wasn't experienced enough to even judge the budgets that Rose submitted, to tell whether they were on target. Suffice it to say, we went way past that $53,000 finishing *Go Fish*. In the end, Guin and Rose split a five-figure modest sum. They moved to New York, where they *really* couldn't afford their apartments. Rose went to work at the Strand bookstore.

Certainly, that money was more than Rose and Guinevere had before *Go Fish*, their long shot that miraculously paid off. I don't begrudge Pierson or his fee. He met filmmakers when they were heavily in debt on their credit cards and desperate to get their movies finished and seen. His premiums were percentages off a pipe dream, paid only when it came true, and the fact that he had a run of great successes (including selling *Roger and Me* for $3 million to Warner Bros.) is a reason to think he was worth it. How could you turn his "finishing" money down? Rose, Guinevere, Tom, and I had nowhere else to turn.

You try to make the process reward you, but money costs money. You're always trying to figure out a situation where getting your movie sold will cost you a little bit less. If people give you $50,000 for your movie, getting $50,000 back isn't enough for them. They've taken a risk, and they want to be compensated for that risk. It's a price I pay every day. Even Pierson burned out. He closed Islet and checked out of film producing. He ran a movie theater in Fiji for a while, and now he's in Austin teaching film to would-be producers.

For the most part, talent gets paid with a second chance. Rose went on to make *Bedrooms and Hallways* and *The Safety of Objects* and is one of the creative forces behind *The L Word.* Guin, who cowrote *American Psycho* and *The Notorious Bettie Page,* has a real acting career. The both of them have plans to make a *Go Fish* reunion movie called *Go Fuck Yourself.*

FEBRUARY 2004

Producer's Diary, II

9:30 A.M. I've got to find out who has the rights to *Avenue Q,* a terrifically bent musical about gay Muppets with real problems. I saw it last night and noticed James Schamus from Focus there *alone.* When an executive sees something by himself, it means his juniors have already seen it and he's scouting to option it. Why was Killer so late to this?

We weren't. Jocelyn Hayes, Killer's elegant development executive, heard about the show long before the reviews flooded in. She knows the buzz on everything and everybody, which is why we hired her. A few years into the gig, she's brought a flood of new writers (like playwright Keith Bunin) and projects (like a Pee Wee Herman biopic) into the company. She informs me that she *did* tell me weeks ago about *Avenue Q*—how does she seem to know everything, always, weeks ago?—but that I didn't listen.

"Look, Jocelyn," I told her, "if you wanted me to notice, you needed to come in here in a Muppet suit." I dispatch her to suss out the rights.

11:15 A.M. In today's *Variety,* there's a story that the Motion Picture Association of America (MPAA) has decided to ban "screeners" of films. It figures. The first year I'm a voting Academy member, and they want to take away my favorite thing about membership.

For the past twelve years, at Christmas time, distributors have blanketed all the members of the Academy with free copies ("screeners") of the films in contention for Oscars. It's a convenient way for people to see the movies they're voting on, since the last two months of the year have turned into an avalanche. In 1989 thirty-seven movies were released in November and December. Last year eighty-two films came out during the same period.

Free DVDs and videos are the only practical answer. But Jack Valenti, the president of the MPAA, now says that the film industry loses $3.5 billion each year in piracy. Of sixty-eight titles sent out last year, he says, thirty-four were digitally pirated, which says something about the percentage of studio movies that are not absolute crap and people want to copy. Valenti thinks that by banning screeners, he can stymie piracy at the source.

But there's far more at risk culturally and artistically than profits if this ban goes through. Come Oscar time, screeners are the only way many of Killer's films get noticed at all. For independent films with modest, and short, theatrical distribution, screeners have become a necessary avenue for getting our movies seen by the Academy voters. We're in the game largely *because* of screeners. There are plenty of places where Academy members live that Killer films don't get to. In a way, the ban is elitist. It's saying, "If you don't live in New York or L.A., too bad for you." It'll significantly curtail our production possibilities. If independents are pushed out of the serious Oscar race, there will be no way for places like Killer to attract talent to work on our films because there'll be no chance for an award—the big carrot at the end of a very long stick. If the MPAA took that away from us, they'd be taking away any hope that riskier independent films will get made. It would be devastating.

Ted Hope calls from the Baltimore set of *A Dirty Shame*, the John Waters movie we're producing together. He worked as a political organizer as a kid. He's *loving this*, mostly because, as a producer on a movie that's going smoothly, he doesn't have much to do. He wants to know whom we can round up to come out against the screener ban. We flip our Rolodexes, corralling folks. Before the day is through, we'll have Altman, Steve Buscemi, Selma Blair, Hilary Swank, Chloë Sevigny, John Waters, and Tracey Ullman signed on.

11 A.M. Wigs, our accountant, has some bad news on the Where-did-our-money-go? front vis-à-vis *One Hour Photo*. We finally got the profit reports from Fox Searchlight, and he's spent the last few weeks poring over them. But he can't find any holes. Killer isn't owed any money. I'm disappointed, but there's nothing else we can do. We've got to move on.

11:15 A.M. Pam is on the phone with an executive at HBO, talking about figures for *Mrs. Harris*. They've got our most recent budget, but they've been dragging their feet about green-lighting it. Then the executive lets slip, "Well, on a film like this, budgeted at twelve million . . . " Pam's eyebrows go up. It's the first time we've heard an approved number, that we've got the OK. When Pam hangs up, she announces to the office, "It's happening."

This is it. This is the peak experience for producers. Your film is going to get made. But you've already spent months, years even, talking and behaving and believing that the project you've got is just about to start production. You live with this imaginary urgency to make people make decisions. Then when the decision finally gets made, it never feels like an accomplishment. It slips out. *It's happening.*

11:30 A.M. Michael Cunningham wrote the novel. That we know. But the question is, Who wrote the film *A Home at the End of the World*?

The director Michael Mayer has been friends with Michael Cunningham from back when Cunningham was a bartender having trouble getting anything published and Mayer was a young theater director. In 1999 Cunningham won the Pulitzer for *The Hours*. and his problems went away. Right after, knowing that Scott Rudin had optioned *The Hours* for the screen, the producer (and former actor) Tom Hulce optioned Michael's second book, *A Home at the End of the World*, for his friend Michael Mayer. Tom came to us to produce it with him, and we hired a talented, twenty-six-year-old playwright named Keith Bunin to adapt it. Rudin paid David Hare six figures to adapt *The Hours*. Keith wasn't even a member of the Writers Guild, so his fee was negotiable. We paid him a low five figures for the adapted screenplay draft, including one rewrite, and gave him a bonus payable when the film went into production.

A Home at the End of the World is not an obvious choice for a movie, since it functions as four connected novellas about the same characters. On top of that, film is not theater. In theater, the writer is king. A director cannot change a playwright's words without permission. This relationship is reversed in film: the writer works in service of everyone else (actors, directors, producers, studios). But here, Michael Mayer had directed Keith's plays before, and now Keith was writing for him. Their roles were reversed. This took some getting used to.

By July 1999, Keith produced his first draft. He'd figured a way to compress the plot, find a protagonist, and effectively structure a film. But the characters had lost some depth. He turned over a second draft in November 1999. I think it usually takes three drafts for a script to get there. The first draft of a screenplay has energy. The second draft, by trying to fix all the problems of the first draft, tends to be a muddle. The third draft corrects the overcorrection and hopefully improves what works in the first place.

When Tom Hulce read Keith's second-draft version, he thought it had moved too far from the book. Michael agreed. The strength of having a single protagonist also diminished the poignancy of the love triangle. On top of that, Michael Cunningham wanted to take a crack at it himself. So on May 15, 2000, Michael submitted his own first draft, which was about a hundred pages too long, not entirely in screenplay format, and very faithful to his own source material. As he said, "Some movies just need to be three hours." By July we had a second draft from Michael, which was much shorter but not quite there yet either.

At this point, Michael Mayer, the director, stepped in. Having directed *Side Man* and *Thoroughly Modern Millie* on Broadway, Mayer pushed for a much more emotional and intimate script. By July 30 he did an "amalgam" of the two versions. In a giant cut-and-paste, he took the Cunningham script and fed in the Bunin. (At one point, one of the interns erased the whole thing, but that's another story.)

But now the script was laden with long paragraphs of description that Michael Mayer had written. We did a reading of the script at the Chelsea Studio. Typically these readings, with a volunteer cast, are held so that the filmmaker and writer can hear the words spoken out loud. Billy Crudup read Bobby, the lonely, searching drifter, and he was remarkable. We cast him from that moment as our ideal Bobby. (Unfortunately he didn't agree and passed.) Patti Clarkson read for Alice, the mother, and Kyra Sedgwick read for Claire, the female lead.

As good as the reading was, Brad Simpson still thought the script dragged. I trust Brad's notes. A tall, brainy East Villager and Brown grad, Brad first came into Killer's orbit when, as a teenager, he wrote

Todd Haynes a gushing fan letter about *Superstar.* (Todd rediscovered it years later when he moved to Portland, much to Brad's intense embarrassment.) Brad started at Killer as an intern and graduated to associate producer and co-producer, along with Katie Roumel and Jocelyn Hayes. All three work closely with Pam and myself. From his years of semiotics at Brown, coupled with a keen story sense, Brad has a gift for breaking down a script, seeing where it needs to grow. He was our proto "head of development" before Killer really had secured the money to hire writers and pay for rewrites.

Brad argued that *Home*'s first thirty-five pages were set in Bobby's childhood, and you can't meet your full-grown leads forty minutes into a movie. So Keith came back and did a polish in June 2001 to resolve the structure questions. Michael Mayer wanted to kick-start the film by introducing the leads—living in bohemian New York—right off the top and flashing back and forward. He called it "the *The Way We Were* version." It didn't work. Michael Cunningham came back in and he and Michael Mayer condensed the early childhood material and tightened the middle. The script went through at least twenty revisions before we got to a script we could shoot. Just for the record, *Boys Don't Cry* went through a similar trek.

But now that *Home* is getting edited—and we need to deliver it to Warner Bros.—we've got to settle the screen credit issue. Michael Cunningham, obviously, wants credit. It's his book, and he wrote half of what you'll see on screen. But the other half belongs to Keith Bunin, who found the structure to hang it all on. According to the Writers Guild, any writer who contributes more than 50 percent of the script to an adaptation deserves screen credit. If Michael disputes the credit, we'll have to go through the script and ID just where every bit of plot and dialogue came from. To keep it simple, what we've got right now is "Screenplay by Michael Cunningham," and Keith may have to have his heart broken. Unless he fights it too.

But Keith makes things easy for us. Turns out he's doesn't want his name on the movie—even though it would help his career, even though it would raise his rate as a screenwriter and reflect a little bit of fame his way. After he's watched a preview, he tells us, "For my first screen credit, I don't feel like it's mine." *Whew.* We'll keep him busy. He's already turned in his newest draft of *The Extra Man*, from Jonathan Ames's novel. It's really good. Just one more draft and I think we'll be there.

12 NOON We've been developing *The Notorious Bettie Page* for seven years, making it a contender for longest film development at Killer (along with *Boys Don't Cry* and *Savage Grace*). It's been derailed several times—once by director Mary Harron's first child, once by Mary's second child, and once by *American Psycho*.

A few months back, Mary found, in her mind, the perfect Bettie: Gretchen Mol. It looked like HBO was eager to finance the film at $6 million, but they had some doubts about Gretchen. HBO went so far as to allow us to do a big casting search to see if there was anyone else out there, besides Gretchen, to play Bettie. But we finally came to an impasse: HBO's confidence in Gretchen just wasn't as high as Mary's. And Mary made it clear that *her* Bettie Page movie was going to star Gretchen. Our movie that was about to be green-lit was set back to flashing yellow.

So we did what we always do: we smashed the budget down to $3 million. Then we went out and secured half the money from the foreign sales company Fortissimo, whom we've worked with a lot. We landed the other half from the Independent Film Channel. Jonathan Sehring, the head of IFC, was really excited about the project, had no problem with black and white, and was enthusiastic about Gretchen.

Both Pam and I felt a distinct uneasiness about making this film for half our budget. The cut would mean serious compromises. But if that was what we had to work with, to make the movie Mary wanted to make, so be it.

Just as we are about to finalize terms, HBO calls today. They've been thinking and thinking about it, and they realize they've made a mistake. They want to do it at $6 million with Gretchen after all. We haven't signed any contracts, so I've got to call Fortissimo and IFC and let them know. I suspect Fortissimo will be fine: $1.5 million was a lot for them. They're probably thinking, *Whew*. But Jonathan at IFC will be pissed. I feel bad. I'll tell him the truth: making *Bettie Page* at $6 million is better for the movie. That's what's important.

I call Jonathan, and he *is* furious. "This isn't cool," he says. "I thought we had a deal." But at the end of the day, I have to do what's best for the movie.

1 P.M. You can't offer the same part to two actors at the same time. But you can definitely stir the pot. We're out to Sean Penn for the role of Truman Capote in *Infamous*. His agent says he's interested but his schedule might not be workable. He's getting the best reviews of his life for *Mystic River* and, like any actor, he wants to do a big movie next to boost his quote. Hence, some action film called *The Interpreter* is giving us headaches. It hasn't started shooting yet, but Sean is committed, so it's just pushing off the potential start date of the Capote project further and further. This is mission creep.

Doug McGrath, the writer/director behind *Infamous*, knows Jude Law's English agent. We sent her a copy of the script last year; since Sean had never explicitly said yes, we thought it would be all right. At the time, Jude was too busy to even think about playing Capote. But now his schedule is opening up and he's reading projects again. The agent likes Doug, likes the script, and this is a huge asset. Every star is different: some actors read everything that gets sent their way; others let their agents and management decide for them. Often, the response is different at different periods in an actor's career. The young starlet turning down roles right and left will probably end up taking every one she can get by the time she's fifty. We've heard that Jude has a long relationship with his English agent, so it feels like the best way to get to him.

We got word that Jude's in town to shoot some final scenes for the bad-boy romantic comedy *Alfie*, and that his agent was willing to meet Doug and get a sense about whether *Infamous* is something Jude would want to do next. Doug did the meeting, and the agent passed the script upward.

The result? We get the call. "Jude passes." You could spend your life trying to secure a star to a project.

2:30 P.M. Jocelyn finds out the story on *Avenue Q:* the creators have sold the rights to television. So we're out of that picture. Another chase that leads to nothing. At least we can tie up a loose end.

3 P.M.   I want the rights to adapt Brad Land's memoir *Goat*, a terrifically written, scary little book. In it Land tells the story of joining a fraternity; during the hazing, a repressed memory begins to surface of an attack on him and his brutal abduction by a pair of fraternity brothers years before. I see it as a guy's *Lovely Bones*, about the way that violence threads through male culture. Now twenty-seven, Land just got profiled in *Entertainment Weekly* and is getting a ton of attention. Other producers and companies are bidding for the book.

It's going to come down to Land himself: he'll choose the people he wants to adapt it. I know that if I can get him on the phone, he'll understand why his book should go to me. So I convince Land's agent to give me his number, somewhere in small-town South Carolina. When I get him on the phone and explain who I am (he's actually heard of Killer!), he says in this great southern drawl, "Well, I'm just tickled to hear from you."

I know Killer will be outbid if it comes down to money. Our discretionary fund is barely enough to keep us in the game. Warner Bros. itself could have decided to option the book (and attach us to develop it), but they passed on it. Really, I don't need Warner Bros. I have a feeling that Land will care more about being involved, about the project's keeping its integrity. That's what Killer can offer. "Look, I know it must be tempting to hear certain numbers from studios, and if all you want is the money, go for that," I tell him. "But let me send you some DVDs of our movies so that you can see what we do."

He's a sweetheart on the phone. He'll watch the DVDs and I'll follow up. I ask him who he thinks would make the best adapter for the book. "David Gordon Green," he says, naming the young North Carolinian filmmaker behind *George Washington* and *Undertow*. So Brad's no bumpkin: if he knows David Gordon Green, he knows movies. I have a good feeling about this. (A week later, we hear the news: the rights are ours.)

4 P.M.   There's a report on AOL that Colin Farrell ran up a bill of $64,000 for a fourteen-day hotel stay while shooting *Alexander*. When he ran up a bill of $4,000 during the *Home* shoot, he happily paid for it.

Chapter 3
Unreleasable

A new level of amateur—Financing <u>Kids</u>—Firing your star,
babysitting your cast—A partner comes on board—The two
Brandon Teena stories — "Brandon wouldn't do that"—
Debating the MPAA

LESSON: TALENT CAN COME FROM ANYWHERE.

Justin Pierce was found hanging in a room at the Bellagio in Las Vegas. I heard about it during the *Hedwig* production in Toronto, July 2000, and even though I wasn't exactly surprised, it was really sad news. Everybody who knew Justin knew he seriously struggled with drugs and alcohol. And that he had no safety net. I remember that on the next to last day of the *Kids* shoot, I had to find a lawyer to bail him out of jail for gay bashing, of all things. He had so much energy but never quite figured out what to do with it.

When Larry Clark cast him in *Kids*, Justin was just another smart-mouth eighteen-year-old skateboarder in Washington Square Park. At the time, he was squatting in the basement of a building he called the Dungeon up on 176th Street. Justin had grown up in the Bronx. But when his parents divorced, he dropped out of school and spent his days on his own in the park, boosting beer. We paid him scale to star in *Kids*, about a hundred dollars a day, and it was still more money than he'd ever seen. No doubt, the movie changed the scale of Justin's life, the scale of what he thought was possible. That movie transformed Justin from a delinquent to an actor, gave him a future and a reason to get written about. Many of the unknown kids in *Kids*—like Rosario Dawson and Chloë Sevigny and Leo Fitzgerald—have gone on to big careers, and Justin was on his way too. He understood direction; he tried things different ways. He scored an Independent Spirit Award for *Kids*, his first performance ever.

For a while, I saw Justin around New York, and he was never anything but polite. I saw him at the premiere of *Total Eclipse*, Agnieszka Holland's movie about Rimbaud and Verlaine. This was before Leonardo DiCaprio was a big star. Justin and the rest of the *Kids* kids showed up at the after-party at the National Arts Club on Gramercy Park, presumably guests of DiCaprio's. It was quite a sight to see them with their skateboards and low-hanging jeans in a private club with gilded portraits on the wall.

But he was a lost soul. After *Kids*, he moved to L.A. and landed roles in films like *BlackMale* and *Next Friday*, though *Kids* was clearly a high point. If you want to make provocative films, you have to deal with provocative people. But how far is too far? Larry Clark broke every rule I knew about film production, like hiring street kids like Justin as leads or asking the female star to take off her shirt during rehearsals. It made for a dangerous atmosphere, not one I think I'd necessarily like to repeat. But I'm thankful to Larry for showing me that you could rethink practically every element of filmmaking and do it your own way. The result was rich and bold.

At this point in my career, I'd started to branch out. With *Kids*, for the first time, I was making a movie for somebody who was seeing me as a producer not a friend. The professional demands on me forced me to really examine what the job was. When you're committed to artistic filmmaking, you've got to behave, in some ways, like an artist. You have to continually challenge assumptions: about what works, what risks are worth taking, how movies reach people, what stories are appropriate to tell.

Kids was, without a doubt, one of the most difficult productions I've ever gone through. I'd worked with first-timers before, but the kids of *Kids* took the challenge to an entirely new level. Trying to make dozens of authentic (and authentically irritating) New York teenagers show up on set and stay put—teenagers who were going through their question-authority period—was hard, especially when our director defended and conspired with his cast. For a few weeks that summer, *Kids* felt barely on the brink of control.

When we finished the movie, we were told it was "unreleasable." It's never good news to hear that your distributor wants to dump your movie, that the MPAA thinks your film is reprehensible. On the other hand, it's vital to keep testing the boundaries of "acceptable" stories, since who's deciding anyway? The most dangerous movies Killer has made are the ones that reflected the real world back with the least amount of artifice: *Kids, Happiness, Boys Don't Cry.* I wouldn't call these films "realistic"; nothing on screen is. What they are, are stories without clear heroes or redemptive "arcs." People may or may not get what's coming to them, and those plots spook an industry premised on wish fulfillment and getting the girl. Our movies divide the room in a business where audiences are supposed to *agree.*

The HIV Hook

When I had my first meeting with Larry Clark, he was a long-haired photographer and former heroin addict. He'd done time in a penitentiary. (In 2003 he punched the British distributor of his film *Ken Park* during a "political argument," so I guess he's still working some stuff through his system.) He became famous through his two semi-autobiographical photographic collections—*Tulsa,* about junkies in rural Oklahoma, and *Teenage Lust,* about the randy life of high schoolers. (One of his photographs is titled "Prostitute Gives Teenager His First Blow Job.") When he rolled into our lives, he'd gone sober and was actually trying to exercise. I remember how, at fifty-one years old, Larry would run up the three flights of stairs to our SoHo office in one straight shot.

It's obvious from his photographs and the movies he's made since *Kids:* Larry is fascinated by puberty. He used to say that he always wanted to make a great American teenage movie. He would complain that back in the 1950s, when he was a kid, the teenager movies at the time were all fakes, movies like *City Across the River*, in which adults played teenagers. He had favorites like Jonathan Kaplan's *Over the Edge*, a more verité precursor to *The Outsiders*, because it used "real kids" at the right age. (Matt Dillon was fourteen when he starred in it, his first film.) Larry wanted to make a teenager movie but "from the inside."

In the summer of 1993, Larry was living in an apartment downtown and frequenting Washington Square Park, where he came across smart-aleck raconteur Harmony Korine taking photographs. Harmony, either eighteen or twenty years old, depending on when you asked him, had grown up on television and old movies. He thought of himself as a prodigy. The two became fast friends. They made a study in contrasts: whatever the indiscretions of his youth, Larry is a big strapping guy, and Harmony is a skinny little guy. They looked like *My Bodyguard*. But Harmony became Larry's entrée into the world of the park, his ambassador to the skaters. One day that summer, Larry called Harmony, asked him to come over, and pitched this kid the concept: a movie by teenagers about real teenagers. He wanted a John Cassavetes-esque take on New York city kids. He asked Harmony if he wanted to write a script. "I've been waiting all my life to do this," Harmony told him. He went home to his grandmother's apartment and wrote the first draft of *Kids* in three weeks.

When they brought the *Kids* script to me, they'd already tried to raise the money through the AIDS charity the Red Hot organization, which had helped them come up with what they were calling "the HIV hook." In the original version they had, the plot of *Kids* was so verité that it went nowhere. The dialogue was incredibly fresh, and Harmony was obviously very talented. But *Kids* didn't tell a story as much as stitch together random scenes, much like a Clark photograph come to life. The whole narrative-plot thing didn't (and doesn't) remotely interest Harmony. A writer named Jim Lewis had composed the wraparound narrative line about a "virgin surgeon," Telly, determined to deflower as many virgins as possible, thinking he can't get HIV that way. Except he already has it. Meanwhile, his ex-girlfriend, Jennie, finds out she's positive and tries to stop him. With HIV woven in, the story had motion and stakes instead of just anthropology. Larry and Harmony were convinced that this "HIV hook" would make *Kids* more sellable as a cautionary tale.

We needed money, someone to finance it. The script bounced around Miramax. They were interested, but when Disney purchased the company in 1993, we all knew that that their mission and output would change. I had one meeting with Richard Gladstein, then an executive at Miramax, to pitch it. We all met at Larry's White Street loft. Here was the pitch: twenty-four hours in the life of a group of New York teenage skateboarders, all nonactors and therefore cheap, shooting five weeks in the summer. We were angling for $1 million. Just then Justin Pierce waltzed in, wearing baggy pants with the crotch sunk to his knees. It was 1993 and it was the first time I'd seen that look done to such perfection, the first time I'd met Justin. Two years later you'd see it everywhere. In Larry's mind, Justin had already been cast as Casper, Telly's best friend and a loose cannon. Justin *was* Casper. Clearly, Larry knew the world he was after. These pubescent kids were becoming his close friends.

Gladstein was sold on it, but to everyone else at Miramax, *Kids* was too far off the map and a surefire ratings nightmare. (The film begins with a "thirteen-year-old" girl losing her virginity to Telly and ends with Telly's best friend, Casper, raping Jennie.) Miramax passed. I told Larry, "I'm really sorry, I want to make this movie with you but I don't seem to be able to get it financed." Meanwhile, Todd Haynes's *Safe* was financed and ready to go into preproduction. So with great reluctance, I said to Larry, "I've got to focus on *Safe*, but keep me posted. I want to stay involved."

A few months later, Larry called. The script had made its way to Cary Woods, an independent producer in New York who had made *Rudy* and *So I Married an Axe Murderer.* (He's since gone on to produce Harmony's follow-ups *Gummo* and *Julien Donkey-Boy.*) Cary had come across a pair of twentysomething venture capitalists who were looking to invest in movies and had a few millions to part with. Cary had earmarked the money to make Alexander Payne's *Citizen Ruth* (then known as *The Devil Inside*), but he loved the *Kids* script. Larry called me in L.A. to say that he'd found $1.5 million from Cary to make the film: would I still produce it? No question. I sat down with Cary and told him that I felt like I'd developed the project and wanted a co-producer credit. I prepared myself for a fight. But Cary said, "No problem." Usually, it's not that easy.

Casting was the first hurdle. Larry was determined to use local kids, warts and all, so we had production assistants canvass the city handing out open-casting flyers at nightclubs and along the Lower East Side. When you're looking for real kids, they don't necessarily come to the casting calls. Larry found Rosario Dawson sitting on her stoop. Larry let Harmony get involved in casting minor parts. At one casting session for one of the female parts, Harmony told the actresses that whoever would kill our office cat (the fleabag office cat that lived in our boxes and bottom desk drawers) would get the part. One girl picked up a pen and said, "Where is the animal?"

We did cast one real actor, Mia Kirschner, the Catholic schoolgirl/stripper from *Exotica*, to play Jennie. She was nineteen and had already worked with Atom Egoyan and Denys Arcand (*Love and Human Remains* and *The Barbarian Invasions*). Larry said he felt OK using an actress to play Jennie because she wasn't a real "character," so it was fitting that she was played by "an actress."

As a starlet flavor of the month, Mia had a schedule that was booking up. We only needed her for a week of the shoot. But a week and a half before production, we still had no firm stop date from the film Mia was in before ours. Since she had so little time to prepare, she asked Larry to get her a video camera so she could shoot her own footage of kids in New York—"research" for her role.

By early July, it was becoming increasingly clear that Mia was not fitting in. Larry decided she wasn't worth the trouble. Chloë Sevigny worked down the block at the hipster boutique Liquid Sky and was friends with Harmony and the rest of the parkies. She'd grown up in blue-blood Darien, Connecticut, and detested it, moving out to Brooklyn when she was eighteen. When she showed up at the *Kids* casting call, she was infamous. She'd already been plucked off the street to be a model for *Sassy*. She'd been an extra in a couple of videos for Sonic Youth and the Lemonheads, but then Jay McInerney saw her on the street, followed her to a rave and a fashion shoot, and produced a seven-page profile of her in *The New Yorker.* While we were shooting, he dubbed Chloë the "Downtown It Girl"—a moniker she hated. She'd stood up McInerney a couple of times for interviews, which only proved to him that she was so "it" she didn't care about being "it." She landed a small part in *Kids,* via Harmony, but now Larry wanted to give her Jennie. "I don't know why I didn't see it before," Larry said. "Chloë's perfect."

So, for the first time in my career, we were going to fire our star. I talked to Lauren Zalaznick, my co-producer on the film, to decide how to do it. Lauren is an old friend of mine from Brown. She had worked on a couple of Hollywood movies, including *Compromising Positions* and *Morgan Stewart's Coming Home,* as a director's assistant, so she had, in my mind, studio cred. (She was also our resident computer genius; she actually understood Lotus 1-2-3. For the production, she sat at her Toshiba laptop that was the size of a suitcase and counted our beans.)

Together we decided to make Larry make the call to Mia. "They're either going to be on the phone and talk for a really long time," Lauren forecast, "and if she's smart, she'll say, 'You can't fire me, I'm the right person' and talk her way back in. Or we'll get a call in two minutes from her lawyer saying, 'Who the fuck do you people think you are dealing with?'" And that's what happened. Suddenly Lauren was on the phone having a hysterically funny conversation with Mia's lawyer. "You can't do this to her, you amateurs," the lawyer said. "Mike Ovitz is her agent and he's going to call you." Breathlessly, Lauren and I waited to hear from Ovitz. Needless to say, we never did.

The kids proved to be easier to cast than the minor characters. In addition to wanting a *real* double amputee for one scene, Harmony and Larry were also insistent about having an actual nursing mother play Telly's mom in a breast-feeding scene. We also couldn't find a ten-year-old kid to play Casper in the flashback where he witnesses his parents having sex and mistakenly stabs his father.

"This Is Just Bullshit, Girly"

During rehearsals, we gave all the kids beepers. It was our only way of keeping in touch. (This was 1994, and the only cell phones were car phones.) But having a beeper didn't mean that they did anything about it when it went off. Early on, Justin Pierce had a court date scheduled for some misdemeanor and we needed to get him to the courthouse. He went missing and his beeper (already his second; the first was destroyed in a "skateboard incident") was "not working." He turned up at a girlfriend's house. We finally got him down to his appearance and scheduled for community service on the three days he wasn't needed. We were constantly playing ad hoc guardians. Pam, as the line producer on the film, had to keep writing notes for Daniel, one of the kids in the park, to excuse him from detention. She called the school and spoke to somebody from Family Court Services who'd heard about the movie. Except once she got him exempted, he would come and hang around the office during casting sessions and annoy us. But these kids had no other place to go.

Of course, we had extensive meetings about the sex scenes. Every actor signs a "nudity rider" to his or her contract about what the actor has agreed to reveal. The rider has to get very explicit, though sometimes actors will spontaneously take a risk. In *A Home at the End of the World*, Michael Mayer convinced Colin Farrell to go full frontal, even though that wasn't in his contract. Robin Wright Penn, on the other hand, refused to show anything. For *Kids*, most of the actors we showed pretending to have sex were of age except Leo Fitzgerald, who was seventeen, and one of the girls, who was fourteen. As the "virgin surgeon," Leo's character is pretty much a heat-seeking missile. We had crotch pads for everybody and closed the set. It was all very professional. Chloë and Justin were friends, so that scene, at the end, was even easier. But our lawyers were paranoid because even showing minors *looking* like they're having sex is a felony in seven states. They argued that the film would be seized and not released if we portrayed minors engaging in sexual activity. Naturally, this made the investors nervous.

Our lawyers advised body doubles, but Larry hated the idea. His whole oeuvre is verité style. He doesn't like being told what he can and can't shoot. Pam asked Larry how he planned to film the scene where Hamilton Harris, one of the kids, exposes himself at the Carmine Street pool. Was Hamilton aware of what he was expected to do? Larry told her that Hamilton hadn't even looked at the script, that he'd just show up and do what Larry told him to. That's pretty much how it worked.

We didn't want the kids to feel pressured, but Larry could be a powerful father figure, especially to Justin. In some ways, all directors have to cast a spell over their cast. If the actors start to doubt a director's authority, they can undermine the whole movie. But kids like Hamilton or, even more so, Justin, who'd been homeless for years, whose parents had said good riddance, thrived in a highly controlled environment like a film set. Justin was willing to go anywhere that Larry and the script pointed him. Most of the kids were, in fact, from middle-class families and had to call their mommies if they were going to be home later than eight. They had structure. But ones like Justin found a structure on the film set that was missing in their lives. And they just gave themselves over.

Over the course of the shoot, Killer kept a diary, to document some of the insanity:

July 17, 1993

It's 12:30 and we're desperately trying to get in touch with the Virgin Girl. She isn't at home, isn't answering her beeper, didn't show for her fitting. Finally, she calls the office to say that she doesn't feel well and just wants to let us know she's not coming in for her scene. "This job doesn't work like that," we say. "Get your ass in here. If you're called to the set, you get to the set."

She comes in. She got her neck pierced and it's infected. Well, that explains it. It looks disgusting. She doesn't feel well. Harmony makes jokes about the grips pulling out the piercing with pliers. Larry doesn't want any of the kids to have piercings. He wants them to look young, not like jaded sluts. So Kara Raynaud, the makeup woman, just unscrews it and cakes over the infection with makeup.

Eventually, we move inside and start her scene—which consists essentially of her getting seduced and later screwed by Leo. Except we're shooting in the bedroom of a house owned by born-again Christians. The scene gets loud. We're just praying the owners don't know what the sounds mean.

July 22

Two of the kids steal a pair of promo'd Airwalks from the costume designer's *personal bag* in the wardrobe trailer. Everything, her petty cash, her wallet, everything is in the bag and they take that too. Exile Ramirez, the assistant costume designer and graffiti artist, catches them. The kids play stupid; he gets everything back.

July 26

The office cat gets captured and used in the scene where Telly kicks the cat. He doesn't actually kick him; he kicks the wall behind the cat, and the cat runs. (This turned out to be one of the most controversial scenes in the film on release!) We leave the cat carrier open in the office, and the cat sleeps in it all morning until its call time. At least we have one performer who shows up on time.

August 2 and 3

Extras nightmare. We can barely keep track of them all. Larry keeps telling people to come back, that they'll get paid. He keeps pulling various freaks from the park and putting them in the shot. No one knows he's done it and he expects the production to have money and gets angry when we don't. All of the kids, meanwhile, are dying of thirst in the sun. One fat friend-of-Harmony almost started a riot among them when we ran short of pizza at lunch.

August 8

One of the actors tells Larry that somebody from Killer called his mother and insulted her, so she's not giving her son his money. We call his place to see if his mother is, in fact, getting his paycheck and to gently suggest that she give her son some of it so that he can decide how to spend it. We are paying him for his services, as much as it sometimes seems like *we* should be getting paid to take care of him. But we don't have much control over the relationship between mother and child, so we leave it at that.

August 12

Steven's apartment scene: this is a total, utter nightmare. The kids are tired and wired and completely out of control. Some of them shoplift from the grocery store next to the building. Other kids, who aren't in the scene, come by to hang outside, drink beer, and skateboard while we are shooting. The cops finally come and nearly arrest some of them.

One of the kids, Nick Lachman, is turning into our nemesis. Pretty much a runaway (as far as we can tell), he came out from San Francisco on the bus at Larry and Harmony's insistence and won't work unless he's paid in cash. This idea has spread like wildfire, and suddenly all the kids also get wind of the notion that if they speak in a scene, they get upgraded to the day-player rate of two hundred dollars a day. Now they're all clamoring for cash. Of course, Nick is written in for one cameo, and when his scene comes, he's nowhere to be found. We shoot it without him.

We close the set for the rape. Chloë gets on her crotch pad. Thank God Justin is close enough to Chloë—they were friends from the park long before the film—that he's tender and gentle about it. We let the actors dictate the conditions. I think what's most upsetting right now are the tiny details: when Justin throws Chloë's legs over his shoulders, you can see she's wearing little-girl socks. The irony is that based on this scene alone, we could get an R rating. When we shot *Swoon*, the one chaste scene of two fully clothed men humping each other got us an NC-17. If it's women, you can show pretty much whatever you want. The biggest annoyance is the couch. We've already established it, so we can't remove it from the scene. But every time somebody sits on it, it sounds like sneakers on a gym floor or serious gas.

Other highlights: One of the kids really vomits for his scene. Supposedly, he ate all this bread so he could barf it. His big moment. We get walkie-talkied to come to the set because one of the set dressers smells pot smoke. The problem is that the *Kids* set is completely permeable to the world outside. It's not a set as much as an extension of the street life most of these kids are living. Larry wants it to feel as naturalistic as possible. But as the producers, we're responsible for keeping the set a drug-free workplace.

August 20

We're on the rave scene at the East Village club the Tunnel. The whole cast payment issue has gotten out of hand. Lauren decides that Harmony shouldn't get paid to play "Fidget," a bit part, his club kid cameo. When Harmony hears this, he gets angry and tells Larry. Larry then confronts Pam, saying, "This is bullshit, girly. He's gotta be paid if he's going to be an actor in this film." And Pam says, "But this is really low budget and he's the writer and you're the director and that's how it works. Don't bully me about that stuff. I'm just watching the pennies here." And Larry says, "This is bullshit." And Pam says, "I'm outta here," and leaves. By the time she gets back to the office, we have flowers waiting for her.

Justin shows up, trashed. He got in a fight and broke his wrist. When one of the assistants went to take him to a doctor, he disappeared. He wasn't even on call. As we edge closer to the end of the shoot, he's getting desperate for attention. He can't see a future for himself after the film. We dispatch Granz, a PA, to keep him away from the set. Granz takes him to a bar for beer—Justin is twenty-two—and brings him back drunk. We fire Granz.

August 23

The nadir. Justin's roommate calls: Justin got arrested. It was bound to happen. He got drunk, stoned, went to his girlfriend's house and threatened her. Then he attacked a passerby on the street, calling him a "faggot" and swinging his skateboard. His girlfriend called the police, and now he's in jail someplace.

In the final days of the shoot, the production feels schizophrenic. We're scheduled for night shoots, so we're on split calls; we start at three in the afternoon and quit at three a.m. Tonight we were sup-posed to do a series of subway scenes on the Times Square shuttle (the subway the city lets you use for filming). But with Justin in jail, we have to cancel—a major headache. With our star locked up, we have no movie. I have no idea what to do. I don't even know a lawyer who can deal with this. I know lawyers to close an apartment or land a record deal. But jail?

Fortunately, the British documentarian Nigel Finch calls me. He's in New York casting for *Stonewall* (my next film), and I ask him if he knows a lawyer. He gives me the name of a big-time New York criminal lawyer who is a nightclub singer on the side. Nigel did a documentary about him. So I call this lawyer, who sends me to one of his protégés, who asks, "OK, where is Justin in the system?"

I say, "I have no idea. I don't even know what 'the system' is."

I tell him everything I do know and we negotiate a price for his work. Within an hour, he calls back and says, "Justin's at this jail, he'll be released at this time, he'll have to reappear . . . " He just negotiated it all.

We don't get Justin out in time for the shoot. We have to resched-ule everything.

August 25

The subway scene, starring the Torso Guy. A small flash of human-ity: Harmony changes his mind about the Torso Guy's character. In the script, he has some lame dialogue about losing his legs in Viet-nam. Harmony decides he should say a little ditty: "I have no legs, I have no legs, I have no legs, I have no legs." Just because he's a torso doesn't mean he shouldn't be joyful. It works. Somehow, we're done.

There have to be two wrap parties because the crew refuses to attend a party with the kids, plus most of them are not of age and the crew wants to drink. A lot.

Postproduction

Though Miramax had already passed on the script, Harvey bought worldwide rights to *Kids* for $3.5 million. Cary was savvy enough to know that the film would raise red flags with Disney, Miramax's new corporate parent. But at the time, Miramax was the only distributor with any track record releasing NC-17 films. They'd brought out Peter Greenaway's *The Cook, the Thief, His Wife and Her Lover* and *Scandal*, the poster children for flouting the MPAA. Harvey and Larry believed that, with cuts, an R rating was a possibility, though remote.

The film, unrated, played Sundance and the competition at Cannes. By the time Disney got a chance to look at *Kids*, the controversy around it was already swirling. No sex had happened on set, but some audiences were convinced it had. Disney got nervous and told Harvey that Miramax couldn't release it. Harvey wouldn't back down, so he up and created an independent releasing arm, Shining Excalibur, just for *Kids*. When the MPAA slapped it with an NC-17, Shining Excalibur released it unrated. It was just the kind of unconventional move that suited a film that didn't fit in anybody's box. The lesson of it, for me, was this: there are many ways to make a movie. Sometimes inexperience creates the right amount of fearlessness, which creates the right alchemy to make a great film. I wouldn't want to do *Kids* again. But it worked. And out of the chaos came Killer Films.

Producing is a lonely business. You're alone with your problems. You can feel like the weight of the world is on you, especially with millions of dollars at stake. Unlike other businesses—which get to diffuse their responsibility—film producing, especially my style of film producing, has a short list of people accountable. I was making peanuts to produce a film that would take two or three years to finish. I could barely stay afloat. *Swoon* director Tom Kalin and I had partnered wonderfully on *Go Fish* and *I Shot Andy Warhol*. But in 1996, Tom, as comfortable with thinking about films as he was with making them, decided to take teaching gigs at Yale, Brown, and

Columbia while he researched and wrote a Robert Mapplethorpe/ Patti Smith project. He interviewed every surviving person he could find. He spent five days with Patti in Detroit and months at the Mapplethorpe foundation. But the film never came together, and its demise was heartbreaking for him. He stopped producing.

I needed to keep working; I needed the money. But I didn't want to be on my own. Lauren Zalaznick, my producing partner, got a job offer the last day of the shoot. She came back from lunch and was handed a memo: "Call John at VH1," it read. "You don't know him but he wants to talk to you." She went on to run the VH1 Fashion Awards. (She has since executive-produced *Zoolander* and the doc *Final Cut: The Making and Unmaking of "Heaven's Gate"* and now runs the Bravo Network.)

Before I was going to make another film, I wanted somebody else to worry about what I was worrying about. It's essential, really, when dealing with finicky distributors. Recently, two weeks before production was supposed to start on John Waters's *A Dirty Shame*, New Line and the bond company told Ted Hope, my producing partner on it, and me that we couldn't shoot because we hadn't worked out Johnny Knoxville's "stop date" for his insurance. We had already sunk an enormous amount of our own personal money into keeping the film alive, paying preproduction costs. We couldn't sink any more. So it was great to have somebody there to ask, How will we get out of this mess?

Pam Koffler came through my door to work as a line producer for Tom Kalin on a short film. After *Swoon* came out, the fashion designer Geoffrey Beene wrote Tom a fan letter, saying he loved the movie, and would Tom direct a pet project? So Tom and I hired Pam to help put together a film in honor of Beene's company's thirtieth anniversary. She'd been an assistant director, a script supervisor, and a postproduction supervisor. It was obvious on that shoot that Pam was tough and smart and hardworking. We hired her to be the line producer for *I Shot Andy Warhol* and then again for *Stonewall*.

Watching her work, I recognized immediately how well Pam's personality complemented my own. She's a nice, straight girl from Yale married to a cinematographer. She has an attention to detail that I just don't have. She knows how to count the pennies. Most important, our tastes overlapped significantly. After nearly ten years together, it's still very rare that Pam falls in love with something that I don't fall in love with too. And this compatibility works in terms of both film and business. We agreed that it made sense to run as open a company as possible—no doors to any office, no private spaces.

So, in 1995, Pam Koffler became my partner in our new company, Killer Films. We ripped off the title from the Cindy Sherman thriller *Office Killer*, which was our first producing gig together. We grew to five people—Pam, myself, and three twentysomething, former unpaid interns: junior producers Eva Kolodner and Katie Roumel, who operated on set, and my assistant Brad Simpson. We were weensy. But the benefits of working with Pam were clear almost instantly. She has a calm to counter my volatility. I know she's often frustrated with me when I hang up on somebody, put a relationship in jeopardy, or make a mess that she has to fix. Her point is What's the point of making somebody hurt or angry? But I can't always help it. I remember hearing about some absolutely horrific agent move, committed in pure avarice and vanity.

"Oh, it's so horrible to watch people get rewarded for bad behavior," I said to her.

Pam answered, with equanimity, "You are *so* in the wrong business."

Spotlight: Bob Berney

PRESIDENT, PICTUREHOUSE FILMS; FORMER PRESIDENT, NEWMARKET FILMS (*THE PASSION OF THE CHRIST, WHALE RIDER, MONSTER*)

Distribution, and the Release of *Happiness*

I started out by running an independent theater in Dallas called the Inwood, which was a bar, hangout, and movie theater—an oasis in that weird culture that is Dallas. It still exists, but now the Landmark chain owns it. You wouldn't just watch a movie there. You'd have a drink there before the movie and then lounge around and talk about it afterward. I used to hang out in the lobby and talk to audiences to see what they liked. There were some definite surprises, like *Kiss of the Spider Woman*, which ran for a year. Merchant Ivory, of course. Anything edgy would work there in a big way because there was just no other outlet in Dallas. People consciously wanted to support the Inwood. I compared running it to owning a PBS station, because people perceived it as a public service but really it was a business. And the pleasure was that even though it *was* a business, the perception was that you were doing people a favor.

I made the jump into movie distribution, which is really just relationship building with exhibitors, and since I'd been one, I knew what the issues were. You have your Rolodex, your history with people, and a sense about what plays where.

I first met Christine on *I Shot Andy Warhol.* I was working at Orion Films at the time, the studio that had done *Dances with Wolves* but then went bankrupt. They were trying to build it back up as an independent company after being a studio. Struggling Orion decided to make a deal to buy the struggling distributor Samuel Goldwyn, which was supposed to release *Warhol.* Samuel Goldwyn was in a major fight with the company that had financed it, American Playhouse, and was threatening to dump *Warhol* to video. Christine was in the middle of that.

I saw *Warhol* and really liked it, especially Lili Taylor's performance and Jared Harris, who played Warhol. So we did a poster that was Warhol-inspired, with Lili (as Valerie Solanas) in the Elvis pose, and a primary-color, silk-screen look. We all liked it, but Sam Goldwyn hated it and there was a growing conflict between Orion and Sam Goldwyn that looked like it might swallow *Warhol* as well. But we just went forward and released it before all the shit hit the fan. It made $1.8 million, not bad, but I still think of it as a "rescued film."

Next time I met Christine, I was working for a company called Banner Films (*Go*) that had decided not to distribute films after all. So I had absolutely nothing to do. I got a call from Christine, who told me about the trouble they were having with *Happiness.* Universal, the parent company of October, had decided not to release it. Christine and her partners on the movie—James Schamus, David Linde, and Ted Hope—had taken it back and were going to try to distribute it themselves. Would I help? I flew into New York and met with them and Todd Solondz too, who knew an amazing amount about theaters and had very specific ideas. Most directors don't care about distribution, but Todd seemed to know every theater, everywhere. You'd look at Saint Louis and Todd would say, "It's got to play at the Tivoli."

One main problem we had was the poster. *Happiness* was an ensemble movie—Lara Flynn Boyle, Dylan Baker, Philip Seymour Hoffman, and so on—and that's always difficult to cram onto a poster. You've got contractual obligations, so you can't just have one person, but you can't put all of them on or it looks terrible. October had developed a campaign using Barbie dolls of each of the characters, but it made the movie look really ominous and creepy, especially considering there's a pedophile in it. Ted Hope asked the graphic novelist Dan Clowes to come up with something. Now, in that era, illustrations were taboo. They were the kiss of death. But Clowes did a really cool illustration of the cast all looking minorly aggrieved that, somehow, let Todd's humor come through.

Most studios never evolve their campaigns. They just try to go big, and if it doesn't work, then screw it. Take *Van Helsing* as an example: the poster looked like they were throwing everything at it, hoping something would hit: werewolves, Frankenstein, Dracula, a bat creature, and Kate Beckinsale with flaming red tassels on her chest. It didn't work. At the same time, *Hellboy* had insane ideas, was much weirder, but you bought into it more because they showed you less on the poster. So much of movie marketing has to do with the underlying mythology. Warhol, ancient whales, the weird power of Polaroids to capture memories—you can have an outrageous film, but what's the underlying mythology that you buy into? At Newmarket, with *Memento, Monster,* even more with *Whale Rider,* we kept changing the image, and I think that always helps find new audiences. At first, we marketed *Whale Rider* as a New Zealand art film with an elegant image of the whale. Then, once people saw it and said, "I want to bring my kid back to this," we released the posters that had the girl jumping around. We turned it into a family movie.

The release of *Happiness* was essentially me with a phone and my operations guy. I would ring up people and say, "We've got this great film!" I called Greg Laemmle, who, with his father, owns and operates nine different art-house theaters in L.A., including West Hollywood's Sunset Five, one of the most successful alternative theaters in the country. I convinced him to watch a tape of the film, and he said, "I love it but I think my dad is going to be totally freaked out." Then, since *Happiness* had won a critic's prize at Cannes in May, we'd slotted it into as many festivals as we could—Telluride, Toronto, and the New York Film Festival—to get as much free exposure as possible. At Telluride, Bob Laemmle, Greg's dad, saw *Happiness* and told me, "I think it's the best film I've ever seen. But my son, he's really conservative, I don't think my son will want to play it." That was *Happiness* in a nutshell. People were almost afraid to say how much they liked it.

Finding the right place and time for your opening day is vitally important. At base level, the success of your movie comes down to box office "thresholds," relative to each market. Your movie has got to make enough in three days (the weekend) to keep exhibitors' faith. In New York, if your movie earns $15,000 or above, that's good. If it makes $25,000–30,000, that's really solid. It's when you get below $10,000 that you've got a problem. What you want is for the numbers to go up from Friday to Sunday. When your numbers are low, and you talk to the exhibitor to keep the movie in theaters, you have to come up with every possible excuse—"It was raining!" or "There was a parade and people couldn't get to the theater!" *My Big, Fat Greek Wedding* never made more than $10,000 (reached in its twentieth week of release), but it ran for over a year. So it also depends a lot on the faith of the exhibitors. You have to keep finding pockets of people. The critic Frank Rich said *The Passion of the Christ* wouldn't work in New York because New York was so secular. But it was the number one gross at the AMC Empire right on Forty-second Street. Why? Because it had a huge Latino (read Catholic) audience.

It can be difficult to find audiences, since they're not always where you want them to be. Gay-themed films don't always succeed in San Francisco, for example. That's because it's a "critic sensitive" city: if the critics are supportive, the audience for art-house movies follows their lead. Seattle, Ann Arbor, Providence are all critic sensitive, especially since they're near universities. Certain critics can turn the tide on a film. Anthony Lane, in *The New Yorker*, for example. If he reviews something positively, a whole set of regional critics will fall in line. We had a film called *Together* by Lukas Moodysson, and I was having a tough time convincing exhibitors to take it. But after Lane reviewed it positively, everything changed. On a national basis, Ebert still has real influence. He reviews everything and puts indie films first.

We opened *Happiness* in six theaters, and based on the press, we made $34,000 per theater on average that first week. That was great. We tried to build on the urban markets, where it was getting good reviews, and then head to the mainstream suburbs and multiplexes. It played well in the art houses, but it didn't really cross over. It did great at the Inwood but didn't work in Plano. It earned around $2.8 million. We didn't have a follow-up poster for *Happiness*, a way to change the campaign, and that might have affected the release. We might have used the controversy more. I've learned since that people will pay double to see a movie if you tell them Hollywood or the government doesn't want you to see it. This strategy worked spectacularly for *Fahrenheit 9/11* and *The Passion of the Christ*.

In a real way, exhibitors know better than the studios what works for their audiences. When I saw *Memento*, I loved it and thought, Audiences love puzzles. But the guys who made that film couldn't get it released because all the distributors thought the ending was too uncompromising. This hesitation just didn't make sense to me. So I joined up to get it released. It played for nine months, earning steady amounts (its biggest week was its eleventh week of release), and made $25 million. I caught *Whale Rider* at the Toronto Film Festival, where most acquisition people just walked out. The film starts slow, and they didn't see the payoff. I stuck around. When the whole audience gave it a standing ovation at the end with tears in their eyes, I thought, This is fairly obvious. Let's get this. So I chased down the sales rep. *Whale Rider* played for six months and got an Oscar nomination for Keisha Castle-Hughes. I'm proud of the way these movies have long lives.

Two Brandons

You have to stay open to finding new talent, anywhere, and cultivating it. With *Boys Don't Cry*, we had two discoveries: a new director and a new star, and their clash over the lead role almost brought the film down on itself.

In 1995 *Go Fish's* Rose Troche had tipped us off to a Columbia grad student named Kim Peirce and to her partially completed thesis film called *Take It Like a Man*. These days, many graduates of NYU and USC have agents and managers already. But back then, Kim was simply a self-possessed amateur determined to tell a story. She'd read, like many of us, the brutal story in the *Village Voice* about a teenaged girl named Teena Brandon who had passed as a boy named Brandon Teena in small-town Nebraska and was later raped and murdered for it. Kim's thesis film was experimental and pretty but didn't show any command of narrative. It was also, true to form for our business, held hostage by DuArt film processing labs when she ran out of money.

Kim Peirce looks like a smaller, more compact Jennifer Connelly—dark hair, piercing blue eyes, leather pants worn with some regularity—and she talks like a superbright graduate student. Yasujiro Ozu this. Scorsese that. And John Ford this other thing. I think every major body of world cinema was referenced in the making of *Boys Don't Cry*. "Brandon Teena *is* Pinocchio" is one of Kim's declarations that stays with me. Sure, these film references could be pretentious, but even in those first meetings we had with her, Kim spoke like a real movie director: connecting characters to the classic types. If she couldn't talk about lenses or film stock, Kim could communicate in terms of cinema in a way that everybody understood. It always blows my mind how little so many burgeoning filmmakers know about their own craft. Kim really was a movieholic. She had seen everything. To me, that is usually a sign of someone who's for real. It made her very attuned to classical story references and structure. "You know when, in *Alice in Wonderland*, Alice falls into the rabbit hole?" Kim would say. "Teena crosses over into Brandon like that." She had an ability to make people feel smart, which is especially a gift when dealing with actors. Put her in a room with anyone, and he or she will come out feeling connected.

More important, Kim's passion was unimpeachable. You can't fly in the face of such abiding ardor for telling a story; that's exactly why Killer exists. One of the great things about first-time directors is that the story they want to tell is the one they have been dying to tell their whole lives. For five years, Kim had nursed this story into a script. She'd been out to Nebraska and interviewed Lana Tisdel, Brandon's girlfriend, by herself. That kind of passion can always help gloss over the inexperience of a first-timer.

On the other hand, she was thirty years old, had never shot a movie, and was clutching a script in need of significant pruning. If we surrounded her with experienced cinematographers and editors, she'd be fine. If the script was too big, that was all right too. Sometimes you need to shoot everything so that you have the palette to paint with.

My rule is that your ambition should always be greater than your money. You want to walk the delicate line between no holds barred and the bottom line. Pegged at $1.7 million, assuming a nonunion crew and a cast of unknowns, *Boys Don't Cry* was going to be about as low-budget as possible and yet high enough to allow us to pay people. Hart Sharp, the duo of producers across the hall who later produced *You Can Count on Me* and *Nicholas Nickleby*, agreed to finance the full $1.7 million. In fact, the money they put up for *Boys Don't Cry* was earmarked for Kenneth Lonergan's *You Can Count on Me*. But when that deal initially fell through, they still wanted to make a film. The money they'd raised was burning a hole in their pockets. The hitch was that they couldn't secure all of it by our start date.

Doesn't matter, I said. We'll find the money while we're shooting. I felt pressure because I knew a secret: we had competition. I'd found out that Drew Barrymore was in the middle of developing a Brandon Teena story with Fox Searchlight. For their project, Fox had bought the rights to a true-crime book about the murder by Aphrodite Jones, and when they heard that we had our own Brandon Teena story, Fox threatened us, saying, "You don't have the rights you need to make this movie, and we do."

When you deal with nonoriginal material, this kind of thing is inevitable. Killer has made a number of films from true stories, so we bump up against rights issues all the time. It's a dicey area and was especially so on *Boys Don't Cry*. Generally, when you're talking about a public figure, enough is in the public domain—newspaper and magazine articles, for example—that you don't *have* to acquire the rights. Much of your subject's life is already out there. By the time we started this project, Brandon Teena had been the focus of a number of articles. Arguably, her story was public domain.

But with the unfamous, the unknown criminals and local heroes— of whom Lana Tisdel was one—you're going to want to acquire the "life rights." Producers acquire them, all the time, for three main reasons. First, having the rights protects you when you want to dramatize information that you haven't been able to corroborate beyond a single source, like a book or the person himself. That material is the property of that writer or that person, and you can't just take it. They'll sue.

Second, if there are multiple books or multiple perspectives on a single issue—the Cuban Missile Crisis, say, or Truman Capote's writing *In Cold Blood*—it's best to buy rights to *one* of the narratives, the one whose perspective you'll be hinging your story on. Facts are easy to verify, but it's the point of view or "take" on a situation that usually draws a filmmaker to a project. In this case, you'll want the rights to protect you from someone who could say, "You stole that from *my* book." You just point to your source and say, You're wrong. Your lawyers will tell you: make *sure* that the book you have is the book you need. You've got limited funds and you don't want to option more than one book.

Sometimes, though, you end up with multiple rights. In the fall of 2004, Jocelyn Hayes came across Jean Nathan's fascinating biography of eccentric 1950s children's author Dare Wright. Wright was famous for a series of dark and weirdly poignant books about a character called the Lonely Doll and her relationship with two teddy bears—a father and son—who come to live with her. Wright herself was separated from her father and brother when she was three years old, and she lived with her obsessive mother, who pretty much kept her as a child even as Wright matured. Wright died in 2001. I loved the book and paid the publisher for the rights. Meanwhile, another producer, named Elizabeth Karlsen, separately optioned Wright's life rights from her estate. Fortunately, Killer ended up collaborating with Karlsen on our film *Mrs. Harris*. We decided to team up on *The Lonely Doll* as well, so we wouldn't have competing projects. Now Julian Schnabel is attached to direct and a screenwriter is coming up with pages.

The last reason for buying rights is the most popular: if you do it first, someone else can't. You're staking your claim to the material. This doesn't mean that there can't be competing projects. With *The Notorious Bettie Page*, Bettie herself had already signed away her life rights to documentary filmmakers. So we optioned a book titled *The Real Bettie Page*, the *Enquirer* version of the Bettie Page story. There was stuff in it that we could use, and we wanted to keep it off the market.

You might want someone's life rights to be able to alter them, to have the creative license to show things that didn't take place. Effectively, you're buying the person's cooperation. (Dead people no longer have the right to privacy. But be wary of the estate's suing you for defamation.) Sometimes you need to edge into territory that a person wouldn't want revealed: drug habits, abusive marriages, maybe just a terrible singing voice. If you don't have the life rights, your subject can sue you for defamation. But usually with life rights, the relationship is more of a collaborative partnership. You're paying a person for his or her stories, photos, and ability to shed light on areas where the history isn't clear.

Buying rights can get expensive. Most often, at Killer Films, we purchase an "option" for them, meaning that we'll pay a little now and pay more for them in the future—when we have an approved budget. That way, we spend money when we have it. The total cost for rights is usually pegged to a percentage of the budget, around one or two percent, but that depends entirely on the market. If you've got people bidding on a popular property, the price will rocket up. Small players drop out early and typically only the studios can afford the highest price tags. On the other hand, if you want to option an article written a few years ago, then you're in a much better position to get the rights for an affordable price.

Waiting helps, if you can handle it, partly because of the ways options work. Usually producers will buy three years' worth of an option. You pay for the first twelve months, and then at the end of that year, you renew for another year. At the end of that year, you can renew again. Why string it out this way? Because once you get the rights, somebody has to actually write a script. Then it needs to get revised, go out to actors, find financing. It takes a while. By coming up with a three-year term for the option, you have the rights for long enough that you can do something with them, but should it all fizzle, you can walk away.

Fortunately, Killer producer Eva Kolodner and Kim had gone back out to Nebraska and had Lana Tisdel sign a release for the information she'd given us and for the stories about Brandon. This release, in effect, was our defense.

But in the case of Brandon Teena, it turned out there was a web of competing rights. On top of the Drew Barrymore project, another producer, Don Murphy (*Natural Born Killers*, *From Hell*), had Brandon's *mother's* rights and the rights to the documentary about the crime called *The Brandon Teena Story*. He had set up a project at New Line with Neve Campbell attached. We were all trying to tell Brandon's story, each of us with the rights to a different aspect of it. Because Brandon was dead, it was an open question whose story was "true." As I've learned, over and over, the best way to fight off competing projects is to get some kind of rights—a toehold into one version of the facts—and then make the best film you can, first. (Months later, after the film was edited, Don Murphy was so furious that he tried to intimidate us from screening the film at the Toronto Film Festival. He threatened to sue the festival for defamation of Brandon's name. I can remember sitting in my hotel room, signing the paperwork to indemnify the festival—meaning pay them back—if the suit went through. We screened the movie anyway, and eventually the suit got dropped.)

In retrospect, Lana Tisdel had no reason to sign a release. But people outside Hollywood get seduced when film people come calling: it's the simple power of having someone pay close attention to you. It's naïveté, really. The fact is that a story like this is very well documented in the press and court transcripts. If it had come down to it, we might have made the argument that no life rights were necessary.

With Lana's story in our hands, we ignored the other projects and pushed on. I knew we couldn't be the second *Boys Don't Cry* out there. The market wouldn't bear two movies about a murdered transsexual released at the same time. Fox had a huge advantage, since they already had Drew Barrymore. To catch up, we were in desperate need of a star.

For two years, we had been casting a net nationwide to find a Teena Brandon—a young woman capable of believably playing a guy and charismastic enough to pull off being a check-forging hero. We hired Kerry Barden (*Seven, Bad Boys II, The Cider House Rules, I Shot Andy Warhol*) to do the casting, and he and his associate Jennifer McNamara put hundreds of young women on tape. You hear about casting calls like this, for *Annie* or *Harry Potter*, but you don't realize how exhausting it can be to look at hundreds of actors (and transsexuals), trying to find the right person. Talented actors came and went (Fairuza Balk, for example); we started to wonder if we'd been too picky. In the best case, someone comes through the door you've seen for five seconds on tape and you know you're done looking. During her casting interview, Hilary Swank told Kim she was twenty-one and from Lincoln, Nebraska—Brandon's hometown. Both were lies (she was twenty-four and *born* in Lincoln but raised in Bellingham, Washington). It didn't matter; if anything, lying was a very Brandon Teena thing to do.

We had half our money and a competing project in the wings from a studio and a star. But all of a sudden, we had our Brandon. It was all we needed.

The Bluest Eyes in Texas

We shot in the outskirts of Dallas. (Is there anything in Dallas *but* outskirts?) As soon as we had dailies, John Sloss and I took the footage to Jonathan Sehring at IFC Films, who'd been circling around the project forever. The dailies made him jump. The people at IFC were looking for a reason to invest and immediately put up a million dollars. If they hadn't, the film might have collapsed. First hurdle, jumped.

Then came the Hilary-Kim conflict. As a first-time director, Kim was impressively articulate and strong. She knew what she wanted. Sure, there were moments when she was overwhelmed by the pressures of a low-budget shooting day: "OK, it's dawn, you've been working all night, the sun's about to come up, and you're not done yet. What do you do?" It's hard to be clear-eyed and correct in those circumstances. But Kim never flagged. She could outlast anybody. No one questioned her strength.

Except maybe Hilary. Everybody was staying at the Doubletree Suites—a cookie-cutter motel that had no trees or suites. During the costume fitting at the hotel, Hilary asked sweetly, "So can I have my dog stay with me in the trailer?" And Killer's on-set producers Eva and Pam looked at each other. There *were* no trailers. Her dressing room was a shower curtain propped up on two metal C-stands.

Hilary wasn't a diva. I know certain actors who make sure it is in their contract that the people who drive them to the set each day cannot speak to them. Think about it from their perspective: it's exhausting to have to be nice all the time. I remember walking past the set of *Great Expectations* a few years back and seeing a PA measuring the ground from De Niro's trailer to the set because, contractually, he didn't have to walk too far to work. Hilary didn't have the résumé to pull that. But she had come from a certain level of L.A. production—*The Next Karate Kid* and a bunch of television— where everybody gets trailers on any size movie. She brought her Lab, which caused problems at the motel, and her husband, Chad, came to visit.

Kim was convinced that the dog and the husband were taking Hilary out of the role. She didn't feel Hilary was immersing herself thoroughly enough into Brandon. "You can't bring your husband here," Kim told her. "He's distracting you." But we all knew it was a difficult role. Whatever Hilary needed to comfort herself, Kim had to allow her.

This tension wasn't just about Kim and Hilary. It was about Kim and Hilary and Brandon, and who knew him better. Kim would give Hilary some direction, and Hilary would answer, "Brandon wouldn't do that." Kim's passionate reactions would escalate right away. Part of managing Kim as a director was making it very clear that it does not serve anyone for the director to be in a hostile relationship with the lead. You've got to find harmony. When they came to the brink, we broke down the options: 1. We could fire Hilary—definitely not an option. We don't have the money or time, and she's amazing. 2. Hilary does it Kim's way—but if she won't, there is no way to force her. 3. We let things cool down and shoot the scene later. 4. We shoot it both ways and see how it looks.

One of the central relationships during production is between the director and the star, because that star sets the tone for the entire set. If your star doesn't respect your director, you've got a riot from the bit players to the gaffers. And it's the worst thing in the world to be on a set when you feel the breakdown of respect for the director. While we didn't come close to that kind of chaos on *Boys Don't Cry*, Kim's intensity could never quite be matched by the people around her. The passion that made her an ideal director for the project made her demanding and exacting—a tough combination for a film with no money to spare.

There are only a certain number of pages of dialogue you can shoot a day, somewhere around three or four. (It's a smaller number of pages for action movies, which require more elaborate sets.) Physically, you just can't do more setups and breakdowns than that. On *Boys Don't Cry*, we aimed for six pages a day. We raced through the script. The shot list for a day of production breaks each scene down to its proportion of the page: one-eighth, one-half, etc. Line producers also count the literal footage of film shot per day, a number between four and five thousand feet (more takes means more film). This way they can do the quick math to determine whether the production is paced right. Are you shooting enough? Are you shooting too much? Too many takes? *Boys Don't Cry* looked way over schedule. Kim had huge, impressionistic sections of the script—Brandon Teena in a cornfield, wearing his varsity jersey, meeting his father in a dream, etc.—that she wanted shot. Normally, a bond company, the insurance agent that contracts producers to deliver films on time and on budget, would have made us cut the script down or told us, You can't shoot all this. But using a bond company is the film financier's prerogative (they're paying for it), and with *Boys Don't Cry*, Hart Sharp didn't use one.

Everyone was getting nervous, given how long our postproduction was clearly going to be. There was pressure on us to make a sale of the movie. I knew that if I could get distributors—the same people who had already turned down the script—to watch the footage, the film would sell itself. Any doubts they'd had before about this *90210* alum Hilary Swank or her believability as a man would be, at that point, moot. In lumberjack shirts and pegged jeans, Hilary more than passed. She was hot. She was mesmerizing. It was now January 1999, and my lawyer John Sloss and I took twenty minutes of Kim's footage to Sundance. We called up distributors, showed up at their condos with a VHS tape, and said, "We're going to be leaving Sundance with a sale."

I was amazed when we showed it to our competition. Lindsay Law at Searchlight watched our footage, confessing that his own Brandon Teena project had stalled out. It pays to be tenacious. Lindsay said to me, "You make us the offer." A film with a budget of $1.7 million we sold to them for $5 million. Lindsay Law called Drew and told her that her movie was dead. She was devastated. (So this Sundance gambit can work beautifully. Other times, not so well. With *Party Monster*, Killer's club kid murder story, no one bought.)

When Searchlight came on board, we decided to use some of the money to shoot one critical scene: a postrape scene between Brandon and his girlfriend Lana. Lana (Chloë) comes to see Brandon (Hilary) in a shack outside the house. We needed to see some kind of acknowledgment and Lana's response to the violence. The question was Would they make out or not? Would they have sex or not? Would Brandon take off her shirt and show her boobs? Kim wanted Hilary to take off her top. She wanted Brandon to show Lana her feminine sexuality. But Hilary didn't think Brandon would do that. *And* we'd already had Hilary sign a nudity rider that limited us to showing certain things in certain scenes. She had the right to refuse everything else.

As usual, what you think is going to be the hardest (the rape) isn't, and what you think is a no-brainer trips you up. The rape was fine productionwise and performancewise because everyone was so psychologically prepared. But this new scene came too late, after the production had pulled up stakes. And Hilary didn't want to do it Kim's way. Her refusal was less about modesty than about classic "creative differences." She shot the scene with her top on.

Then the twenty-two-week postproduction turned into a yearlong marathon. The complicating factor with *Boys Don't Cry* was that there were so many potential versions of this story. For many stories, there is one movie you can make from that material (more often, less than one). Other times, you've got multiple films you can make from the same material. Todd could have made four different movies out of everything we shot for *Happiness* and *Storytelling*. Kim had developed the material for years, made her student film from it, shepherded it through countless revisions. She had the age-old director's frustration: she wanted every version in the final version. The problem in editing *Boys Don't Cry* was that even when it was two hours and forty-five minutes long, it still played to audiences. It was an incredible experience for them. When you have a movie that plays, how do you convince a director that it could play better?

We have a saying at Killer: it's not the length that's the problem, it's the *perception* of length. A short film can feel long when motivations aren't clear, transitions don't match, or the proportions of the story are off. It doesn't matter if your movie is ninety minutes. If people feel like it's two hours, then you've got to fix something. *Boys Don't Cry*, at heart, was an excellent story with great performances. What it wasn't was an "art" film, and that took some adjustment for Kim. For example, Kim had fallen in love with the symbolism of Brandon's varsity jacket—whether it was on and what that meant for his gender identity. The jacket itself was trying too hard as a symbol. People asked, "Why is the jacket on here and not there?" We ended up having to reshoot a scene of Hilary taking the jacket off just so that we didn't have continuity problems. Then we had footage of Brandon meeting an apparition of his father with light emanating out of his head in a cornfield. None of this was serving the story, but at that point, Kim was in love with all of it.

The rape scene was particularly difficult. Initially, it went on for a good five minutes. It was excruciating. Kim's response was "Deal with it. If that's what happened to Brandon, then the audience should go through it." Of course, the response to that is "Kim, people don't go to the cinema to 'experience' five minutes of rape." How could we balance it so that people feel the horror without becoming numb? Kim wanted to stand her artistic ground. A lot of times young filmmakers debate it in their mind: "Should I be the kind of filmmaker who absolutely refuses to budge because of art? Or should I just bend?" I've worked with both. With *Happiness*, a film with two ejaculations, Todd Solondz wouldn't bend. So James Schamus, the executive producer on the movie, wrote a letter in defense of the film. The MPAA just laughed him out of there. (We went out unrated.) It took a while for Kim to find her process, but it entailed screening the film seventeen times, trying to find the right pace. The rape ended up about two minutes long, but you felt every second.

The editor is your first line of defense against your darlings. But even editors can get lost in their film. This is why you so often see two editors in the credits; the first editor starts by cutting the movie identically to the way the screenplay is written. Then the director and editor begin playing with it, dropping scenes, playing scenes off new characters. When it comes time for the final finesses and adjustments, that first editor can't see what the film needs anymore. Tracy Granger, who'd edited *New Jersey Drive* and *Mi Vida Loca*, had taken *Boys Don't Cry* as far as she could. We replaced her with Lee Percy, a former Juilliard actor who jumped into editing with *Troll* and the *Re-Animator* and progressed through *Blue Steel*, *Single White Female*, and *Reversal of Fortune*, one of the most brilliant pieces of editing from the 1990s. After months, Kim's four-hour epic came down to size. We finally found the movie.

Meeting the MPAA

When you are done editing, when you are ready to exhibit your film, this is what happens: you submit your film first to a group of parents

who watch the movie somewhere in Southern California. These reps
from the Motion Picture Association of America will give your film a
rating. But they won't tell you what for specifically. It's not as if
three sex scenes equal an R. No doubt, there's a double standard in
terms of female and male nudity, but the judgments are even subtler;
plenty of movies have penises in them that are not NC-17. *Velvet
Goldmine*, for example. The rating depends on what the penis is
doing. When we submitted *Boys Don't Cry*, it received an NC-17
because, the MPAA said, "in general there was an overall intensity to
the film that we found disturbing."

Kim didn't understand what the NC-17 meant, which tells you
something about just how single-minded she was. It's fairly well
known now that the NC-17 rating is the marketing equivalent of lep-
rosy: some newspapers won't run ads for your film, and theaters
won't show it. When you get an NC-17 rating, you can go back and
try to cut to an R. Sometimes repeatedly. Jane Campion's *In the Cut*
had to go back to the MPAA thirteen times before it finally garnered
an R.

Obviously, we knew the rape scene, when John Lotter (Peter
Sarsgaard) attacks Brandon Teena, sent up red flags. It always did.
But Kim had finally come to a "final" version of it and wasn't about
to start snipping away. But what else would we have to contend
with?

Instead of cutting *Boys Don't Cry*, we decided to fight the rating.
In person. When there is a disagreement between the filmmaker and
the ratings board, a filmmaker and a producer go before the MPAA
board in Los Angeles. Together, you watch the movie at the screening room at the Directors' Guild in Beverly Hills. Afterward you get
up, face eleven MPAA reps—schoolteachers, businessmen, parents,
etc.—and have a parliamentary debate: fifteen minutes of your side,
fifteen minutes of rebuttal, ten minutes of you, ten minutes of them,
five minutes you, five minutes them, then questions. Then they huddle and decide. You need a two-thirds majority to win.

We sent Kim and Brad Simpson, the head of postproduction for
Boys Don't Cry. Brad had developed a close friendship with Kim
during the editing process. While Brad hadn't been there on set during the shoot, he knew the movie inside and out, walking it through

the cuts. Kim trusted him. And like Kim, Brad is a gifted talker. But at the time, maybe he was a little too punk for the MPAA. He looked like an East Village waif who'd spent a few too many nights at Brownie's. So Fox Searchlight took him to Banana Republic and bought him a blue button-down shirt and beige khakis. Kim went to Agnès B. They made a good team.

On the plane over, Brad and Kim reviewed the rules of the MPAA dispute game. The main rule is that you can't bring in the outside world or other movies. No outside context. In your defense, you talk about the film and what's on the screen. Because the MPAA is an "advisory organization" that gives families advice on whether kids should see a certain movie, if you want an R, you need to make the argument to them that a child should be able to see this film with a parent. You need talk about your film, parents. Your film. Parents.

Brad and Kim made up a detailed outline. Kim would go first and talk about the structure of the film (fifteen minutes), and then Brad would talk about how Killer hoped people would respond to the film (ten minutes). Kim's argument was that in the film, John Lotter is a bad guy, what he did was terrible, but he's also charming and seductive. That's what's so awful about the rape. The film didn't glamorize it; there was nothing sexy about it. We felt that what you see Brandon go through was actually the best depiction of how "normal" things can spiral into violence.

When they arrived in Beverly Hills, a woman rep from the MPAA greeted them and told them that the board wanted to screen the film without them. Brad asked, "So what should we do while you watch it?" And the woman said, "Well, there's great shoppin' here just up and down Rodeo Drive!" Brad just looked at her. "What are you talking about? We can't *afford* anything on Rodeo Drive!"

So they window-shopped. They went for a walk and came back two hours later. Kim gave an intense fifteen-minute presentation, and then a male rep from the MPAA stood up. "Well, I think we've all watched the movie," he said. "We can see why it's NC-17. It's all up there on the screen. We're under a lot of intense political pressure right now, and it's a really big thing to overturn the ratings board and we don't want to do that." He was referring to *South Park* and the fact that the MPAA was getting hammered for giving it an R.

"There are congressional hearings going on and we cannot overturn the ruling now," he said, finishing. And sat down.

Brad's jaw dropped. This guy had done exactly what Brad and Kim were expressly told *not* to do—bring up the outside world and politics. He hadn't made an argument except that "It's all up there on the screen." Brad and Kim looked at each other. Then it was Brad's turn to speak.

He faced the board and, on automatic pilot, he delivered his ten minutes about how we really hoped parents would take their kids to see this movie and talk about gender identity and crisis and hate crimes in America. "We know this movie is probably not going to be in multiplexes," he said, "but we also know that no one was going to come out of this movie and want to rape someone. They're actually going to come out with a deeper, more complicated understanding of this violence." In the sea of eleven faces watching him, there were four nodding women, a ninety-year-old priest, and the rest were stone-faced men. And he knew they were screwed. You need two-thirds of the room to overturn the ruling, and they weren't going to get it.

There was supposed to be two more back-and-forths. But the guy they had been debating said, "I have nothing more to say. Don't overrule it," and there was no more debate. No questions either. Brad and Kim left and waited in the lobby for the decision.

"That was ok, wasn't it?" Kim said.

"That was a problem, Kim," Brad said.

"A good problem or bad problem?" Kim asked.

"Bad."

The rep came out and announced that five people had voted to overturn and four had voted not to. Brad and Kim had the majority, but they didn't get the two-thirds. They lost. There was no appeals process beyond this. This was the appeal. For directors, this is rough. Once you've got your edited film that you think is perfect, it's impossible to think about cutting anything, especially with an anonymous board of people forcing you to do it. When the MPAA told us to recut *Happiness*, Todd Solondz refused. When you've done something serious and artful—not violent schlock—the double standard of American values about guns (fine) and sex (nope) in our media feels all the more senseless. Kim fell apart.

"Oh my God, what just happened?" Kim said. "What do we do next?" Brad told her, "We cut the film."

We told Fox Searchlight and they were livid. Invoking the "outside world" is verboten in a ratings dispute, and it was clear *Boys Don't Cry* had been sucked into the political fray over *South Park*. The studio called the MPAA and raised some hell, but there was no choice. We had to cut the movie. But the MPAA said just resubmit two scenes, the ones that they found the most upsetting: the rape scene and the sex scene between Lana and Brandon.

The second was a surprise. Finally we had specifics, but we weren't sure what they were talking about. Screening the film again, Brad noticed this tiny moment when Brandon goes down on Lana. When he comes up, he wipes his mouth just a little. Brad had watched the film twenty five times and never noticed it. But it's the kind of sex content—partly gay sex content—that puts the MPAA into a boil. So we nipped those frames out.

Next came the rape scene. Nobody wanted to change a frame— not Kim, not Brad. Not me or Lindsay Law. What we had was terrifying and hard to watch. To shorten it would diminish its power. So we cut as little as we thought we could get away with. And we resubmitted *Boys Don't Cry* to the MPAA, telling them that "we'd cut it significantly." We weren't lying.

And it got an R.

Chapter 4

Pitching, Buying, Begging, Stalking

*Insanity on La Croisette—Good Cannes meetings and the
other kind—"You Only Want To Go to the Party That Didn't
Invite You"—Where are the movies?*

LESSON: AT THE CANNES FILM FESTIVAL, EVERYBODY'S A PROSTITUTE.

This is not classy. This is not one endless première. It is not one long
unfurled red carpet from Le Croisette to your name printed on a little card on a seat in the Palais next to Soderbergh and Binoche for
an Un Certain Regard screening. At the Cannes Film Festival, there
are too many prostitutes, curdled buffet tables, nine-dollar bottles of
water, dog turds, and lobster-faced film producers to even begin
counting. For ten days in May, Cannes is coarse, and maybe one of
the most reassuring qualities of the festival is its proof at last that
the French can be as tacky and gauche as the rest of us.

If you want to see Cannes as I see it, you have to start in "the
Bunker," the teeming, underground convention center beneath the
Palais du Cinéma. The Palais, situated on a jetty at the edge of the Medi-
terranean, is the city's cathedral of film. It's about as majestic as a
movie theater can get. The Bunker is the basement. Don't be dis-

tracted by the twenty-two films in competition for the Palme d'Or. The real business of Cannes is the selling of thousands of movies— chilly Japanese dramas, Korean action movies, Brazilian whatevers— down below in the teeming international Cannes market. Walk through the Bunker and you could be in the Javits Center, you could be at a trade show, you could be anywhere. In booth upon booth of the Bunker, producers shill their movies to sales agents, and sales agents sidle up to distributors, and distributors sniff out what producers are cooking up.

The whole world is at Cannes. There are other film festivals and markets, of course, and most often, the festival you take your film to is dictated by when your movie is done. If you finish in winter, you submit it to Cannes. Fall, you try for Berlin. Spring or summer, Venice. Subject matter also helps. We knew *Hedwig and the Angry Inch*, with its story of an East German transsexual, would play better in Berlin than Cannes. As the most important international festival, Cannes is the premier opportunity to broker these deals because everyone is here, wandering the Bunker. It's a clamoring, chaotic environment, a blizzard of themed tchotchkes, giveaway souvenirs, televisions previewing the schlock that makes up the majority of movies released every year and most of the films looking for financing.

The city reflects this market. For five days, aboveground Cannes is overrun with grade Z films. Along La Croisette, the broad boulevard that abuts the water and runs up to the Palais, all the grand hotels are invisible, covered in banners and scaffolding that announce straight-to-video movies being shot. So a hotel like the Majestic, one of the nicest in the city, gets covered in signs for *Spiders 2*, *Point Doom*, *Skeletons in the Closet*, and *The Heart of the Warrior*. Want to cross the street? A pink convertible filled with topless women promoting a film called *Bad Guys* cuts you off. Wondering why the traffic is at a standstill? Arnold is here, promoting *Terminator 3*, with a bunch of female cyborgs (not topless), and all the paparazzi want a snap. Walking up and down the Croisette is like running some surreal obstacle course. Filmmakers from around the world promoting their film try to shove flyers in your hands as motorbikes whiz and weave around the hordes of stargazing tourists. You pass old friends and future meetings as you walk up and down the street, lowering your head when you spot someone dangerous—a distributor you fought with, a financier who dropped the ball on a project, or a filmmaker whose script you passed on.

Cannes Rule 1: Keep watching the ground, as France does not seem to have pooper-scooper laws.

It's May 2000. Brad and my assistant Laird have arrived first and succeeded in stepping in dog shit twice. Each. They've set up a mini Killer office off the Croisette and left their shoes at the door. Pam and I arrive off a direct flight from New York, and while Brad and Laird scrape their soles, we pause briefly to freshen up before heading to the accreditation office to retrieve our badges. The Killer team is four people, which is very lean, comparatively. We push past someone wearing a sandwich billboard advertising *Spiders 2*. Pam asks me how much Killer would have to pay me to walk up and down the Croisette wearing a billboard and handing out flyers for one of our movies—say, our ballet drama called *The Company*, to be directed by Bob Altman if we can get it financed. I say $5,000. Brad and Laird say they'll start raising the money.

After getting our accreditation, we stop by the FilmFour offices to pick up our tickets for their lunch, which starts in thirty minutes. FilmFour is a British production company that partly financed *Velvet Goldmine*. This lunch, which takes place every year on the roof of the Noga Hilton (one of the anchor hotels on La Croisette), is always a treat, filled with British filmmakers and producers with whom we have close relationships. No Hollywood insanity—just brilliant, sarcastic people with bad teeth and acid tongues, chain-smoking. Alas, at the office, we are told that even though we were invited, it is too late to pick up our ticket, so we will not be able to attend. What?

> *Cannes Rule 2: Keep watching the ground, as France has an inordinate number of small dogs on leashes.*

We walk back toward the Noga and, as we enter, have our first celebrity moment. A car in front is being mobbed by screaming young girls taking pictures. We push past, trying to act like we're not looking (as we fancy ourselves to be unimpressed by celebrity), but we notice one another straining to see who's arriving. It's little Haley Joel Osment! Brad, watching him wave, accidentally steps on a small poodle.

> *Cannes Rule 3: Do not expect to have great food just because you are in the South of France. Every big lunch in Cannes is a buffet, and the main ingredient is mayonnaise. Shrimp, cucumber, crab, pasta—all warming in the sun.*

We push past the very official-looking Frenchman in the lobby of the Hilton checking tickets for the FilmFour party and ride up to the roof of the Noga. One barrier down, one to go. Aha, the publicists working the door know us and like us. Less of a hassle just to let us pass. We glide in without tickets. I sit down with *Metropolitan* director Whit Stillman. He says he just finished his novelization of *The Last Days of Disco*. You'd think directors like Stillman would have better things to do than write novelizations. But look at it this way: give them a chance to spend more time with their characters, and they'll take it. Pam and Brad check out the mayonnaise buffet and come back empty-handed. Why did we want in here so badly?

> *Cannes Rule 4: People will sometimes get up and leave in the middle of a movie or a meeting. Get used to it. Cannes was founded on principled rejection.*

Our first day at Cannes is pretty light. After lunch, we have two quick meetings. These days, our work takes place mostly in conference rooms at hotels along La Croisette. We've graduated from the Bunker. Each of the hotels has restaurants on the beach across the street, umbrellas and tables and sand, and when financiers are feeling generous, you'll end up getting a free meal and some sun. Most companies—well, the ones that have had good years—rent "villas," three- and four-story houses that double as offices and sleeping quarters. Most of the time, we go to the money. We're the ones begging.

In all the glare and glad-handing, it's easy to forget that Cannes started as a kind of political protest, a real-world *J'accuse*. In 1939, with Renoir's *Grand Illusion* the leading contender to win the top prize at the Venice festival—the original international festival—the German and Italian judges split the top prize between a German film (made under the aegis of Goebbels' ministry of propaganda) and an Italian film directed by Mussolini's son. The French were disgusted. The festival was a mouthpiece for the Axis, they argued, and they withdrew in protest. To design a festival without political bias and repression, French critics and filmmakers created the Cannes Film Festival (and promptly canceled it after opening night, when France declared war on Germany).

Nearly thirty years later, the festival almost imploded. In 1968, with the rest of France convulsing with student marches and strikes, the leading avant-garde filmmakers, including François Truffaut and Jean-Luc Godard, protested the festival's bourgeois orientation. Henri Langlois, founder of Le Cinémathèque Française and leading advocate of the New Wave, had been fired, and they felt the state turning against their movement. Out of the controversy, the festival created the Director's Fortnight to open up the festival to "little-known filmmakers and national cinemas, without concern for budgets or shooting formats." It's the fringy grab bag of the festival. In 1974, when *Mean Streets* screened at Cannes, it went to the Director's Fortnight and was soundly ignored.

Many films screen "out of competition," from *Hollywood Ending* to *Star Wars Episode II*, so there's not really a threshold of quality. It's a way for studios opening summer movies to use the publicity of Cannes (in May) to launch a film. The section Un Certain Regard, created in 1978, is more of a survey of global cinema, so there are no prizes. It started out as a way of drawing in films about other art forms and more contemporary history. The competition is, by far, the festival's most prestigious section, but the Palme d'Or does not guarantee box office. For every *Pulp Fiction* that wins, there are five *Billy Augusts*. What's *Billy August*? Exactly. The fact that a movie ends up mentioned in papers across the world does not translate into a distributor's picking it up.

Screenings at Cannes can be terrifying: the audience does not hold back. When *Girlfight*, Karyn Kusama's indie about a teenage boxer from Brooklyn, was screened at the Director's Fortnight, amid the applause, one lone man stood up and booed. The audience shouted him down viciously.

The films in competition are shown in the grand Palais du Cinéma, a theater with a screen the width of a Wal-Mart. It's strictly black-tie. As your movie begins, you sit completely still, praying for silence. A cough can echo forever in the big hall and set off a whole chain, so that it sounds like a TB ward. But it gets worse. The seats in the Palais are heavy and jolt up when you leave them, making an audible thud. That's the sound you dread most. In a bad screening you hear many thuds—every thud sending an earthquakelike spasm through your body.

My first couple of times at Cannes, I had to make up my schedule long before I went and then just hope that the meeting I had set up ten days ago with an executive I'd never met would actually be on the Carlton Terrace at 10 a.m. I had to leave notes for people at their hotels, assuming they even slept, but that was about it in terms of controlling things. Cell phones changed Cannes just as they changed L.A.

In these meetings, we tout our past successes, our record of fiscal responsibility, our buzz, then go through our projects (around a dozen) in active development or production, dropping names like Altman, Todd Solondz, and Mary Harron. Sometimes those meetings are great: high-energy, exciting, engaged—the kind where we ourselves are actually reminded how cool our movies are. But the opposite can happen too, and it's demoralizing.

A Great Cannes Meeting

I show up on time with my partners and the director. The company we are meeting with is on time as well. We order drinks. It turns out they have read the script! *And* they have prepared questions and concerns to discuss with the director! We proceed to have a lively, engaged conversation. They a) express genuine interest in getting involved, b) seem to actually have money to invest, and c) do not seem in the least bit fazed by the amount of money we are asking for. We end by clinking glasses and vowing to be at Cannes next year with this very movie. Icing on the cake: they pick up the tab for the drinks. I have had this meeting maybe once or twice in twelve years.

A Good Cannes Meeting

We show up late but they are running late too. The Big Cheese immediately confesses he has not read the script ("I'm sorry. I wanted to. You know how it is!") But the second banana has read it and likes it. We proceed to basically pitch the project to the Big Cheese while the second banana asks the director some pointed questions. They express cautious enthusiasm but with some caveats, such as a) "We need at least one more huge star," b) "That's not the final version of the script, is it?" c) "Nine million dollars! Wow, we thought closer to five," and d) the even Bigger Cheese still has to read it. We split the drinks tab and leave. If we are lucky, the following *won't* happen (but it usually does): we leave the meeting and immediately run into someone who says, "What were you meeting with *them* for? They don't have a pot to piss in! They lost everything on [last year's indie disaster]!" I have this meeting often.

A Lousy Cannes Meeting

We show up late, breathless, hot, and sweaty. They are even later. Finally they appear. The Big Cheese (probably someone who prides himself on being "frank") sits down and says something like "We are really trying to do higher concept movies here at Such and Such Co. This seems a little small for us." We all try to convince him of the universalness of our movie, and he listens politely but answers his cell phone twice while we're talking. After a few more minutes of conversation, it becomes clear that he has not actually read our script. His second banana smiles at us sheepishly. At the end we shake hands and get a lukewarm commitment from Big Cheese to take a look at our project sometime in the indefinite future. We didn't even get drinks. This kind of meeting also happens a lot.

A Terrible Cannes Meeting

We show up on time at Big Company's office, probably at the Majestic or Carlton Hotel. We are greeted by a pretty young thing who tells us the Big Cheese's meeting is running late and would we mind awfully waiting a bit? We all sit down in the waiting area, not quite big enough for us all. After twenty minutes she comes back and says Big Cheese just can't get out, she's awfully sorry, but he said for us to meet with Seventeenth Banana instead. So we troop into a room with someone who looks about twelve years old and says, "Hi! So who are you guys exactly?" We start to explain Killer Films while he smiles and nods and glances at his BlackBerry. "Well, cool! Nice to have met you! I'll be on the lookout for that project!" and out we go. I simmer on the Croisette: "Don't they know who I am!" We take a collective deep breath and head to the next meeting. We have this meeting too often!

Signs that your meeting is going nowhere fast

Bad Location: Instead of at a busy bar, at a decent table, or on a terrace, you're in someone's unkempt hotel room surrounded by dirty laundry.

Absence of Honchos, or the Seventeenth Banana Problem.

Ignorance: The people with whom you are meeting have no idea what the meeting is about, schedule almost no time to be with you, or maybe don't even show up.

Yawns: A terrible sign—despite the fact that no one sleeps here. Yawns are especially bad news from people trying hard to make it look as if they're not yawning.

Interruptibility: A minion slinks into the room in the middle of your pitch to remind the honcho of the next, far more important meeting/phone call. This means that before you sat down, the executive has told his assistant that this is an "interruptible" meeting. The worst is when you're pitching to a group and the key executive simply gets up while you're talking and, without explanation, leaves the room.

Boredom, Your Own: When all of the above start to happen, and when you begin to bore yourself with your spiel—I feel like I'm chewing food that has already been eaten—it's time to wrap it up and cut your losses.

And get to the Moulin de Mougins. Every year, the IFC (one of the principal investors in *Boys Don't Cry* and a great supporter of indie film) throws a big dinner at the Moulin, which is a secluded restaurant in Mougins, about a half hour outside Cannes. For me, it's one of the high points of Cannes. The dinner is an odd mix: local cable operators from across the United States dressed in suits mix with a group of indie film types. The young star of *Girlfight*, Michelle Rodriguez, and director Darren Aronofsky drink champagne and talk to a guy who is in charge of satellite sales for Cablevision.

It's always the same menu. I get the truffle. We skip out before dessert to meet actor/writer/director Tim Blake Nelson for a drink. We submitted his unflinching, bleak *The Grey Zone*—a film about the Jews who were coerced to help the Nazis in the camps—to the Cannes competition because it was the kind of movie that needed the imprimatur of a festival to get people into theaters. They rejected it. Still he's here with *O Brother, Where Art Thou?* We have drinks and are in bed by 3 a.m. Setting our alarms for 8 a.m., we are ready for our first full day of nonstop meetings.

Cannes Rule 5: Five hours of sleep is a lot of sleep.

We wake up after a couple of hours of hard sleep. I leave first; I'm being interviewed by Charles Lyons of *Variety* for a cover story that's supposed to run today. Killer Films is forming an alliance with Jody Patton and Paul Allen's production/finance company, Clear Blue Sky, to make *Far from Heaven*. This is (we hope) big news. I have to make sure to stress Killer's ongoing partnership with John Wells Productions, which *Variety* has failed to mention in the last two stories it has run on Killer. Given what John has done for our company, these oversights are painful.

We fill the morning with meetings and, in the afternoon, Pam swelters in a tent in the *Variety* pavilion moderating a panel on Financing Independent Film. She's flanked by eight guys (Rick Sands of Miramax, Russell Schwartz of USA, and Jonathan Sehring of the IFC, among others)—the only woman on stage. "Despite how it may appear from this panel," she begins, "there are women who spend their lives raising money for independent movies." Rah rah!

During the panel, Brad and Laird call around, trying to figure out our evening's activities. On any given night, there are a dozen parties in villas, on the beach, and on boats that are strictly invitation-only. Some are planned in advance and some are spontaneous. And any party that has a limited invite list, no matter who is throwing it, becomes a hot ticket. (The *Velvet Goldmine* party we threw at Cannes was incredibly exclusive; people were actually beaten down by security guards as they tried to climb over the fence.)

Cannes Rule 6: There is always some other great thing happening that you have not been invited to.

Cannes breeds this feeling, no matter how secure you think you are. You walk around sensing that, at any moment, there is a lunch, a party, a press conference, a meeting that you have been excluded from. You try to stay above it, but then someone says, "I'm heading off to the Luxembourg Film Financing Website Lunch!" and suddenly you're back in high school.

A primary example of "You only want to go to the party that didn't invite you": Darren Aronofsky's second feature, *Requiem for a Dream*, is showing tomorrow. We casually ask producer Palmer West if there will be a party (the point, of course, is to cadge an invitation), and he says, "Oh, just a really small dinner for the people who worked on the movie." Fair enough. Then, later on, Micah Green of Sloss Law asks if he'll be seeing us at the *"Requiem* bash." Ouch! Killer is off the list! I mean, we're already going to other parties—and, I might add, far cooler, more exclusive ones. But we spend the afternoon obsessing over why we didn't make the *Requiem* cut.

The rest of our day passes in a haze. We have pitch meeting after pitch meeting, and they all start to blend together. Brad takes notes just to keep straight who is interested in what.

Cannes Rule 7: If you can—even if it is only for a few hours—don't forget that you are in the South of France.

Exhausted and sunburned, we make plans to escape Cannes and have dinner at the Colombe d'Or, an old farmhouse/inn in the hills past Nice. Relaxing with amazing food and good wine, we avoid talking about the festival.

Four hours later, we wonder where to conclude our night. After parties or dinners, we usually end up at the Petite Majestic, a tiny bar away from the Croisette that stays open until dawn. Around one or two every morning, people head over and the crowd spills into the street. This is the most egalitarian place in Cannes: anyone can go to the Petite Majestic; there's no bouncer at the door. Schlock filmmakers, lower-level executives, and major stars all stand in the street drinking big glasses of beer.

The other extreme in late-night options is the bar at the Hotel du Cap. We know people who have been coming to Cannes for years and have never made the cut for the du Cap. The entrance to the grounds is strictly guarded by large men with muzzled dogs and a list. The list is more terrifying than the dogs. If you aren't on it, you don't get in.

The Hotel du Cap is legendary for several reasons: They do not accept credit cards—cash only. This means hotel guests have to wire the money for their stay before they get there. The drinks are astronomically expensive. The bartenders seem to have a hard time keeping a straight face as they tell you that will be thirty dollars for your glass of Evian. Legend has it that one major talent agency's du Cap bill was over $1 million.

Set on a cliff in Antibes, the du Cap is an imposing structure. It is also the primary spot for stargazing. We end up at the du Cap because Tim Blake Nelson is staying there. Ethan and Uma (pre-divorce), Nick Nolte, and George Clooney are there. The thing about George Clooney is that he looks in person just like he does on screen. Some stars have a team of stylists and collagen experts and pocket Botox to keep them attractive. Not Clooney. The rest of the crowd is a mixture of industry bigwigs (New Line head Bob Shaye, Miramax's Harvey Weinstein), hangers-on who can't believe they're in the same room as all these celebrities, and a surprising number of women who seem to be practicing the world's oldest profession.

Pushing through the bar past this insane scene, we settle on the terrace with Frances McDormand, Joel Coen, and Tim. This is a Killer sort of crowd. They are glowing after a good screening. Frances reminds me that she worked for me in a short for Killer in 1995, Tom Kalin's *Plain Pleasures*. As if I would have forgotten! Tomorrow she plans to travel to Nice to go thrift shopping and tells us about the great French nightgowns and fabrics she collects from the sixties and seventies. Some women with bleached hair, stilettos, and Moschino clothes sit down next to us. Pam wonders if they are prostitutes, and Frances says, "Hey, there is a fine line here."

Cannes Rule 8 (maybe the most important): In a market like this one, you can't really accuse anyone else of being a prostitute.

We spend the evening talking on the terrace and getting people to buy us drinks. The trick is to get on the tab of a bigwig. We get a reporter from *Variety* to buy us a round. Next Laird approaches the bar and tells the bartender to put our drinks on the tab of a big-shot film executive staying at the hotel who is presently ringed by ladies on the other side of the room. The bartender asks Laird to point him out. Laird points over to Brad, who smiles at the bartender. Laird returns to the table with four drinks (tab: $125). Truth is, the big shot would probably not mind that we charged drinks to his room, but he would be stunned that the bartender did not know what he looks like.

Cannes Rule 9: Never pay for anything. In a town where an ice-cream cone can run ten dollars, you can save your child's college tuition by having distributors and foreign sales companies pick up your dinner or drinks tab.

As we head out around 3 a.m., John Lesher, then a UTA agent (who now runs Paramount Classics), asks us if he can buy Killer lunch at the du Cap on Tuesday. Taking note of rules number 8 and 9, we quickly rearrange our meetings for the day so we can take him up on the offer. One must keep one's priorities straight.

I'm up early to the usual flawless, hot, sunny day and an apartment full of snoring co-workers. Pam is the next one conscious—which is generally the case, since we're sharing a room. We stumble out into the sun in search of *Variety*. Killer Films' deal with Jody Patton and Paul Allen's Clear Blue Sky is supposed to be announced today: we're anxious to inspect the placement and to make sure that our other deal—with John Wells Productions—is also there. It is: front page! Too bad it's beneath an announcement of a digital deal between GreeneStreet Films and United Artists. Harrumph. Our lawyer, John Sloss (he brokered the deal with Clear Blue Sky), says not to worry. We should ultimately feel very satisfied. Job well done.

Cannes Rule 10: You will look like shit by the end. Embrace it.

It's our third straight day of pitching our slate, and we're starting to flag. After a few days, everyone you meet develops a sort of demented stare: they're exhausted, hot, and often hungover. And when you look in the mirror, you don't always recognize the bleary-eyed person staring back. A few people somehow manage to avoid this deterioration. We bump into Manny Nunez, a talent agent at CAA, and marvel at how rested and put together he looks. He says it's his Cuban roots, but we all believe that CAA has discovered some sort of antiaging elixir. Or maybe it's some sort of packaging deal with the devil.

Today our morning meetings click—especially the 10 a.m. with Alliance, a large Canadian distributor and foreign sales company. Charlotte Mickie, who has been trying to do a project with us for a long time (she worked hard to convince her company to get involved with *Boys Don't Cry*), clearly made this session a priority. It was well attended, focused, and productive. We have one script in development with them and leave with a clear sense of what else they have their eye on.

Then it's off to the American Pavilion, an enormous tent on the waterfront for American festival attendees. It's really just computers and a buffet table with some imported celebrity chef like Mario Batali and Bobby Flay getting ignored because nobody has the time to eat. We try to check our e-mail. Annoying, because no one honors the ten-minute limit on the public computers.

Quite hungry by now, we pile into the car and head off to the du Cap for our lunch with John Lesher. The lunch scene at the du Cap is pure calm at the center of the storm. Casual fabulosity. Spectacular views of the Riviera, really good food, crisp white wine, and an excellent angle on Harvey Weinstein and Sean Penn in private laughter. Lesher is fun company. He represents a host of cool directors we want to hear gossip about, but he is discreet and most of the gossip comes from us. Still, we get nuggets. Meanwhile, I share the asparagus risotto *avec* black truffle with Brad. Pam and Laird do La Grande Bouffe (only one trip each). We all finish with wild strawberries and cream. Now we're fortified for an afternoon of meetings.

Running late for our 3 p.m., stuck in what Brad calls "beach traffic," we use the time to fit in phone calls. Laird calls his friend at Miramax for contact info on the guy we're running late to see, but the conversation quickly segues into party reports and the contents of festival goody bags. Brad—who really shouldn't be talking on the phone because he's one-handing the wheel on some narrow, curvy Riviera streets—checks in with Jocelyn, Killer's development exec, who tells him that for some reason domestic issues of *Variety* do *not* mention Killer's deal with John Wells Productions. He freaks out, begins to shriek, and we grab the phone before he drives us off a cliff into the sea. What a Cannes legend that would have made.

The Last Day at Cannes with Killer Films

Pam, Brad, Laird, and I crawl up and down the Croisette, continuing our pitch meetings, taking turns being "on." We've had two front-page stories at this festival: our slate of films for the next year and our deal with Jody Patton and Paul Allen's Clear Blue Sky. Our Oscar nominations and award for *Boys Don't Cry* inform everything. We had credibility before, but we still needed to shop Kim Peirce around for years before we'd raised a scant couple of million to make that movie. Now more people trust us when we say we know that a director has "got it." They want to be in business with us.

We even meet with Kinowelt, which is sort of like the Miramax of Europe, only bigger. Kinowelt pulled its money out of *Safe* at the last moment in 1993, and there's been bad blood since. But after some initial coolness (they say it was my fault, I say it was theirs, etc.), our meeting goes terrifically. Of course, that doesn't automatically translate into a deal. (In fact, they've since crashed and burned.)

Many international distributors vanished in the late 1990s and early 2000s when the TV resale opportunities in Europe dried up. Each year, another company dies, but a new one shows up in its place. There's a constant churn, from British Film Council money to German funds, so you have to keep reinventing the wheel. To be successful, you have to stay one step ahead of an ever-shifting market. For this reason, you hear a lot of promises at Cannes, but follow-throughs are harder to come by. People here are not quite themselves. There's an edge of unreality to all your business dealings. Even the most dismal places for meetings have views of the Riviera. Back in one's grim office, things might look different.

On the Croisette I run into James Schamus. He's in his bow tie, a tad sweaty in the relentless sunshine. James is delighted with the review of the new Ang Lee movie *Ice Storm* in *Variety:* it is, he says, as if he'd written it himself. I'm happy for him. It's good to see one movie starting out with a bang. James congratulates us graciously on our deal with Clear Blue Sky, although he does manage to slip in that he knew about it before the official announcement. How could he have? But that kind of insider information is the real currency in the film world (like a few years later, when I got tipped that he was going to run Focus).

One thing I haven't mentioned yet are the *movies*—ostensibly, the reason we're here. That's because we've been so busy running from meeting to meeting that we've pretty much resigned ourselves to not seeing any.

The buzz this year is that there's "nothing to buy" and that the acquisitions execs are just going through the motions. Their attitude is "I must see movies in order to pretend that my company is doing something other than spending inordinate amounts of money to sell last year's leftovers."

You get this cynicism regularly, at every festival. This is partly because there *is* less to buy. Independent film financing has changed drastically in the last decade, such that most of Killer's "independent" films are presold, meaning we have our domestic and international distribution in place by the time we shoot, or else we sell the film during postproduction. We can take advantage of the intense competition among the mini-majors (Miramax, New Line, Lionsgate, etc.) for good product and make a deal before we even get to the festivals. By the time Cannes rolls around, the film is no longer for sale.

As we get ready for dinner, we talk about how Cannes is its own world, with its own vocabulary, rituals, and daily newspapers. Nothing outside show business has meaning. For two weeks, you're clueless about unrest in Iraq, but you are keenly tuned in to the status of the next Almodóvar. Cannes is delirious with contradictions. You'll spend a whole day on a yacht, pitching various investors and distributors, and while everybody's talking about their millions, your head is spinning and you're thinking, "Lock your eyes on the horizon!" with a smile plastered on your face. Fortunately, nobody is paying attention to you. They're looking at Helen Hunt, next to you in a dazzling cream-colored suit, pitching *her* movie while a band of bad French lounge lizards are serenading the disembarking passengers of the humongo *Queen Elizabeth 2* that just docked two inches from the yacht you're on . . .

———————

Cannes is also something of a yardstick for me. I've been coming here for over ten years, and each year my experience reflects the changes in my career. The first year, I slept on the floor of someone's hotel room and my meals were the little hors d'oeuvres at the parties I managed to scam my way into.

And I actually went to see the movies.

Then I got to stay in hotels but I shared a room. Then I didn't have to share a room (or a bed!) unless I wanted to. Then my movies showed in competition, and I got to wear a suit and walk up the red carpet. Then I actually got invited to parties and didn't have to rely on friendship with the publicist at the door to get in. Then people called me to try to set up meetings instead of the other way around. Now— this is the most amazing change—I occasionally pick up a check.

I've lost something too. I don't stay out as late. In the old days, I'd go to parties until 2 a.m. and hang at the bar of the Petite Majestic until 5. The year that *This Boy's Life* was screened, I sat outside the Petite Majestic at 3 a.m. watching the late CAA agent Jay Maloney, who represented Spielberg, Scorsese, Kubrick, and Tom Cruise until cocaine got the better of him, chat up Leonardo DiCaprio. The sense of serendipity is gone. I used to gasp when I found myself three feet from some movie star or legendary director, but it's all familiar now: the same cast of characters, the same parties, the same little quiches. Business as usual. Has the festival changed or have I? Probably both. As we head to our last dinner, on a yacht, I am oddly nostalgic for that earlier, more guerrilla Cannes. I wonder if I'd sleep on the floor to get it back.

Spotlight: David Linde

HEAD OF UNIVERSAL STUDIOS; FORMER CO-PRESIDENT OF FOCUS FEATURES (*BROKEBACK MOUNTAIN, LOST IN TRANSLATION, THE PIANIST*)

Making Sense of International Sales

One of the most startling changes to the American film industry in the past decade is just how many movies get released in a week and how the increase has affected specialty-title films. The market has become intensely competitive. Take a look at the list of the top twenty movies in a given week in the summer of 2004: *Collateral, The Village, The Manchurian Candidate,* and *De-Lovely* are all pursuing the same adult audience at once. You've got movies like these taking away filmgoers from specialty-audience movies like *A Home at the End of the World.* It's wild. Since it's become more competitive, it's become more expensive to distribute films. Open up the *New York Times* on a Friday, and the first six movie pages are big ads for major studio and "indie" releases. Distributors have become ever more reliant on how the film "opens," which ratchets up the costs of advertising the film and getting it out there.

So now you're paying more for advertising and it's front-loaded with the initial release of the picture. And since you're spending so much money so quickly, publicity (which is relatively inexpensive) is of paramount value. That, in turn, means increasing star value and securing the highest-caliber cast you can get, since they're (beyond the quality of the film itself) the best guarantee of media attention for a specialty title. It can be a very cooperative way to make a movie. Independence tends to breed the original and quality drama that actors often seek.

In a reaction to all this escalation, high concept has also begun to take hold in the indie world as one alternative to star casting. Typically, you associate high concept with Hollywood, but two of the most talked-about movies of 2004 were *Open Water* (lost at sea, sharks circling!) and *Napoleon Dynamite* (weird underdog who doesn't swear!). Most recently, *The Grudge,* which was an independently conceived and financed film (but distributed by a studio), hit it out of the park. A few years earlier, *Crouching Tiger, Hidden Dragon* did wonderfully for us—we were Good Machine then—as well.

Interestingly, a trend that has emerged simultaneously in the international marketplace is an increasing interest in local productions. It's not unusual these days to see local, relatively inexpensively budgeted films gross tens of millions of dollars in a single country. *Good Bye Lenin!* grossed $41 million just in Germany, and those are no longer unprecedented numbers. *Hero* made $125 million outside North America and $26 million in China alone. These are enormous numbers and represent theatrical box office only. You've got DVD and television revenue after that. Accordingly, a lot of overseas distributors, instead of buying American independent features as they used to, are getting involved in local productions themselves. That trend is decreasing the market for American drama, which is largely what American independent film is.

These overseas markets are quite distinct from the U.S. market. Just as one example, in Europe and, to a lesser degree, Japan, the director can also be the star because there is much broader recognition and appreciation of the filmmaker than there is in this country. So certain star directors—most of whom do not work in English—can attract an immense amount of publicity coverage for the distribution of a film. The specialty market overseas also tends to be somewhat less dependent on marketing expenditures than we are in the United States, which takes away some of the competitive (monetary) advantage of the American studios and their product. This further fuels the market for local productions and films by name directors because overseas distributors have easier, almost preferred, access to that kind of material. That reality further decreases the interest in independent American dramas. Given this kind of marketplace, how do you differentiate your production?

Back we go to the cast. Let's think about it: a distributor has two dramas, both of which he or she likes but one with an A-list actor attached and the other without. In this environment, which one would you choose?

How do producers like Christine Vachon enter the international marketplace with their projects? There are several ways. First of all, they can sell the worldwide rights to an American company (like Focus Features) proven to be an effective distributor overseas and domestically. Second, if she doesn't have that American deal, she can seek financing from an international sales company that operates only overseas (like Fortissimo, Capitol Films, or Celluloid Dreams) or one of their affiliated financiers. Third, there is a variation on that second strategy. If she has a film with a name director and a proven track record, she may be able to (with some help) secure a few key overseas distribution deals that will provide the financing cornerstone the film needs. Once it's proven there is overseas interest in the film, an American company or sales agent is motivated to step in and finance the picture. That's exactly what we did at Good Machine with Christine on *Happiness*.

There is also a newer alternative that has recently materialized, one that allows a producer to access ongoing television deals that studios maintain overseas. Very generally, every studio has its own international theatrical and video distribution divisions as well as "output deals" with overseas pay and free television networks. These output deals are effectively an agreement with a pay TV service (like HBO) and/or a free TV outlet (like a network) to license a certain number of movies every year from the studio. All studios want these output deals because it's their way to secure revenue in a risky business. The level of revenue is usually based on the theatrical performance of each film, but these deals will also include a minimum or "floor" price that the studio will receive no matter what the performance of the film. The revenue of all these deals together can result in an aggregate "floor" of millions and millions of dollars—again, no matter what the performance of the picture. Several of the studio-based specialty divisions use this mechanism to calculate the minimum value of a film in considering it for production or acquisition. As with everything, there is a potential downside. If a film is made in part based on its minimum overseas television value, there is less motivation to release it *theatrically* overseas.

Let's take Germany as a possible example, where there is one pay TV service and multiple free TV broadcasters. The hypothetical American studio that has bought Christine's movie has an output deal with the pay service as well as with one of the broadcasters. Those deals allow for up to, let's say, twenty movies to be licensed by the studio to the output partner each year. If the studio doesn't make twenty movies, then its specialty division gets to "put" its movies through also.

This is the mechanism that provided the financing for *A Home at the End of the World*. John Sloss, who represented Christine and the other producer of the film (Hart Sharp Entertainment), first went to the leading international sales companies, none of which offered enough money to finance the picture. So he went to

Warner Bros. and negotiated with them. Warner agreed to buy the movie for domestic release (through their specialty division, Warner Independent Pictures) and separately guaranteed the film access to their overseas output deals. Because those deals have an aggregate "floor" and are guaranteed, John was able to secure the financing of the picture in a loan against the minimum revenue from those deals.

Letter from L.A. I

ONE DAY IN JULY

Cancel the studio screening?—Working Variety*—There is nothing more important than Julia Roberts—We keep a secret*

A Very Rough Cut

From the way Hollywood sells itself, you'd think studio lots were all backdrops and celebrity sightings. What they really are is Midtown laid out sideways: blocks of low-level buildings, housing office after office of executives, marketing people, D-boys and D-girls, etc. Every now and then you catch a little shingle advertising the odd star's "production company." That's the perk stars get as payback for doing the studio's schlock. (You don't have to be Tom Cruise to snag one; even Seann William Scott has a production company with a bungalow.)

The Warner Bros. lot in Burbank is nicer, classier, and older than most—a small, sand-colored city, with a commissary, upscale restaurant, and a view of the L.A. "River" sluicing along a basin the width and depth of a roof gutter. For some reason, the tallest structure on the lot is an ancient-looking, freestanding water tower that probably slaked the ponies of *Intolerance*. Most of the surface level consists of either enormous, windowless boxes (the actual shooting lots) or parking spaces, each with its own stenciled curb reading, "This Space Reserved for ..."

I've flown in from New York to show the rough cut of *A Home at the End of the World* to Mark Gill, the new head of the recently christened

Warner Independent division of the studio and the guy responsible for distributing our movie. We've got a first-look deal, which means Warner Independent gets the first shot at making our movies. *Home* will be the first of the partnership, and the first film for the division, so a lot is riding on it.

I first met Mark back when he worked for Miramax as the head of marketing. He's about my age, really tall and striking in a long, lanky way. He started off as a reporter at *Newsweek,* jumped into PR, and did the usual stint in the trenches at Miramax. He played a large part in the advertising campaigns for *In the Bedroom, Amélie,* and *The Talented Mr. Ripley.* According to my friend and colleague Ted Hope, who worked with him on *In the Bedroom,* he's a great co-conspirator; all independent producers, when they work with studios, need executives who can help you navigate the inevitable politics of corporate institutions. Still, when I knew him back then, I found him guarded and cold.

But then he graduated sideways to become a producer at a company called Stratus Entertainment. I ran into him at Sundance this year, having not seen him since he left Miramax. He sat in front of me at a screening, so I said hi, cordially. But he just turned around and beamed hello. He was a totally different person, so relieved not to be working for Miramax anymore. And I thought, You take the guy out of that context, who knows how nice he can be? Clearly, something worked, because now he's in charge here at Warner Independent Pictures, as of two weeks ago.

There must be hundreds of these screening rooms at Warner Bros. The regulation hugely comfy plush armchairs, check. Wall-to-wall carpeting, check. Lighting soft enough to hide any nips and tucks, check. But there's only one in which Tom Hulce is having a breakdown. This one. Our co-producer on *Home,* Tom was a huge asset. He was the director Michael Mayer's closest ally and ambassador to the film world. After directing *Side Man* and *Thoroughly Modern Millie* on Broadway, Michael wanted to try his hand at a movie, and for first-time directors, it can help to have a veteran at their side. Since *Amadeus,* Tom has become a respected theater and film producer. Shadowing Michael almost every day on the Toronto set, Tom acted as a sounding board for Michael's ideas and ran interference when necessary. If Katie from Killer took care of all the logistics, Tom protected Michael's creativity.

With Mark out of the room for a moment, Tom says to me, sotto voce, "I think we need to cancel the screening."

This was Mark's first chance to see a cut of *Home*. We weren't going to cancel the screening. "What are you talking about?" I say.

"Watch this," he says, and plays the tape. The dub of *Home* that we got from our editing facility looks awful, washed out and nearly unintelligible. Killer, by accident, has submitted a *terrible* quality VHS for projection, the version of the film put together on Final Cut (not Avid). It looked like the garage-budget version of a film that was already low-budget. (Of course, most executives at studios are used to film screenings, not tape anyway.) After a month and a half of filming and weeks of editing, what we've got to show makes Colin Farrell look like a gray smear with a soundtrack that sounds as if it's coming through a subway grate.

"Since no one will be able to tell which characters are which," Tom says, "do you think I should just stand in the back of the room and shout out their names?" We try to get a techie to fiddle with the image, but once he makes the switch, the image is a lot better, but there is literally one track of sound. You can hear dialogue and a little, tinny bit of music.

At that point, Mark, John Wells, and a couple of junior Warners executives join us. I can see Tom is completely unnerved. You don't get any more top than this brass and he's afraid we're about to get judged. But I decide, Fuck it; even if the video looks bad, at least it shows there's room for improvement.

"Hopefully the performances and the compellingness of the narrative will overcome some *slight* technical difficulties," I tell them. Little do they know. Amazingly, they don't walk out. At the end, Mark gives the usual encouragement: it's got great potential. He has some notes: he thinks we meet the main characters too late in the movie; he thinks there's a stronger performance lurking in Colin's Bobby. He wants a couple of days to gather his thoughts. But most importantly, he says, "I can market the shit out of this."

Competition

I'm meeting up with the very funny Doug McGrath, who adapted and directed *Emma* and just finished directing *Nicholas Nickleby*. His new script is now in the middle of a feeding frenzy. Appropriate that we meet at the Warner's commissary.

Doug's script recounts the story of Truman Capote writing *In Cold Blood;* it's one of the best Killer has ever developed. It focuses on the intense bond Capote formed with the incarcerated killer Perry Smith, one of two drifters who killed a family in 1959. It's witty, poignant, an unclassifiable mix of true-crime documentary and love story between what Doug calls "a near-dwarf and a mass-murdering other near-dwarf." (Both Capote and Perry were short.) New Line is into it. Miramax wants it. It's the ideal Killer film, and we're seeing if Warner Independent will agree to finance and distribute it. As part of the first-look deal, we have to show it to them, but they've passed on everything since *Home.* In my thinking, Warner Independent was created to make this kind of movie: it has a literary pedigree, it's performance-driven, and it's way cheaper than *The Matrix* and *Harry Potter.* Two weeks ago, Killer had a totally different slate of upcoming projects in *Bettie Page* and *Mrs. Harris.* HBO snatched those up, then zip, everything changes.

This is where Richard Lovett, one of the partners at CAA, comes in. Lovett started out in the mail room and climbed his way to the top of CAA in 1995. He brought Spielberg, Tom Hanks, and Julia Roberts to the CAA client list, and he's credited with softening CAA's image—less sharky and more subtle. I made sure to send him a copy of the script, and last Friday night he called me to say that he loves it and that he hopes I don't mind, but he went ahead and *slipped it to Julia Roberts.* There's a pivotal part in the film for a Harper Lee, the author of *To Kill a Mockingbird* and one of Truman's closest friends. When Truman went to Kansas to research *In Cold Blood,* she accompanied him. Capote was a squeaky-voiced, tiny little man, and she was his "ambassador to normalcy." When a partner at CAA—the topmost level—loves a script, it spreads through the entire company. It's like having this giant amorphous borg want to service you in any way it can. Julia read it and said, "I want to do a meeting with these people." So it's scheduled for this afternoon.

Except that this can't come up at the commissary in our meeting. We can't create false expectations about this becoming a Julia Roberts movie when we don't even know for sure that she's interested. Moreover, if we talk about Julia Roberts, the scale of Doug's movie changes irrevocably: it becomes a star vehicle and nothing less than stars will do. Doug honestly did not want to make a $30 million movie or a $25 million movie or even a $20 million movie. He knows that, given his material, for a studio to turn a profit, this movie can't cost too much. (His *Emma* cost $6 million and made $40 million, turned Gwyneth into a star, and made Doug a hero at Miramax.) So Julia stays off our agenda.

Instead, we chitchat with Laura Holstein (John Wells's head of features), and Kevin McCormick, a Warner Bros. executive, who say they're interested, contingent on our finding a cast. It's clear the picture would go through Warner Independent Pictures, since even though Doug's a proven commodity, the mood of the picture is dark and close to being—if not actually—gay. But they see what we see in it.

Fortunately, Laura and Kevin are on to casting ideas. We draw up a list of potential Trumans and shoot high: Tom Hanks, Sean Penn, Jude Law. I don't think Tom Hanks will do it because he's already done gay, but you never know. Doug nixes Nicolas Cage because "he's too big"— Capote was five foot one—but chews over Mike Myers as a possibility. By the time Jake Gyllenhaal's name ends up on the list, we know we're done for the day.

Ms. Roberts

Doug and I get ferried to the CAA offices on Wilshire by the most starstruck intern I've ever met. It's sort of nice to be recognized, because it's rare, but she seems a little overenthralled with her gig. Doug picks up that she is having, as he later described, "a personal G-spot moment." She says, "We're going to CAA? Who are you meeting with?" I think, Oh no. I don't have a driver's license. I need her eyes on the road and her lips together.

Julia only left ICM two months ago, and CAA is eager to put out every welcome mat it has. (The fact is that Richard Lovett, one of the five partners at the top of CAA, even passed this quirky, literary script to Julia as an attempt to show her that they'd be different from ICM.) Still, Doug is extremely skeptical and protective of his script. Julia's involvement would certainly simplify things; we could make it with *Maggie* Gyllenhaal playing Truman at that point. But she'd also throw the balance off. *Infamous* is Truman's story, and using a megawatt bulb for background light might not work. Plus, Doug needs Harper Lee to be different from the society swans that surround Capote; she was not a glamorous woman. Doug doesn't see any way around that.

We collect ourselves in a third-floor conference room at CAA with the requisite tray of a thousand slices of kiwi and kumquat. Julia walks in, by herself, looking like she just came from her house without doing any extra fuss. Doug's a little gaga but he's hiding it well. She comes in and shakes hands and looks us in the eye; Doug chalks that up to good breeding.

Now some producers go into these meetings with elaborate Machiavellian strategies to coerce stars into their package. That's never worked for me. I advise people meeting talent to just say how they feel. Keep it down-to-earth. Anything else will sound forced.

So at first, there's just chitchat.

"Where are you from?" Julia asks Doug.

"I'm from Texas," Doug says.

"Oh, I'm so relieved,' she says. "Because I thought you were English because of *Nicholas Nickleby* and *Emma*." (Rumor has it she had a bad time on a British production. Maybe she was thinking, Just what I need, another English jerk to ruin my day.)

Doug then says, "Where are you from?"

"Smyrna, Georgia," Julia answers.

"Oh, I've heard of that," Doug says, and then he pauses for a second. "I guess I've heard of it because you're from there."

Do I talk about Killer? Does she know about our films? It isn't the time or place for me to ask or tell her. I interject occasionally, but Doug can more than easily handle his side of the conversation. If anything, when he's nervous, Doug has a propensity to chitchat a little too much. That's what I'm there for: to keep the business on the table.

The thing is, there's not much business to conduct. Julia is not the one who can tell us when she's available. That's what her agent does. She's not "attached" to this picture until we have a Truman locked in, and we don't. I just want her and Doug to have a meaningful conversation about the story and how they see it. She suggests some names for Truman. She's a fan of Billy Crudup and has been angling to act with him for a while. "Did you see him in *Elephant Man* on Broadway? He was amazing," she says. Doug tells her he loved Billy in *Arcadia* and had him audition for *Emma*. But is Billy too internal for Capote, a complete extrovert? Doug wonders.

We're there talking for an hour and a half. Julia mentions that Harper Lee disappears from the script a bit; once he's visiting Perry in prison, Capote calls home, but he only talks to the society ladies and never to Harper, who returns to New York. "I began to feel a little hurt that he wasn't calling me," Julia says. Good point. Doug nods. She shouldn't disappear. She's the main humanizing factor to Truman. Julia has some suggestions for where Harper might return to the story, but they are smart and appropriate. She isn't saying, "Maybe I could sweep out Perry's cell or something?"

Then I realize we're supposed to have a meeting with Mark Gill back at the Chateau Marmont at 5 p.m., in five minutes. I can't just take out my cell phone and say, "Excuse me, Julia, something a little more important just came up." In my insular little film world, frankly, *there is nothing more important than sitting in a room with Julia Roberts*. It would be rude, even though she probably wouldn't care. It's the actors who are insecure about their stardom who are like "Peel me a grape." She is more like "Isn't all this fame just funny?"

So we finally exit the office. Now, the CAA offices were designed by I. M. Pei to be a huge atrium. There's a hollow center that goes up to the top floor. The bottom two floors ring the lobby. The general purpose is maximum stargazing; you can look from the banister and see who is coming in, and from the lobby you can see who's walking around. We start heading to the office of Richard Lovett, Julia's agent. And suddenly, all the agents start sweeping out of their offices. It's like she's a queen surrounded by her court. The metaphor isn't that far off. With a $20 million per picture paycheck, Julia personally puts $2 million into CAA's coffers with every movie she makes.

Not telling

We race to the Chateau Marmont, and I alert Mark's people that we're going to be a half hour late. He's fine about it. We arrive and find him in the vaulted, cathedral-like sitting area in the hotel. I tell him we were at CAA.

"Oh, what about?" he asks.

"Just talking about various actors," I answer, keeping it vague.

Fortunately he doesn't ask and we don't give off a special Julia glow. We have a great meeting. Mark did the marketing campaign for Doug's *Emma,* so there's already a relationship. He wants to talk about *Infamous.* He's got some script notes; there are documentary interview segments, with Norman Mailer and others, sprinkled throughout the script. Are there too many of them? Doug doesn't disagree. He's just not sure which ones are unnecessary.

"And also, they're the least expensive thing to shoot," Doug says. "We're going to do them all in a studio in one day. And they might turn out to be important linking pieces when we cut the film. It'd be foolish not to shoot them." Good answer. Mark also thinks the section where Capote struggles to fit into small-town Kansas runs too long. "You can cut fifteen or twenty pages out of that," says Mark, and I see Doug recoil, like *You* try cutting fifteen pages. "I'll look at it again," says Doug, "but I don't think we can cut a fifth of the movie."

"How much are you thinking?" he asks.

Fifteen million, I say. He nods. It's not like he's about to hand us the money with a "Yes, go shoot it." The whole notion of a studio "green-lighting" a film has changed. It used to be that studios would say, "We're making this movie," and they'd go through as many actors as it took until they got someone. Now you're never really green-lit until you have a cast. And we haven't even begun the search.

"Well," he says. "This is a stunning script. I want to make it."

Postscript: Julia got pregnant with twins. Her due date turned out to be right in the middle of our shooting schedule. We moved on to Sandra Bullock.

Chapter 5
Crashes and Burns

A director passes (then fails) the Director's Quiz—Writer Vs. Director—What a bomb feels like—Life on the development conveyor belt—How Kirsten Dunst made, then unmade, a movie—Breaking the producer's triangle

LESSON: LEARN TO WALK AWAY.

A Cautionary Tale: The Problem Director

It was only after the movie had come and gone and done precisely $45,465 worth of business that Pam got the letter from the Director.* It was formal and apologetic. It read like one of those twelve-step letters, where you're supposed to ask forgiveness of all the people you've been awful to, a chance to tell them that you're clean and sober and struggling, off whatever you were on. I felt bad for the guy. But honestly, his self-destructiveness had made our lives hell and nearly ruined Killer's first studio-financed film.

When I think about this middle period in Killer's life, I see a

---

* Name withheld. Why? Because Pam told me to. We don't want this guy to come after us.

string of object lessons in learning to walk away—what I now know is an essential skill for a producer's survival. If we saw the warning signs of this ill-begotten flick, we didn't heed any of them. We were overeager, with a studio relationship to nurture. We needed a project in the pipeline. But sometimes the deal, the project, the star isn't worth it. It took me ten years to learn how to hold on tenaciously. Now I needed to learn how to let go.

When we met him, the Director had written and directed a great, low-budget indie with a dreamy, understated quality that we liked. He came to us with a script written by a successful Hollywood rewrite guy, a passion project, and the script was undeniably fresh and weird—the kind of story Killer could get into. The Director and the Writer came to us as a team. Or rather, they *represented* themselves as a team. In fact, the Writer was, contractually, a producer of the film primarily to protect his script. And as a producer, he'd be able to visit the set and supervise the production. Warning sign number one.

Typically, when new directors or producers come into Killer's office, we'll have a friendly lunch to check them out. Pam and I joke that we should give new directors a quiz to assess whether they can handle the job. It's really just one question: Have you been able to maintain a long-term relationship in your romantic life? Because if you can do that, you can probably maintain professional relationships. It's not always true, but it's the best test we've found.

Obviously, you want a solid, trusting creative relationship between the director and his producer (and, in this case, writer). It looked like these two had that. Still, we did our homework, a background check. You always want to call around to see if the team is consistent, if the same people who worked on the director's last movie are willing to work with him again. As far as we could find, a lone costume designer was the *only* person sticking with this director. The rest of the movie was going to be a complete reboot.

That's not completely uncommon; cinematographers, lighting designers, line producers all need to keep working, especially at indie pay scales. They can't wait around for a project to get green-lit or they'd starve. So they move on, and the fact that the team would be new didn't worry us too much. Then we called a well-known producer friend who had invested in the Director's first film, but he didn't raise any red flags. Pam called the distributor of his first film, another way of finding out how a person behaves in the process. The distributor said, "The Director is assertive and clear and fights for what he thinks is right. He's not obstructionist." They liked his first feature, and when things go smoothly, nobody notices the problems. A good outcome colors everything.

Not one told us that the Director was, as we came to learn, a mess and unproduceable. No one. I can't explain it really. I guess they thought that he'd changed, grown up. Maybe we just met him at the bottoming out of an addiction we never fully understood. Only when we emerged bruised and battered from the production did people start to come out of the woodwork to tell us the truth. It was only then that we got a letter from the producer friend, saying, "I'm really sorry I wasn't honest with you about what a nightmare it was to work with the Director. I just made an assumption that with producers of your stature, there's no way he would have been able to carry on those same highjinks that he did with us."

Pam and I have worked with demanding directors before. The word on music video director Mark Romanek was that he was *very* difficult. He'd gotten a rep of being a perfectionist, taking days to make a three-minute film. You can't do that on a movie, with crews and lights and craft services wilting away. The real issue for Mark on *One Hour Photo* was adjusting from a ridiculously high-end environment of boutique video production. He was used to a $7 million budget to put a single song on film. He was going to make *One Hour Photo* for $13 million. That reduction was going to hurt, no matter how you approached it. But any grief we experienced came from Mark's determination to make his film as good as it could be. When he was faced with a compromise, he was used to not compromising. That was going to have to change.

It's easy to think of these compromises as a problem exclusive to low-budget films, but sacrifices happen at every level of production. I read an interview with director Ron Howard (*The Missing, Apollo 13*) and his first AD, a guy he's worked with over and over. Howard made the point that he uses this guy because the AD helps him to compromise, even on a film budgeted at $78 million like *A Beautiful Mind*, to make a decision when they're on set and the sun is going down. Since Ron Howard is so invested at every level in his film's future, he notices where the money is going. If there's money being wasted, he doesn't like it. He has a producer's way of directing that balances the craft and the economics, the same as in any Killer production. Howard isn't alone. Most directors who stay working do so because they know when to bend. During the *Company* shoot, for all Bob Altman's blustering about "I don't care what it takes, make it happen," he was totally mindful of the budget. We never went over.

In preproduction, we realized the Director had big designs on the Writer's script, plans for changes that the Writer was, no surprise, not happy about. The Director had in fact started rewriting it with a friend in secret and not told anyone. Every morning the department heads would get rewritten pages. The Writer would see them and say, "What the fuck is going on? This wasn't the deal." And it wasn't. Early on, perhaps suspecting that there would be trouble, the Writer specified in his contract that he couldn't be excised from the physical production. Meaning, he had a legal right to come to the set. What could we do? We needed a script to shoot the movie. The Director, meanwhile, cooked up this paranoid fantasy that the Writer was trying to creatively take over the movie and stopped talking to him. Letters from the Director's lawyer and the Writer's lawyer starting flying back and forth. The Writer called us to say, "You are in breach. Fix this." We could see the lawsuit coming.

The Director and the Writer couldn't be together. The Director would evaporate if the Writer came anywhere near him. It got to the point that the Director just stopped showing up. In the last days of preproduction, you typically have a big meeting where all the department heads come. The AD reads through a scene-by-scene discussion of every component and how the film is going to come together. We'd rented a church hall because Killer's office was too small. Everybody, including the Writer, was there, but the Director was nowhere to be found. He'd seen the Writer in a folding chair and ducked out. It doesn't get any more irresponsible than that. I thought, What the hell is going on? Somebody pinch me.

These days, I would just say, "Later, bozos." But then we were afraid. As our first studio movie, the project would be looked at as an example of what Killer was capable of. We weren't making much money on it. Looking back, I think the real reason we didn't just pull the rip cord was that we were convinced that we had to support the Director. Defending the director was Killer's raison d'être. We had to prop up the Director as best we could. And if we were going to ally ourselves with one of these two people, it *had* to be the Director because he was the one who had to say, "Action."

This wasn't why I got into this business. Any questions about the craft or the creative process fell to the very bottom of the priorities list. Every day, our first chore was to make sure the Director didn't walk off the set. One day, the Writer showed up and the Director vanished. We had the starlet in a two-hundred-degree set waiting for the Director to say, "Let's do another take," and he disappeared.

Somehow, miraculously, we got the film in the can. We got *a* film in the can. But the Director alienated the studio. He was so uncooperative and ungrateful that his behavior influenced the studio's perception of the film. At this point in the process, it's crucial to maintain a positive relationship with the studio because their passion about your film colors everything—how much time they'll spend working on the poster, how much they'll listen to the director's nagging about the poster, everything.

Then the film tested poorly. The studio dumped it in a couple of theaters. We never spoke to the Director again after the film was released. Pam was in Bulgaria on the set of Tim Blake Nelson's *The Grey Zone*, and it took an e-mail from her mother to remind her that the film was actually in theaters. That's never how we feel when a movie comes out. The film lasted three weeks and barely made a blip.

Months later, a new set of producers called us, doing their homework on the Director. They had a film they were trying to set up and wanted to know what he was like to work with. We were honest. When he didn't get the gig, the Director called us. We didn't take the call.

Shagged by The Shaggs

The lazy Susan spins. An interesting project comes through your door, you fall in love, and the lazy Susan spins again and it's gone. Ninety-five percent of projects in the film industry are in some form of development shuffle. Occasionally, Killer is where a great project lands after a long, circuitous trip. Other times, we're just another spoke in the wheel.

In 2002 Katherine Dieckmann came into our office with a homeless screenplay. She'd been a book critic at the *Village Voice*, a video director (for R.E.M., Aimee Mann, Wilco, and the Indigo Girls) and had made one very heartfelt, virtually unseen first feature called *Good Baby*, with Henry Thomas and David Strathairn. She's a downtown hipster who wears one of those cropped black hairdos like Uma wore in *Pulp Fiction*. She'd actually written one of the first, big pieces about Apparatus, back in its infancy, for the *Voice*. It was a clip we sent out everywhere.

Artisan Entertainment, the company that rode *The Blair Witch Project* to millions, approached her to write the story of the rise and fall of the Shaggs, a terrible, all-girl sixties folk-rock band. The Shaggs were three sisters whose father forced them into bad haircuts and matching plaid suits because he thought they would be the new Beatles. They were so bad and unlistenable that they're modern. (The *New York Times* deemed the Shaggs' first album, *The Philosophy of the World*, "the best worst rock album ever made.")

They're a cult band now, and all the sisters are currently working as maids in budget motels in New Hampshire. There was some bidding over their story; Tom Cruise and Paula Wagner had optioned Susan Orlean's 1999 *New Yorker* story about them called "Meet the Shaggs," but Artisan went ahead and optioned the life rights of the three Wiggin (aka Shagg) sisters and the music rights (effectively scooping Cruise's deal). In 2000 Dieckmann went up to New Hampshire, interviewed the sisters, and wrote the screenplay.

Dieckmann was attached to direct when Artisan cut the project loose. They didn't want to do it anymore, and we never quite knew why. Artisan was going through growing pains and, with more experience acquiring films than producing them, they may have decided the costs to make the film were too big for the potential payback.

Companies take projects in turnaround from other companies all the time, though it can get expensive. Typically, a studio, say Universal, pays a writer $200,000 to develop a property, say a book that they've optioned for $100,000. That writer takes the script to a certain point. Afterward, Universal will probably pay another writer $100,000 to polish it, and then the studio attaches a director, paying him his $50,000 development fee. So this one project has accrued $450,000 in costs. But then Universal decides, "You know what? We're not going to make this." So Universal puts it on the lazy Susan, and then Paramount takes it off, but at a price. They will negotiate with Universal, who will want all that turnaround cost paid back plus a 15 percent premium on top. Usually there's some room for negotiation because Universal would rather get *some* money back than see nothing from it. Plus, turnaround costs are contingent on the film's budget, and you don't have to pay them until you go into production. It's a gamble everybody makes.

We knew that if we made *The Shaggs*, we'd need to pay some kind of turnaround costs to Artisan, in the neighborhood of $150,000 (to be paid only when our budget was approved). These costs represented what Artisan paid to Dieckmann to research and write the script, to the girls for their life rights, and to the music publisher for the rights to the music. This was the package.

Dieckmann came with a producer already attached, a woman named Rachel Cohen from Artisan. She had carte blanche at Artisan because she'd actually been the one who spotted *Blair Witch* at Sundance and convinced Artisan to acquire it. Though she was still working for Artisan, she loved the project and she wanted to be involved (and was willing to leave her job if she had to). She had no real production experience, so we agreed to produce it together.

Packaging would be critical on this movie: we'd need stars. But attracting them wouldn't be easy with a second-time director whose first film had been seen by practically nobody. Actors want to work with directors with vision. They want to feel a point of view. Just the fact that a director's first film was small or personal isn't a problem for them. David Gordon Green's *George Washington* wasn't seen by lots of people, but the critical acclaim was so strong that, after its release, actors would seek him out. It had a gripping directorial eye and a cast of all nonprofessional actors taking risks. Katherine's first film didn't make as many waves. To actors, she was an unknown quantity.

Casting a star or someone about to be a star (what Miramax calls "future casting") would make financiers take the leap with us. We made an offer to Kirsten Dunst to play the lead Wiggin sister, Dot. She was on the rise, having done *Bring It On* and *The Virgin Suicides*, but *Spider-Man* hadn't opened yet, so she wasn't meteoric. Her agent called us within days. "Kirsten *loves* this," she said. "She wants to meet with the director." Score. We decided that Pam and I would start the meeting and then leave Katherine and Kirsten alone to bond creatively.

We met in Kirsten's suite at the Mercer Hotel. Kirsten was lovely and unaffected. She said it was the best script she had read all year, and she showed tremendous enthusiasm for Dot. I always take an actor's enthusiasm with a grain of salt because they tend to be myopic when it comes to scripts; what they mean when they say "It's the best script I've read all year" is "It's the best part for me I've seen all year." Still, we all got really excited talking about the movie. There is always a point when I am pitching a script when suddenly I get a moment of clarity—when, in my head, the script goes from paper to celluloid. I can *see* it. That happened in the Mercer, and as we left, a voice in my head chanted, "We are making this! We are making this movie!" The timing was good because I was leaving soon after for Cannes, the platform to secure financing for the film. Meanwhile Katherine and Kirsten were having weekly phone calls, discussing the intricacies of Dot's psyche.

Then *Spider-Man* opened and did outrageous business. We got nervous. Would Kirsten even remember us? She continued having frequent "creative" conversations with Katherine. John Sloss, Killer's lawyer, said it was time to pin Kirsten down. Right before Cannes, we got on the phone with her team—a manager, an agent, and a lawyer—and found ourselves in the middle of the age-old indie catch-22: "We can't commit to this movie until it's financed!" they told us. Killer, of course, could not finance the movie without her commitment.

I told Sloss, "I *know* we have her! She talks to Katherine all the time! Let's just go to Cannes and represent that she is attached. We'll get the movie financed and then we'll get her commitment." So we did. We pounded the pavement along La Croisette for *The Shaggs*, repeating "a seven-million-dollar budget, Kirsten Dunst, Katherine Dieckmann, Killer Films, shooting this summer," etc. At a certain point, you have to behave like the train is leaving the station: "Colin Farrell is doing *A Home at the End of the World* and he has to shoot it April first. So some kind of camera is going be rolling on Colin Farrell April first . . . ," even though you have no clue how the hell it's getting financed.

By the end of the festival, we had solid commitments for *The Shaggs*, all pending Kirsten's attachment. But when we came back and called her agent, she didn't call back. Hmm.

Katherine called Kirsten. She didn't call *her* back. Uh-oh.

We called her agent again. For three or four days her agent played the West Coast call-back-when-nobody-is-there game—that is, at ten or eleven o'clock at night. I've been down this road before. The writing was on the wall. *Spider-Man* had changed everything. But we wanted to just hear her say, "This is over." Finally the agent called. Kirsten was bailing.

"She doesn't want to play a teenager," the agent said. "Other commitments have come up." Maybe she was being advised by her manager and agents, after such a colossal success, that she shouldn't have gotten involved with a project as small as *The Shaggs*. Maybe she fell out of love with the project. Actors are creative beings and sometimes they wake up in the morning and they say, "I don't want to play a singer." It's a drag, but it happens all the time.

I wanted to say, *"What happened to 'the best script she's read all year?'"* But all I said was "Kirsten owes it to Katherine to call her and tell her herself." (Kirsten did and asked Katherine, as genuinely as possible, "Do you hate me?" Honestly, I think it really mattered to her.)

It took us a few months to recover from that. There had been this expectation of something big for *The Shaggs*. Now there was a perceived *lack* of a star where there had been one. We had to reassess: Do we want to get another star of that caliber? Do we want to rethink the budget to do the movie for under $5 million and go a different way? We are constantly adjusting our expectations for our films, and it's one of the hardest parts of producing—adjusting to the ebb and flow of different possibilities. The people who were very excited about the project before were excited because of Kirsten as Dot. It was hard to *not* see her in the space where Dot was.

Eventually, we did find other financiers, a company called Hole Digger. They were a bunch of young, idealistic guys who wanted to be producers. They had made *Rodger Dodger* and *The Secret Lives of Dentists*. We started trying to work out a deal with them. They were very into financing the film. They liked Katherine. They wanted to do it for a considerably smaller chunk of change, around $5 million. But then, in the spring of 2003, they invited Katherine and Rachel (the producer from Artisan) out to dinner without us. I knew why: they were going to say, "Why do we need Killer?"

It was a mistake to put Katherine in that position. Any filmmaker will feel, I have to make my film whatever it takes, and I respect that. Of course that's how they feel. Katherine was desperate to make her movie. Rachel was desperate too. But to make Katherine choose between Killer and Hole Digger is like making a child choose between their parents in a divorce.

In my opinion, Hole Digger's formula was bound to fail. These guys fancied themselves producers: they would put up the cash *and* take care of producing the film. They thought because it was their money, Killer was just another slice out of their pie. But when the financiers and the producers are the same person, that's an intrinsic conflict of interest.

Pam and I had a big soul search about *The Shaggs*. We could have fought for it. But as much as it hurt us to get shut out, it was a mistake for Katherine and Rachel to go with Hole Digger, and we believed they'd figure that out soon enough. Somebody has to fight for the overall integrity of the movie, and that's what a producer does.

Katherine went with Hole Digger. We were shut out, but not entirely. Since we controlled the underlying rights (we got them when we took over the project from Artisan), we asked a producer's six-figure fee and our development costs back. The Hole Digger boys called and begged us to be flexible. After all, they argued, Killer attached Kirsten but Kirsten's gone and we didn't develop the material. We don't bring money to the table. And if we're inflexible, the project goes nowhere. They said, "We can make it work for one hundred all in." We thought about it and said, "We can make it work for one fifteen all in." We still haven't gotten our money.

Postscript: After promising to make *The Shaggs* in the spring of 2003, Hole Digger went belly up. So far, *The Shaggs* has gone nowhere.

Spotlight: John Cameron Mitchell,
ACTOR/DIRECTOR (*HEDWIG AND THE ANGRY INCH*)

Getting *Hedwig* to the Screen

Hedwig was born at Squeezebox, the first predominantly gay rock club in New York. Lots of drag queens sang and did covers there. They had a house band that my boyfriend at the time played in with the future *Hedwig* composer Stephen Trask. Now, I had met Stephen long before, on a plane from L.A. We were both trying to get away from the in-flight movie, and he had a book on the gay German filmmaker Fassbinder, so we just started talking. A couple of years later, I was looking for someone to compose some music for a stage piece I'd been working on about Tommy Gnosis, the young rock star in *Hedwig*. And Stephen said, "You should get a gig at Squeezebox doing this material. But you've got to come in drag."

At the time, Hedwig herself was a minor character. She was based on a tranny I knew in Berlin, where my father served in the army when I was younger. The more I thought about Hedwig, the more the idea of her botched sex-change operation emerged and she became more interesting. So I performed bits and pieces at Squeezebox and developed the play with Hedwig at the center. When I started doing it, people were like, "Oh my God, John's gone off the deep end. He's doing *drag*." But people make decisions based on fear, especially of the unknown.

When it was finished, Stephen and I brought on some theatrical producers to mount it. Very quickly after it opened, Jersey Films approached us to produce it as a film, with New Line releasing it. As an actor, I'd done a film for New Line's president Bob Shaye (*Book of Love*), and Stephen's uncle was the head of marketing there, so there were all these positive connections. We agreed. But then Jersey Films wanted to release both the soundtrack and the cast recording. Stephen didn't want to do that; he wanted the recordings released by a specific label that he liked. But Jersey wouldn't bend, so they dropped out. We were left with New Line, who was still interested. So the next stage was to find producers, and the natural choice was to go for the people I knew and respected, which was Killer.

I'd met Christine at Sundance in 1993. I went after *Poison* and *Paris Is Burning* had won awards there. I didn't have any project, I was just an actor. I'd done TV (*MacGyver* and *Head of the Class*) and some film (*Band of the Hand*). I gave Christine a headshot and said, "I'd really like to work with you." She had this ultracool reputation, maybe slightly unapproachable. She couldn't believe my boldness in giving her the headshot. (But I'm glad I did it. It worked!) That year I went to a legendary party in a former church hosted by Mickey Cottrell, who is a well-known publicist-actor-man-about-town. It was gay-oriented when it was kind of unusual to have a gay party at Sundance. I remember Brad Pitt sitting on the porch but not coming in. And John Cusack freaking out. But I met, now informally, a lot of people who became good friends, filmmakers like Todd Haynes. He asked me to be in *Safe* and *Velvet Goldmine*, but I had other things at the time. Christine wanted me to play Warhol in *I Shot Andy Warhol*, but the director wanted somebody else.

Even though Christine doesn't brook fools lightly, she has another, little-known side, which is that of a show-tune queen. She was really into *Hedwig* and I liked the way they made movies: with no bullshit, no egos, grass roots, efficiency, and the extensive use of interns. So a year and a half after the play had been running, we got green-lit to make it, with Killer producing.

Now, I'd gone to the Sundance Filmmakers Lab—when the play opened, they invited me—and there I had collaborated with a cinematographer, Frank DeMarco, who'd made a couple of great documentaries (*Lou Reed: Rock and Roll Heart, Theramin*). It had gone so well that when I was looking for a DP, I said why not go with this lesser-known but proven DP? He and my editor became co-directors with me in a way, since I didn't know much about editing or the camera.

During production in Toronto, Christine was very calming and soothing to my jittery nerves. She's also very protective. But there's a certain point where a producer can't do any more because, ultimately, it's the distributor who releases the film. New Line came up with the great tagline, "Get Hed," and made lots of great foam wigs for promotion. I asked to have Mick Rock shoot the poster; he's the rock photographer who did the cover of Iggy Pop's *Raw Power* and Lou Reed's *Transformer* albums. The only thing I wasn't really happy with—and I think it's always true for directors—was the trailer, which went for a sort of zingy, campy, *Rocky Horror/Priscilla*–type mood. I had some veto power, so I vetoed the narrator's voice-over, which I hated. That "In a world . . ." stuff. But what did I know? I don't know what sells. I just know what I like. And that's why a director never gets to do his own trailer—because he would make it into a short film.

After *Hedwig*, I decided not to go with development deals or take offers to direct things. I just kept seeing people get destroyed by those deals and waste a lot of precious time. I get really depressed if I'm working on something I don't like or if I'm working on something that I know will never be seen. I'm never dismissive of people who've got to do what they need to do to live. But you've always got to be working on that other thing that you care about. To survive, I didn't buy anything after *Hedwig*—no apartment, no car, anything—and so the money I got kept me alive for three years. Now I introduce films on the Independent Film Channel and am working on a new film, called *Short Bus*, even lower to the ground than Killer's films.

When people ask me how do you make a transition into film, I say never make a decision based on what you think people want to see, because it's probably a wrong one. I didn't make *Hedwig* to make money or for any career; it's not a smart acting career decision to play a tranny. For me, the unknown was drag and sex. And that meant it was exactly the place to explore.

Chapter 6
All That Heaven *Allows*

*Todd Haynes's peaks and valleys—We've got Cathy, who plays
Frank?—Enter Harvey Weinstein and Scott Greenstein—
A French twist—The big, bad bond company—Producer
jail—Testing the movie—Bidding for the Venice Film
Festival—Oscar night*

***LESSON: IF YOU'VE GOT TO SCREW UP, DO IT
FOR THE RIGHT REASONS.***

Autumn 2001, East Village, New York City

I wake up with an intense feeling of dread—the kind that roams, that makes you search your mind to remember why you don't want to get out of bed. It's 6 a.m. Next to me, Marlene sleeps peacefully, and Guthrie lies conked out in her crib. Outside, the East Village is quiet.

Then it hits me. I've lost control of *Far from Heaven*, the most expensive film Killer has made. Representatives from Film Finances, the completion bond company that insured the movie, have swarmed the set and taken over the bank account. Bond companies are the way distributors guarantee they're going to get a releasable movie on budget. They're like police officers for produc-

151

ers: screw up too much and they're all over you. Nobody likes to talk about them, since their presence is usually the sign that your film is a mess. The bond company took over Roman Polanski's *The Ninth Gate* when the shoot started to run long, and Spike Lee had the bond company threatening to take *Malcolm X* off his hands. As *Lost in La Mancha* shows, Terry Gilliam lost *The Man Who Killed Don Quixote* to his bond company, and he's still trying to buy back the footage from them. (They want $15 million.)

Right now, Film Finances is cutting pages from Todd's script to save money. They're combing the budget for ways to lay people off, ways that they can pin the overages on me. This is a director's worst nightmare and professional suicide for a producer. Ask anyone from Scorsese to Altman to David Lynch; they'll tell you the bond company will ruin a movie. Like repo men of the film business, they're running my show.

I haven't had a boss since I was twenty-five. Is this what getting fired feels like?

Autumn 2000, Killer Films Office, New York City

In this industry, you've got to learn detachment. At this point, I've taught myself to let go and move on from disappointments. The peaks and valleys are part of the business, and your peak can be your audience's valley and vice versa. But it's easy for me to say that. I've always got a next—a next deal, next production, next release date. I'm never the one *living* in the valley. In 1999 Todd Haynes went into a creative funk after *Velvet Goldmine*. He'd spent six months living in London making a beautiful, difficult, risky film about glam rock only to come back and find out nobody cared about it nearly as much as we did. Not Miramax, who halfheartedly distributed it, not the critics, who called it "overambitious" and "maddening," and not audiences. We spent $9 million—then the biggest budget in Killer's history—on huge sets in Brixton, Ewan McGregor's paycheck, and about five hundred pairs of platform shoes. *Velvet Goldmine* made $1.5 million. That's not great math. So in the fall of 1998, Todd returned to his apartment in Williamsburg, where everybody is twenty-six and always will be. His landlord was about to kick him out. And he sank into a depression. Here he was, staring forty in the face, not where he wanted to be emotionally, and he thought, This is my life?

So he moved to a Craftsman bungalow in Portland, where his sister lives, and Todd started to grow younger. Really. There's an element of living in New York that's about measuring up against your peers. Todd didn't even have an agent; he didn't want one. Competitiveness is not in Todd's makeup. He'd rather sit around with his friends and read Foucault. In Portland, that's exactly what he did. I miss him, but he's so much happier there.

All this to say, in the fall of 2000, I get a call from Todd. We talk every other day, so this is not weird. But it's the kind of call you always hope for, as a producer and as a friend—the call that says the valley is over. "I want to write a script," Todd says. "A kind of Sirkian melodrama." Then he calls four weeks later and says, "I'm done." Usually Todd labors a lot more over things. The script for *Velvet Goldmine*, for example, started out at about 250 pages and went through nine months of rewrites. But this script flowed out. He sends it to me with a beautiful cover drawing he did himself in colored pencil of Cathy, the main character, with a scarf over her head. Very Todd. The script is about a Betty Crocker housewife rocked by the revelation that her husband is gay. At heart, it's a story about a chaotic universe that you cannot control and the tragedy that comes when you try. The script is so simple and flawless, I say, "There's not much you can do to this."

The only thing we change is the scene when Cathy walks in on her husband, Frank, making out with a man. Todd has Frank giving the guy a blow job. On one level, I love it because it is this moment that rips everything open. Douglas Sirk was known for his lush, precise, and highbrow melodramas about characters in conflict with their own impulses (*There's Always Tomorrow, All That Heaven Allows, Imitation of Life*). Usually his movies are very insular and almost painterly. Rock Hudson often starred in Sirk's films (talk about conflicted impulses), and the idea that you'd see Rock Hudson going down on Robert Stack in a Sirk movie is *wild*. But it would have blown Cathy's mind and perhaps our rating. So Todd downgrades the contact to a deep kiss. Other than that, what you would eventually see on screen is the draft Todd delivered to me. Clearly, whatever unresolved issues Todd had with the reception of *Velvet Goldmine* are behind him.

Schedule F and Up

From the beginning, we have our best asset, one that most films in development never come close to: a brilliant star who just might work for what we can pay her—Julianne Moore. Ever since Todd cast her as the environmentally ill mom in *Safe*—after Jennifer Jason Leigh turned us down—they've been close. She'd done soap opera through the eighties, but I first noticed her in that terrific bad-nanny thriller *The Hand That Rocks the Cradle*. She was the one who dies in the shower of greenhouse glass. Hard to miss, really.

Todd had written the part of Cathy with her in mind. Normally I would send it to her manager, Evelyn O'Neill, who is very close to her, and say, "Evelyn, I need Julianne to read this right away." When you're trying to get a film off the ground, you have to say, "Right away." You need to give off the impression of urgency or nothing gets done. In this case, Todd sends *Far from Heaven* straight to Julianne in Rome, where she is filming *Hannibal*. She calls him back and says, "This is a gift. I want to do it." Todd then calls me, and I call Evelyn to say, "We need to shoot this next fall."

That gives me almost a year to put together the financing for *Far from Heaven*, and we're going to go down to the wire, in terms of securing the money by our start date. We figure we'll shoot it in Toronto, which saves all kinds of production costs—given the strength of the American dollar (at that time)—and will still give us the exploding-autumn look Todd wants. He actually wants to shoot the movie the way Sirk did, with rear-screen projections on a sound-stage to heighten the artifice. If there was ever a movie we could shoot in Toronto with no compromises, this would be it. Very slowly, over the phone, I start working out a deal with Evelyn, because obviously Julianne is not going to make a ton of money. Even so, she'll probably be the most expensive line item in the budget. Instead of a single check, Julianne's got to have a good back end—or "points," for percentage points of the profits of the film. But she needs to get paid *something.* The lowest you can possibly pay an actor is Screen Actors Guild "scale," which is $2,279 a week, plus 10 percent for the agent. Schedule F is the next step up: $65,000, from rehearsal through postproduction. After that, you can negotiate anything.

But Julianne isn't going to work for Schedule F. She's just done *Hannibal,* and her quote has shot up to $5 million a picture. But since she tends to alternate big movie, little movie, big movie, and so on, we think we could be the next little movie in line. We also know that we are going to have to pay the actor who plays the husband the same amount, even though the part's smaller. That's how it works in Hollywood: you can never pay the boys less than the girls. I start throwing numbers at Evelyn, sizable six figures but definitely way below what Julianne has gotten used to. The trick is, the higher her rate goes, the higher Frank's rate goes, etc. Some film actors define their work by the price they command. You open up *Variety* and it's all about Colin Farrell's getting $8 million for something or Julia Roberts's getting $15 million. It's all about what their payday is. That's how actors define their success. In a way, how else can they?

With Killer, actors do it for love. That's how we get people like Ewan McGregor to make out with a guy in the freezing cold (*Velvet Goldmine*), John Goodman to work out of a "two-banger" (a star trailer split in two) for Todd Solondz's *Storytelling,* or Julianne to end up in the final frame emaciated, with cysts on her face (*Safe*)— for love. But lots of actors don't do it for love. Some actors just don't care. They say, "You want me to move my ass out of my house and into some tiny trailer and eat your crappy food? Well, this is what it costs." The current film industry orbits around a small number of very expensive actors. (Only 5 percent of all actors, SAG has announced, make over $70,000 a year.)

Directors, incidentally, rarely make as much as their stars. The standard Directors Guild of America fee for directing is $150,000. On a modestly budgeted film like *Far from Heaven,* a writer-director would get paid around $100,000 for the screenplay and

$150,000 for directing. Producers too have their own "quote." A producer like Brian Grazer can command over $5 million a picture. Needless to say, Killer's quote is a lot less and usually follows a sliding scale based on the production. I charge less for *Go Fish* than for Altman's *The Company*, and my partner Pam and I decide how the money gets split up. We don't get paid any other way.

When Todd wrote the script, he had James Gandolfini in mind for the husband, Frank. But matching our shoot with James's availability is impossible. *The Sopranos* shoots for nine months out of the year, and it's going to be impossible for him to carve out the time in the fall. Todd's next choice is Russell Crowe, but Russell's agent tells us that Russell said, "Fuck, I'd play Cathy, but why would I want to play this guy? He's not even the lead." Point taken. So we get it to Jeff Bridges, who reads it and is interested, but apparently you have to court Jeff Bridges. Todd needs to go out to Santa Barbara and take a meeting. But before he goes, Jeff Bridges's agent asks, "Is Todd gay?" Now, I don't think this was meant in a bad way. It was almost a politically correct question: "Is this script being written by somebody who is part of that world?" No big deal, except it has also revealed that Jeff was probably not, shall we say, familiar with Todd's work. "Yes, yes, Todd is gay," we say, hoping it helps. It does. Todd goes out to Santa Barbara, meets with Jeff, and does a cold reading with him. Todd comes back excited.

Next, Jeff engages Todd in a discussion about "more moments of reflection for the character." This could be perceived as an attempt on Mr. Bridges's part to get more scenes for his character, but it connects up with something Todd has been thinking himself. Todd starts saying, "I do feel that there is one more moment I want to give him." I start to think we've found our man. But then Jeff's agent calls. He wants to make sure that we can meet Jeff's bottom line. I know that's impossible. Julianne won't be paid that much.

"He's not going to get that," I say.

And he answers, "That's what he commands."

The conversation's over. Jeff's out. I call Todd and say, "Look, I think we have to move on," and Todd is pissed. These kinds of concessions—and compromises—are inevitable. You can't get too attached.

How Much?

Meanwhile, I'm working out the budget. This is how my math works: Todd Haynes plus Julianne Moore minus the fact that Todd's movies have not been runaway hits. I also have to find a budget that accurately reflects the money we'll be able to raise *and* the amount we'll need to successfully execute a period movie with a luscious palette. Period films pose specific production questions. One big one is "How big is your frame?" If your script features a New York City block in period style, the budget is utterly dependent on whether Julianne Moore is in the shot, whether you are seeing her in close-up or seeing her in a master shot with cars, street vendors, other people in the background. The more you see, the more you have to dress in period, the more you have to pay. Those factors shape the budget immeasurably. Todd has, wisely, written a script defined by interiors: Kathy's suburban home, her husband's office, and two bars—one gay, one black.

I come up with a $12 million budget—including the cast Todd wants and crew—which will be difficult to solicit from a single source. John Sloss, our lawyer, has an idea; the way to get to $12 million is to spread the risk and use a triumvirate of companies. Often Killer films are financed with one North American and one foreign sales agent. The North American distributor makes money off North America, and the foreign sales agent makes money off selling the rights to the film to territories abroad. This time, to amplify the possible budget, we add a third factor—an equity investor—and everybody will put the same amount into a single pot and split the profits evenly.

We first approach Clear Blue Sky, Microsoft founder Paul Allen's film financing company, which is actually run by his sister, Jody Patton. They don't distribute movies. They just put up the cash to make them. They financed Rose Troche's *The Safety of Objects* and John Sayles's *Men with Guns*. Their biggest investment thus far was Julie Taymor's *Titus*. They hired the renowned theater director and Anthony Hopkins to star, and they went to Italy with $12 million. However, they banked on one of the bloodiest, most obscure Shakespeare plays. One year later and several million dollars in excess, the movie came out and flopped. How many smart billionaires get burned in Hollywood? Nobody's immune to failure.

But Clear Blue Sky is still in business, which means they like ambition and they're resilient. They also really seem to have a sense of mission. No one is in business for anything else but to make money, except it feels like Clear Blue Sky is in business to make money *and* to do something more.

The Allens are rich, so they're very suspicious. Everything goes through their consigliere, Eric Robison. He's a very decent guy, but it's like you're talking to the person at the front door who just may, if he feels like it, go walking through Xanadu to let his boss know you're there. At this point, I'm asking for $4 million from three partners and hoping Clear Blue Sky will be one of them. They read the script—it really all does come down to the script, and I know this script is a gem—and they say yes to $4 million. Even better, they don't care about who is going to play Frank, which is one of the best things about them. Typically, if people are putting up money, they have input. The question is always How much?

It's now May and I head to Cannes, where I keep hawking Todd plus Julianne plus this Douglas Sirkian melodrama called *Far from Heaven*. Ideally, we'd have one international distributor, one North American distributor, and Clear Blue Sky. In the bar of the Hotel du Cap, drinking thirty-dollar Bellinis (peach juice and champagne), Sloss and I meet with ARP, run by a French couple, Michele and Laurent. She's a stick-thin, hyperkinetic Frenchwoman with gigantic glasses, and her husband is a heavy-set, formerly handsome man in that Gallic, square-jawed way. ARP distributed one of Killer's previous films in France and were incredibly passionate about it. Michele literally *wept* when it didn't pick up any big prizes at Cannes. (It did win a "special prize" for Best Artistic Contribution.) They'd also done a couple of Luc Besson films that were big hits. They are unflaggingly enthusiastic about *Far from Heaven*—the script, they said, was *"fantastique"*—but they stop just short of signing the appropriate papers to finalize the deal. When I try to get them to sign on the dotted line, they make me feel that I'm being gauche. I believe them. Big mistake.

The Killer Films office staff (left to right): Pam Koffler, Charles Pugliese, me, Michael Wiggins, Jocelyn Hayes, Katie Roumel, and Yee Yeo Chang. (PHOTO COURTESY OF HENNY GARFUNKEL)

ACADEMY OF MOTION PICTURE ARTS AND SCIENCES

8949 Wilshire Boulevard • Beverly Hills, California 90211-1972 • (310) 247-3000
FAX: (310) 859-9351 • (310) 859-9619

December 13, 2002

Officers

FRANK PIERSON
President
ROBERT REHME
First Vice President
ROGER L. MAYER
Vice President
KATHY BATES
Vice President
CHERYL BOONE ISAACS
Treasurer
DONALD C. ROGERS
Secretary
BRUCE DAVIS
Executive Director

Board of Governors

DEDE ALLEN
MICHAEL APTED
KATHY BATES
ED BEGLEY, JR.
CARL BELL
ALAN BERGMAN
CHARLES BERNSTEIN
JON BLOOM
DONY CAMBERN
GILBERT CATES
ARTHUR DONG
RICHARD EDLUND
JONATHAN ERLAND
JUNE FORAY
SID GANIS
DOUGLAS GREENFIELD
CONRAD L. HALL
ARTHUR HAMILTON
CURTIS HANSON
J. PAUL HUNTSMAN
MARK JOHNSON
RICHARD KAHN*
FAY KANIN*
HAL KANTER
KATHLEEN KENNEDY
JEFFREY KURLAND
MICHAEL MANN
MARVIN MARCH
ROGER L. MAYER
WILLIAM M. MECHANIC
FREIDA LEE MOCK
JEANNINE OPPEWALL
FRANK PIERSON
ROBERT REHME*
DONALD C. ROGERS
OWEN ROIZMAN
TOM ROLF
BILL TAYLOR
JOHN TOLL
SAUL ZAENTZ
•
JOHN B. QUINN
Legal Counsel

*Past President

Christine Vachon
380 Lafayette St., #302
New York, NY 10003

Dear Ms. Vachon,

I'm delighted to advise you that the Board of Governors extends to you an invitation to become a member of the Academy.

As you know, the Academy is an honorary association of film artists and craftspeople whose purpose is to advance the cultural, educational and technological progress of motion pictures. The annual Academy Awards, voted by the entire active membership, are given for outstanding artistic and technical achievements. However, our activities encompass much more than the Annual Awards as indicated in the enclosed booklet "A Brief Guide to the Academy."

Membership comprises those who have made significant contributions to the arts and sciences of motion pictures, and consists of fourteen branches. On acceptance of our invitation you will become a member of the Producers Branch.

The dues are $250.00 per year, and you will be billed pro rata from the date of your acceptance through the balance of the year. If you have any questions or wish any information, please contact the office of Bruce Davis, Executive Director. An acceptance card is enclosed for your convenience.

We'd be pleased if you would join the more than 6000 of your colleagues throughout the world who are Academy members, and enjoy and take part in the Academy's many programs and activities which celebrate the art form of which we're all so proudly a part.

Cordially,

Frank Pierson
President

FP:mp
Enclosure

Have I finally made it to the "inside" circle in Hollywood? My acceptance letter from the Academy. (PHOTO COURTESY OF THE AUTHOR)

Hilary Swank as Brandon Teena and Killer Films regular Chloë Sevigny getting intimate in *Boys Don't Cry*. (PHOTO COURTESY OF FOX SEARCHLIGHT PICTURES)

John Cameron Mitchell rockin' onstage as Hedwig in *Hedwig and the Angry Inch*, which he also wrote and directed. (PHOTO COURTESY OF NEW LINE CINEMA)

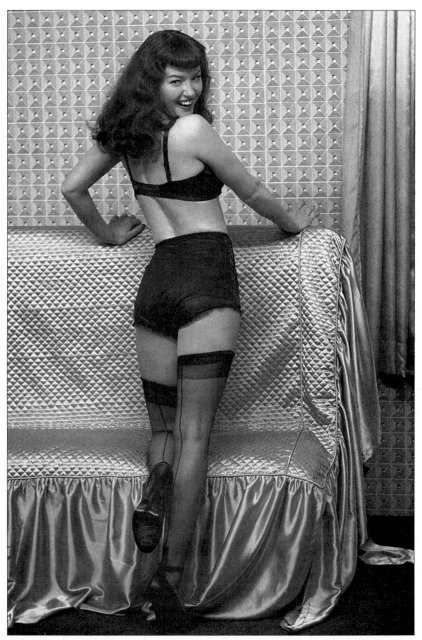

Gretchen Mol doing a fabulous pinup pose as Bettie Page in *The Notorious Bettie Page*. (PHOTO COURTESY OF PICTUREHOUSE)

Julianne Moore with Dennis Haysbert in *Far From Heaven*. Luckily, her pregnancy didn't show at all. (PHOTO BY ABBOTT GENSER; COURTESY OF FOCUS FEATURES)

Todd on the set of *Far From Heaven*. While shooting, great directors like Todd can look at the monitor, pause and think, and see the entire film edited in their minds. (PHOTO BY ABBOTT GENSER; COURTESY OF FOCUS FEATURES)

A very creepy Robin Williams develops Connie Nielsen's pictures in *One Hour Photo*. (PHOTO BY FRANCOIS DUHAMEL; COURTESY OF FOX SEARCHLIGHT PICTURES)

Annette Bening as the very proper headmistress Jean Harris in *Mrs. Harris*, enjoying a drink and the attention of famous diet doctor Herman Tarnower, played by Ben Kingsley. She later goes on to shoot him. (PHOTO BY LOREY SEBASTIAN; COURTESY OF HBO FILMS)

Me on the *Mrs. Harris* set in L.A. with my producing partners: Chrisann Verges, Pam Koffler, and Elizabeth Karlsen. (PHOTO BY LOREY SEBAS-TIAN; COURTESY OF HBO FILMS)

Toby Jones as Truman Capote travels to Kansas with his best friend, *To Kill a Mockingbird* author Nelle Harper Lee (Sandra Bullock), in *Infamous*. (PHOTO BY JOHN CLIFFORD; COURTESY OF WARNER INDEPENDENT PICTURES)

Toby Jones dances with Sigourney Weaver (who plays socialite Babe Paley) in the club El Morocco. Despite shooting almost all of *Infamous* in Austin, Texas, director Doug McGrath perfectly captured the elegance and glamour of New York society. (PHOTO BY JOHN CLIFFORD; COURTESY OF WARNER INDEPENDENT PICTURES)

Above, this is what you think Cannes will be: beautiful vistas, blue sky, and yachts floating in the background. On the left, this is what Cannes actually is: step onto the street and you're surrounded by a maddening mob of Europeans, pushing you aside to get a glimpse of some famous supermodel or action star. (PHOTOS COURTESY OF THE AUTHOR)

Here's the accounting statement Fox sent me for *One Hour Photo*, which was extremely successful in theaters and on DVD. I've blacked out most of the figures for privacy, but as you can see, the bottom line, in terms of profits for Killer, is still zero. We get nothing. Sigh. (PHOTO COURTESY OF THE AUTHOR)

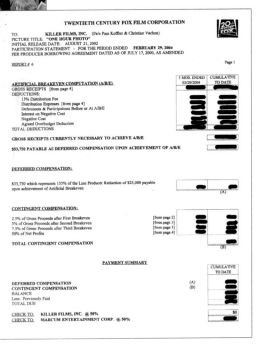

Come August 1, I have to be in preproduction. We've got Clear Blue Sky and French Films Inc., but I'm a little frantic since we don't have our North American partner. Todd is already interviewing cinematographers. We're still leaving Frank a bit open at this point because I know the North American distributor is going to want to weigh in. So we send the script out to a handful of potential partners—Sony, New Line, Miramax, and USA Films, which is a new, boutique division of Universal formed out of the ashes of independent film distributor October Films. (A few years later, it will become Focus Features, James Schamus and David Linde's company.) Two companies bite, USA and Miramax. Harvey Weinstein, co-chair of Miramax, calls me when I'm in the airport back from Cannes. He can just see the Oscar for *Far from Heaven*. He says, "I love this script. It's fuckin' great. I want to do this movie."

This all would have been a lot easier if Harvey had just hated *Far from Heaven*. Todd was still smarting from his last Harvey experience. When *Velvet Goldmine* came out, Miramax was behind it in only the most perfunctory way. In Harvey's mind, there was a commercial movie in there but Todd refused to unearth it. From Miramax's perspective, the film got the release it deserved. Todd felt betrayed. So when Harvey calls me to say he wants in on *Far from Heaven*, I'm conflicted. We can't do it with Miramax because Todd is too angry. He feels too unprotected. If I get down on my knees and say to Todd, "Look, I think we have to do it with Miramax and I will protect you," he would say OK. But the first time Harvey screwed with the movie (which would've happened), Todd would've blamed me, and I can't put my relationship with Todd in that kind of jeopardy. All this said, in retrospect Miramax may well have been the best distributor for *Far from Heaven*, hands down. Come Oscar time, we would have been everywhere. But the production process would not have been tenable for Todd, and I just knew that.

Enter Scott Greenstein. Scott runs USA Films, which is controlled by Barry Diller and partially owned by Universal. They bankrolled Neil LaBute's *Possession* and Mira Nair's *Monsoon Wedding*. Scott was Harvey's deputy until he went out on his own, lost a lot of weight, bought some new suits, and took over USA Films. He's very

Jersey and proud of his Jersey. He's friends with Bon Jovi and Spring-
steen. Like Harvey, he's got a lot of large appetites, and also like Harvey, he's got filmmakers very loyal to him. Steven Soderbergh made
Traffic with USA Films, and he feels that Scott got him his Oscar and
he's right. Steven heard about *Far from Heaven* at a meeting at CAA
long before we even settled the financing. "Todd Haynes is doing a
melodrama? I wanted to do a melodrama," Steven said. We get him a
copy of the script and he loves it. Because Steven is a fan of Todd's—
and a hugely generous filmmaker—he offers his services as an executive producer to Killer (and brings his buddy George Clooney with
him) to help protect Todd from studio pressure. Steven turns out to
be our secret weapon.

But Steven Soderbergh can't cut our deal for us. Over the phone,
Scott Greenstein is working me over. "You gotta close this deal with
me. You gotta close it," he says. "C'mon already." He's getting terrified
that Miramax is gonna scoop him. But he's coming in at $2 or $3 million, which is not the deal we want. Finally, he skips up to $4 million.

When I start waffling, Miramax does what they always do: a full-
court press. Harvey's heard that Scott Greenstein, his former number two, is the leading bidder for the film. This makes him insane. So
he's instructed his *entire* business staff to show up at my office on
Lafayette, which they do, scaring the interns.

"We want to make a deal right now," they say.

"I can't do it," I say.

"We're not leaving here until we have a deal."

"I can't," I say. "We're going with USA."

They taunt me, high school style. "Even if you think it's better to
go with Miramax for the movie?" they ask. "Your director, he runs you
around."

They decide they are going to *sit in the office* until we make a
deal. I say, "Well, I'm going out to lunch," and leave. What else can
I do?

Meanwhile, Scott—sensing that Harvey is on his trail—becomes
so desperate to close the deal that he has called John Sloss and
sweetened the deal with a "signing bonus" that we can use to jump-
start preproduction.

When I come back from lunch, the Miramax team is gone, fortunately. But now they begin calling me. An executive says, "Look, we understand that you're probably gonna do it with USA, but can Harvey have at least one conversation with Todd?" I say, "Sure." I call Todd, who squirms, but I say to him, "You just have to."

The history of the film business is written in phone calls like this one. Todd gets on with Harvey, and Todd immediately says, "We've already closed the deal with USA," which wasn't really true. And Harvey explodes. He screams. And screams some more. Todd is calm. He says, "Harvey, don't talk to me that way." When they finally finish, Todd does not hang up. He waits. And he hears Miramax's co-president of production (and long ago Harvey's executive assistant) Meryl Poster, who has been listening on the phone the entire time, say to Harvey, "Great, Harvey, you just alienated another filmmaker." And Harvey says back, "You know what your problem is, Meryl? You're too soft." We hear, from an undisclosed source, that Harvey later said, "I'm gonna pay ten million to make sure Julianne Moore does *not* get an Oscar." (When this story ended up in Inside.com the next day—the speed was impressive—this is how Miramax covered Harvey's tracks: "A Miramax spokesman said, 'The account is totally inaccurate. Julianne Moore has been in a number of our films in the past and is in a number of our future projects and we've always enjoyed a positive relationship and wholeheartedly support her. We wish Todd Haynes the best on this project.' Vachon declined to discuss the details of the Haynes-Weinstein encounter, but said, 'It was not a hostile conversation and things ended on a very upbeat note. We will hopefully be doing business with them in the future.'" Ah, spin. (Two years later, at the New York Film Critics Circle Awards, Harvey approached Todd and apologized. He even came out publicly raving about the movie.)

Needless to say, we're going with USA Films. The problem is that Scott Greenstein has ideas about casting Frank, lots of ideas. Like Greg Kinnear. Because he'd just had lunch with him. Todd's response is "Nobody is going to be surprised to find out Greg Kinnear is gay." Next, Scott decides that Hugh Jackman should play Frank because he'd just seen him in *Somebody Like You.* Julianne is saying, "I'll call actors for you. I know how hard it is to cast when the girl is the lead."

And it's true. Cathy is the man's part, and Frank, the husband, is the woman's part. Every male actor we send the script to wants to know if he's missing some pages from the script. Meanwhile, I get a call from Jeff Bridges's agent saying, "Is the part still open?" Because Jeff wants to read it again. So we get back into that tango. He takes another month to tell us he's still not going to do it.

Then Julianne's agent calls: the good news, she's willing to work for the money we've got in the budget; the bad news, no Canada. We have to shoot in New York or she's not going to do it because she wants to be near her family—her husband and four-year-old son. This will bump the *entire budget* up. Well, if we shoot in the New York area, at least it's not a runaway production. This is not the last of the revelations from her. We're at dinner and I notice she isn't drinking. I say to myself, That's funny, doesn't she usually have a glass of wine? but I don't ask because, God knows, I don't want to know.

With this ultimatum from Julianne, I've got to call all my partners, Scott Greenstein at USA, Michele and Laurent at ARP, and Jody at Clear Blue Sky and ask for more money. I don't have a $12 million budget that works in New York. The first thing I've got to do is find a line producer who can come up with a budget. The line producer looks at every line of the budget and makes sure it squares. He's supposed to be a friend of the crew, the cartilage between the director's vision and the people trying to make it happen. He also watches every department—costumes, lighting, etc.—and makes sure they stay in line. I get Declan Baldwin, a dapper, Irish Catholic bald guy in his forties who worked on *Storytelling* for me and *The Laramie Project* for HBO. He's very meticulous and polite. Even his mustache is well disciplined.

I'm slowly exposed to a really insidious thing at USA—their "in-house production team." Every studio has one of these in-house teams to help supervise the productions that are using its money. I've dealt with them at New Line and Fox Searchlight. They tend to be people who are a little more conservative than me, but usually they are working to help me get the most for my money. Sometimes, their attitude is "I don't know how you're gonna do this, but let's see if you can pull it off," and if you do, they're really happy.

At USA, the physical production executives, let's call them "John" and "Jen," don't give me the feeling that they are really on my side. Perhaps it's because they're working at a company where the leadership keeps changing. (USA Films had been churning through executives.) I'm starting to feel that John and Jen need to create crises in order to solve them. They'd rather be right than fix a problem. This is a strategy that has clearly served them well—they have managed to keep their jobs through myriad company shuffles—but I'm growing concerned that it won't serve *Far from Heaven* well. Their response to upping the budget by shooting in New York is to say, "We should just recast Julianne." I can't believe it. "Guys," I say, "she's doing it for one-tenth of what she normally gets. If it costs us a million and a half to move the production to New York, we're still getting Julianne for cheaper than her five million. Who do you think we'd replace her with?"

As the financing bounces around, we're still trying to cast Frank. This week, Scott Greenstein is pushing hard for Hugh Jackman, but Todd isn't convinced. Scott also wants us to look at Don Cheadle for the part of the black gardener. Or Q-Tip. Or any rapper he's ever heard of. I let Todd know the ones he absolutely has to deal with. Todd is getting frustrated. He says, "Why the hell can't I just cast who I want?" I tell him, "Because there needs to be some love around the production," which means, Pretend to listen to Scott's ideas. Some of them may even be good. We'll get what we want. This was actually the advice of Steven Raphael, who is our creative production executive at USA, above John and Jen. Production executives like Steven are the diplomats who help you navigate the studio. Good ones are invaluable. He tells me, "This is how you play it. Make Todd hear Scott out about Hugh Jackman or whoever. Have him watch the tapes. But then call Scott at the end of the day and say, 'Listen, I just can't go there.'"

The other factor here is that the balance of power in casting has tipped heavily toward the actors. Nowadays, actors are in one movie and they think they shouldn't have to audition anymore. They're just "offer only." It's a real problem. But if you're Todd Haynes, actors are desperate to be in your movie, and you can say, "You need to come in and read." Our casting director Laura Rosenthal sees Dennis Quaid in *Dinner with Friends,* the film based on the play by Donald Margulies. It's about two couples struggling with divorce. Dennis just shines. At that precise moment, George Freeman, who is Russell Crowe's agent, calls and says, "What about Dennis Quaid? Would Todd be interested?" *The Rookie* had not come out at that point, so the last thing Dennis Quaid had been in that people had noticed was *Frequency.* George shows Todd a bunch of his stuff. When Dennis Quaid married Meg Ryan, she was America's sweetheart, and he was the male equivalent. They *were* Cathy and Frank.

Even though Scott is still saying, "Why don't we get . . . Leo?" Todd really goes for Dennis. And it turns out that Dennis is a huge *Velvet Goldmine* fan. All George had to do is *mention* it, and Dennis is in. Except Dennis hasn't really done low-budget movies. I was afraid he was going to show up, see his trailer, and say, "What the fuck is this?" As it turned out, he loved shooting a lower-budget film since he was used to sitting in his trailer and waiting and waiting. Comparatively, for Dennis, working on *Far from Heaven* must have felt like being in the Green Berets.

Working Toronto

We've got Dennis and Julianne. What we don't have is the money to put them on the screen. It's mid-August, two months before we start shooting. "I have to tell you something," Julianne confesses to me. "I'm pregnant." Now, before production, all actors have to be examined so an insurer can guarantee them. As soon as she did her insurance exam, the cat would come out of the bag. But because the financing is in and out, I tell her, "Everything's just too insane right now, I can't drop this particular bomb. Keep it to yourself and let's let it come out when the exam is done in two weeks."

Meanwhile, every day or two all summer, I've been leaving messages for Michele and Laurent at ARP to get them to sign off on the film. They do not seem to be in the habit of returning calls. On the rare occasions when I get through to them, they insist they are still in on the deal. Sloss even goes to France to talk to them. But as time goes by, they only get more elusive. They send a series of peculiar letters that seem intended to stall for time. By mid-July they go incommunicado. In late August—August being the national vacation month in France—I track them down to a houseboat in the South of France. I speak to one of their kids, who hands the phone over to Michele. Meanwhile, I can hear Laurent screaming obscenities in the background. Clearly, the French do not like to be interrupted during their vacation month. Nothing gets resolved. We hang up.

I pin my hopes on finalizing the deal at the Toronto Film Festival in early September, where I know I will find Michele and Laurent. I have Brad Simpson from our office, now a co-producer on *Far from Heaven*, stake out the Park Hyatt, where they are staying. Brad lurks by the potted trees at the hotel entrance and calls me on my cell phone as soon as they appear. It is time for answers. But when Brad approaches, they refuse to meet with him.

Then, on September 8, 2001, we premiere *The Safety of Objects* at the festival. It's a twisted, suburban drama directed by Rose, who made *Go Fish*. Her new film is woven from A. M. Homes's collection *The Safety of Objects* and stars Glenn Close. (Unfortunately, Homes wouldn't give us the rights to arguably the most interesting story, but that's another story.) Rose pulled it off, we tested it, and the results went through the roof. We anticipate a big sale at Toronto.

But right before the premiere, I get a call on my cell. It's a representative named Rebecca from Film Finances, the completion bond company on *Far from Heaven*, with a crisis. This call is the beginning of months of headaches, threats, and stress.

Completion bond companies assure financiers that a film will be delivered on time and that costs over budget will not be the financier's responsibility. The advent of bond companies came with the collapse of the studio system fifty years ago. As film producers went to banks to borrow money for their films, they couldn't show how budget overages would be met. Banks had learned the hard way that unfinished films have absolutely no value. The original founders of Film Finances, as their website says, were "themselves film producers who had learned that mortgaging all they owned against potential budget overages was not a sound proposition; however, unfortunately, that was the only way in those days to get a motion picture independently financed."

Basically, the bond company is an insurance policy that a film will be made on a certain budget. The company's agents watch the weekly cost reports and wait until you've used up about 50 percent of the contingency—the unallotted part of the budget that is set aside for unexpected costs. Then they come for you and your movie. Let's say you as the producer have been given $3 million by New Line Cinema to make a director's first feature film. You say, "I know this guy can do it. I'm going to keep him on budget. It's going be fine." Just to make absolutely certain, you and New Line (but not Mr. Director because he or she has no say in this whatsoever) agree on a bond company. The bond company comes in, checks your budgets, and has the ultimate say over the movie. They make comments. Usually this is a somewhat symbolic ceremony where they make the art director, the costume person, every department, submit a budget and *sign it*. You're effectively swearing that you're not going to mess up. Of course, you sign it. But ultimately, a budget is just an estimate, a draft, especially on a film.

The bond company can be helpful in the sense that they're a neutral partner, and they can even be a real friend. They're on top of the production as much as anybody else. But they are not invested in any way whatsoever in the artistic merit of the movie. They are not invested in whether it is successful for New Line. Their job is to deliver *this* script for *this* amount of money. As long as you basically make your days and do what you're supposed to do, they leave you alone. If you start going off the track, they start appearing on your film set, making decisions for you.

Now, I've probably given Film Finances over two million bucks over the years from my movies' budgets. (The bond company gets paid between 3 and 6 percent of the total budget.) But I've always worked with a woman named Maureen Duffy, who understands that Killer films are made with a certain leap of faith. She respects what we do. This time I hear fateful words. "Maureen is on vacation. Rebecca Myers* will be your representative for *Far from Heaven*."

In the theater, just as *The Safety of Objects* is beginning, I hear Rebecca tell me that in order for her to bond Todd's movie, Todd and

---

* Of course her name is not Rebecca Myers.

I have to defer *more* of our salaries to put into the contingency cushion. At this point, we've already deferred over 50 percent of our salaries. I have to live on *something*. The film business is the only business that expects you to be so happy that you get to do your work that you'll accept not getting paid. Remember "How about nothing"?

The whole time I'm thinking, Rebecca, you don't know the least of it. Nobody knows yet that we're double-screwed, because we don't even have ARP yet. Or at least we're starting to suspect we don't. Film financing companies get cold feet all the time, but it usually happens before they commit. After the handshake or the signature, my assumption is that they're stuck with us. They'll have opinions—like "We'd rather not have Dennis Quaid"—but then it's about whether the creative elements you're bringing on board are protecting their investment. It's not "Wow, I'm going to bail out." But sometime between May and September, ARP got cold feet. I think they just didn't have the money, so they needed to come up with ways to get out of the deal. The way they did that was to make it *our fault*.

I go back into the theater and watch the rest of the movie, my heart sinking the whole time. Clear Blue Sky financed *The Safety of Objects*, so I think, If we just make a good sale on this, everybody will be confident. The problems will all ease up a bit. After the screening, the Miramax reps are all over Rose. They're outlining the Oscar campaign. It's premature, but that's how Miramax works. Harvey will see the movie tonight; we set up a meeting for the next day to do the sale. Good, we'll make a good sale and everyone will be happy. I go to bed with some sense of relief. But the next morning, ten minutes before the meeting is supposed to start, I get a call from the then-head of Miramax's business affairs, Andrew Herwitz.

"Harvey saw the movie," he says. "He doesn't want it."

Boom. That's that. No deal.

But because Miramax came on so hard, other potential distributors already backed away. What seems to be happening with *The Safety of Objects* is that all the mid-people in every company adore it, but the people at the top are unmoved by it or just don't see its commercial potential. (After Toronto, we make a much smaller deal with IFC for its release.)

As the situation is falling apart, we're scrambling to put a good face on it. It's now September 9, and I'm supposed to fly back to New York for two days to be with my family and then fly back to Toronto on September 11 for the premiere of another of our films, *The Grey Zone*, and some kind of resolution with ARP. I get back to New York, and on the night of the ninth, I talk over the *Far from Heaven* situation with Marlene. Without ARP, we will have to find another backer within a matter of days or *Far from Heaven* will never make it.

Sunday night, the ninth, I know what I have to do. We'll dump ARP and find someone else. I have to go back to Toronto before the eleventh. I've got to go up there as soon as possible. Like tomorrow. I tell my team still in Toronto, "Set up meetings for me with any potential foreign financing entity there, and I'm going to take the first plane out on the tenth." I arrive and hit the ground running. We shuttle back and forth from the two hotel bars—the Four Seasons and the Park Hyatt—trying to make a deal. I'm spraying *Far from Heaven* scripts all over the place and spelling out the deal to whoever will listen, ending everything with, "How quickly can you give us an answer?"

Of course, these companies smell the desperation on me. We're shooting in three weeks and we're missing one leg of a $12 million—nope, make that $14 million if we shoot in New York—stool. But what else am I going to do? Pretend that's not a dire situation? I've got a brilliant movie that's got Julianne Moore and Dennis Quaid in it. I have *something*. But papering a deal like this doesn't happen quickly. For the bond company to close, and for USA Films and Clear Blue Sky to feel that they really have this third partner, there has to be a legitimately tall stack of paper generated. We need a company with a good reputation. I collapse at the end of the day. It's the night of September 10, 2001.

Bright and early on the morning of September 11, I am on the phone with our lawyer John Sloss plotting our next move. Is there *any* other foreign sales company that we haven't approached yet? I am still in my pajamas and the muted TV is on CNN as John and I hammer out a strategy for the day. Then, out of the corner of my eye, I see the first image of the World Trade Center right after the first plane hit.

All I could think about was making sure my family was safe—the phones worked for a while and I managed to get hold of Marlene just as she was racing back to our daughter's nursery to pick her up. As the events unfolded I called Hertz and rented as many cars as I could to get the Killer staff and the directors and actors who were in Toronto with us back to NYC.

What I learn on September 11, among other things, is that our lawyer John Sloss is an insane workaholic. He doesn't understand why people are canceling their meetings. He has a mixed reputation, stemming largely from his tendency to get executive producer credit on movies that he's put the financing together for. Some people would say that's an overstatement of his role. Other people would say it's a tribute to his passion and the fact that he's built up his own practice with his own hands. The thing about Sloss that I like is that he has an intense sense of justice. He has an "I'm on a mission from God" thing about what he does, which I have too. We make a good team. What he does not have is a lot of sensitivity. On September 11, Sloss doesn't understand why FilmFour isn't still meeting us. I tell him, "The World Trade Center fell down. People think the world as we know it may be coming to an end and they want to get home to their families."

As the full horror of the day begins to sink in, a lot of people with us start asking themselves why we are wasting time making silly movies when there are so many bigger issues to deal with in life. All the screenings are canceled, and the bar at the Four Seasons is filled with movie stars and celebrities staring at the horrific images on the big screen. Their glamour is completely usurped. Someone says we should get out of big cities altogether, go live on a tropical island. But I sense that others, like me, feel a need to get back to work, that work is the way to keep our minds focused and sane. *Far from Heaven* hangs in the balance.

The only meeting on September 11 is a screaming match with ARP. Right before we meet them at the hotel bar, John and Jen at USA tell me that they are about to kill the project.

"You can't do that!" I say. "It's going to be a great work of art!" As if that would sway them.

They answer, "Yes, we can, and we will."

Over drinks, prospects dimming to black, Michele and Laurent are speaking French behind our backs, saying, "This is ridiculous, I've had enough of this stupid movie." (They don't realize I speak French.) We are so desperate at that point that we actually put up with this. Laurent ends our conversation with "Fuck you, I'm tired of this," and walks away. *Far from Heaven* is over.

We walk out, depressed. My cell phone rings. It's Jean-Charles Levy at TF1, a representative from the French television channel. We had met with him the day before. TF1 had just made a big deal with Miramax to distribute films in France. "We love Todd's script," Jean-Charles says. "We want to find a way to make it work."

Peaks. Valleys. Same difference.

All this time, we aren't paying any of our bills; we have people in our employ and can't let them go, but we also can't buy them any supplies. Suspicions are brewing that the *Far from Heaven* production is a house of cards on the verge of collapse. We are trying desperately to maintain the fiction that this is all business as usual, because if anybody *does* walk out, the house of cards probably would collapse.

Far from Heaven is made in a war zone. Though we shoot most of it in Bayonne, New Jersey—where Cathy's "house" is—one of the buildings we were going to use has become Merrill Lynch's new headquarters. The sets are built in the converted Marine Air Terminal. *Oz* is filmed right next door, and *A Beautiful Mind* was shot there as well. The physical production people are all over me, complaining that we'll never finish on time or within budget. But the crew wants this to work. Production is dead in New York right now; everything has stopped—except us. We are the only game in town, so we have all the top people manning our departments. And they know something is wrong, since we're paying people but not letting them buy things.

Everybody is jumpy; our days are punctuated by the wail of police sirens, anthrax alerts, and Code Orange. At least Todd is our one saving grace. He's completely calm and focused. Some of the directors that I work with are terrified that someone's going to realize the emperor has no clothes, so they overcompensate in ways that are tyrannical or insecure to the point of indecisiveness. Todd has an absolute, supreme trust in his own abilities, and in the early days of production, Todd always makes his day.

Unapproved Overages

Miraculously, we are reaching the two-thirds-done mark of production and everything seems to be going alarmingly well. We're on schedule, the weather is cooperating, and we're on budget. Or are we? It's almost too hard to believe. We had to scramble for locations that we lost, our costume designer is not known for her frugality, and the combination of September 11 and the delay in financing has created a situation where the only way to solve *Far from Heaven*'s production problems is to throw money at them.

Then Declan, our line producer, calls me. His voice is tight and he sounds upset. "I think we may have a problem here, Christine," he says. "The overage number keeps going up." The overage is how much we've gone over budget and dipped into the contingency, our cushion. Two weeks ago Declan assured me we would have at least $200,000 *left* in the contingency. A week ago he told me sheepishly it was probably closer to $75,000. "How up?" I say on the phone. Declan is silent.

"North of two hundred fifty," he says, finally.

I'm stunned. I hang up and try to refocus—I have to get myself on the offensive, not the defensive—but how? We're $250,000 *past* our contingency. The bond company will know. Rebecca calls and I dodge her. She's reading the same reports I am. She knows we're in trouble. What happened? How did we get here?

You hear a lot about films going "over budget." There are two ways of doing it: approved and unapproved overages. Usually what will happen is while you're shooting your movie, the director will want something that is not in your budget. Let's say he wants some gigantic crane that costs $2,000 dollars a day. You can say, "Look, Todd, we've got a five-hundred-dollar crane budgeted for six days. Can we take four of those days and just get rid of them and use the grant crane for one day only?" If he says yes, then you put that in your cost report and say, "This is my overage, but this is how I'm covering it." In other words, you're not really going over the budget, you're just shuffling the costs around as you go. If you *have* to go over budget—if Todd says, "No, I want both damn cranes"—you call the studio and say, "We need this crane; it's going to make the movie better." Somebody there, usually your production executive, says, "OK, you get your two thousand over."

But it's up to them. Does the studio want to alienate the filmmaker by bringing the bond company in? On *One Hour Photo* I would call up our executive at Fox Searchlight to say, "The bond company is saying we have to stop shooting at ten o'clock tonight because we can't afford any more overtime. But if we do that, the director won't get the rest of the scene and Robin Williams will be furious. What do you want us to do?" Peter Rice would then tell me, "All right, I will approve the additional two hours of overtime." That was an approved overage, which means the studio would have to cover it, not the bond company.

Unapproved overages happen when you don't call the studio, when you don't file an accurate cost report, or when your lead's pregnancy starts to show and you need to keep refitting every costume she has. Now, Julianne's pregnancy, for the most part, is working in our favor. Normally, she is incredibly slim and her face is very striking, but with a little bit of pregnancy weight, she looks much softer and more 1950s. But Sandy Powell, our costume designer, has to deal with the fact that Julianne's body keeps changing. Sandy did the costumes for *Gangs of New York* and *Velvet Goldmine* and won an Oscar for her work on *Shakespeare in Love.* She's rail thin, with bright red hair, and she's one of those people who's so about the clothes that she doesn't see anything else. On set, she would come up to me and say, "I just want you to know that Julianne is eating *cake.*" I'd say, "This woman is an actress. She eats brown rice all the time. She barely gets to eat. How often does she get to be, like, 'Fuck it, I am eating the cake'?"

Even though Sandy came up through the arty world of Derek Jarman, she now lives at a higher scale of economies. If you asked her, "Sandy, how was *Gangs of New York*?" she'd say, "Well, I got this special boot for the extras and it was perfect and period, but the line producer told me that only the *first* line of extras can wear them. Can you believe it?"

Midway through the production, her department's cost estimates versus actual costs are proving to be wildly irreconcilable. As soon as we realize this, we replace her assistant, which does nothing. So we hire an auditor for her department, but the costs keep going up. Other problems crop up. Sandy, with little experience with New York costume houses, has received a large number of miscut costumes that have to be replaced at a hefty cost. Nearing the end of the shoot, Sandy tries to convince me to come up with the money for an alternative evening gown for Julianne for the party scene because she is afraid that the one she'd made was going to make our star look too pregnant. It will cost $8,000 just to have it on hand *in case* we need it. The answer is no. So, ingenuity, independent-film style: Sandy brings in a friend from London who is a "costume shader." Using markers, he literally shades Julianne's costumes so that they take your eyes away from her waist. Brilliant. It works, and at about one-tenth the cost of the gown.

Killer is always straining to push the budget to the absolute limit. As the budgets get bigger, the pressure and the scrutiny get more intense. In total honesty, I really didn't know how close to the edge we were skating, and yes, $250,000 really *is* the edge for modestly budgeted films. But this is primarily a cash-flow problem. It's hard to keep track of money when you don't really have it. Clearly, the bond company didn't know the extent of the problem either or they would have had no choice but to take action. September 11 was having a ripple effect on our shoot that I couldn't begin to measure. September 11 gave us no margin for error. And the only thing the bond company could have done to curtail our spending would have been to cut sets, set decoration, and costumes. So, if I had realized how close to the edge we were, we would never have had a movie as beautiful as the one we got.

Still, Rebecca and the bond company can't just force us to do "whatever" to finish the film. They have to insure the delivery of a film that matches the script and that makes sense. What they *can* do is force us to cut personnel, breathe down our necks about overtime, and make us say no to Todd.

Once I hang up with Declan, I work myself into a righteous frenzy ("After September eleventh and our limited cash flow, it's *amazing* we're as on track as we are!" "Look at what they're getting: it's all on the screen!") I'm scheduled to meet with Rebecca the following morning and hash out what's happening.

Losing Control

At 9 a.m. I'm at a big conference table at our office with Rebecca. The worst thing that could happen to a producer is happening to me. The bond company is officially taking over my movie. Rebecca says, "We don't want to hurt you or the film," "This process can be easy or it can be difficult," "You are here as a direct result of your own actions." When someone says, "We are *very very* disappointed in you" enough times, you stop listening. Then Rebecca starts flexing her increasingly real power. "You are going to have to cut at least two days out of the schedule," she says. I want to say, "Rebecca, over the past ten years I've probably handed at least two million bucks over to Film Finances, and you've *never* had to come in. So why are you being such a jerk about it?" Instead I say, "I don't think we *can* cut our schedule."

She says, "You are not being cooperative."

I answer, "Well, then, I mean I don't know *how* to cut the schedule by two days."

She counters, "You mean you won't."

You get the idea.

Rebecca is trying to terrify me into convincing our financiers that they have to give us more money to cover the overages. The last thing the bond company wants is passivity. The last thing they want is for the producer to say, "OK, fine, you go in, finish the movie, big, bad bond company," because they can't finish the movie. They can't just walk in and say, "You know what, we're done shooting. Everybody go home." They're contracted to deliver the film; that's what they are paid to do. If they have a horrible relationship with the director and the producer just sort of disappears, it's going to end up a nightmare for everybody. In the best-case scenario, what the bond company wants is for the producer to think they are a big, fat threat and that the director and producer will be so scared that the director will say, as some do, "I'll just pay for it. I'll put the rest of my salary toward this crane shot." Jim Cameron did it famously on *Titanic*, and Scorsese did it on *Gangs of New York*. Directors and producers do that all the time because it's so heinous to be working on your movie and have the bean counters come in and start tallying everything. The joke is that on *Far from Heaven*, Todd and I have already deferred so much that we don't have any left to tip the balance.

The rest of the day Rebecca spends walking around the set, telling various department heads that Film Finances is now in charge and I'm not. They take my name off the film's bank account so I can't withdraw any money. That night, I want to crawl into a martini and never come out. This has never happened to me; I know other producers who have been usurped like this. It's like having a DUI on your driving record.

Then the phone rings. It's Todd, hysterical.

It seems we have a new line producer named William,* Rebecca's partner from Film Finances. He's set himself up in an office at the studio. And William has called the assistant director and told him to take Scene 31 off the schedule. (William, I learn, was also caught with his hand in the till when he was producing a TV show a few years ago. He was led off the set in handcuffs. Gossip gets around a set pretty quickly.) Scene 31 is definitely interstitial, something like Cathy looking at Frank through the window, but it is symbolic. Lots of hysterical calling ensues—me to Sloss, Sloss to Rebecca, Todd to Sloss, Todd to USA. At least the crisis allows me to scramble onto some moral high ground with USA, telling them they should have had a creative discussion with Todd before the bond company made the decision for him.

In the final weeks of production in November, the bond company is now all over the set, trying to find people to fire, but we're too lean and mean. We have the union minimum staffing in all departments, so there is no one to fire. To prove they're doing something, the bond company takes away the E-ZPasses from most of the crew

*Name changed.

people—a big mistake, since the crew don't give a shit about saving money for the bond company (and isn't E-ZPass actually cheaper than paying cash at the tolls?). It's just a massive headache, since months later, the production will get hit with "hidden" E-ZPass costs, thousands of dollars in fines from crew vans going through the E-ZPass lane with expired passes.

To their credit, the crew fight back. They won't work for this William guy, and they demand to keep Declan there to be a French collaborator. Every tiny decision—to shoot even fifteen minutes later, to rent an extra light—has to be run through them. Rebecca expresses concern that in the event that there's another terrorist attack, if we let Dennis Quaid go home for Thanksgiving, he might not come back. All I can think, from my pointless perch, is, "If another terrorist attack happens, who cares if he comes back or not?"

This drama makes everybody feel edgy and threatened. The department heads don't want to be on a movie that the bond company takes over: it dents their career. Every time a director sits down and talks to the bond company about whom they want to hire for their next film, the bond company can now say, "Mmm, you know that costumer went really over budget on *Far from Heaven.* I'm not sure we can approve her." Your livelihood is in the balance. On the other hand, Rebecca tells me, "I can't believe how irresponsible Sandy, the costume designer, is. This is going to affect her career." At this point, Sandy has already won one Oscar. I want to say "I'm sure Sandy will cry all the way to the Academy Awards."

Meanwhile, we discover that Declan and Killer's checks were being "held." On top of that, there are around $30,000 worth of Killer expenses that have been put through the AmEx, which needs to be paid each month, no question. These are also being "held." So I call the head of Film Finances in L.A., Kurt Woolner. I say, "What is going on? We need our money!" And he gives me the we're-so-disappointed-in-you line, which at this point I can't even hear any longer. Then he says, "Christine, if you fully intended to spend the contingency, you committed fraud and we're not paying you."

Now, when you're six weeks into a production, you haven't been sleeping much. You're drinking twenty cups of coffee a day and eating terrible food. You're highly suggestible. But I know Kurt is wrong. We may have lost a handle on the movie, but we never intended to blow through our contingency. Right now, the bond company is all about just grabbing money wherever they can and pushing me into a corner. They even scour all the receipts that the producers turn in, looking for hidden cheats they can stick me with. But they can't find a one. (Actually, they hit me with thirty dollars' worth of tolls on an E-Z Pass, but that's it.) I am demoralized. I want badly to just stay home and out of it, but that's not fair to Todd. Film Finances has done a ton of movies with me. Why are they treating me this way? I have never called them in before, and they have certainly had to bail out movies in far worse shape than this one.

Finally, I manage to get Jean-Charles from TF1 on the phone to pledge one-third of our overage—approximately $75,000 to $100,000. Huge relief, but only a third. Now I just have to shame Clear Blue Sky and USA into doing the same. The bond company is getting increasingly aggressive. Last night Rebecca told me she would give me until today to come up with more money, but if I didn't, well, then they would start calling *every* shot. That will kill Todd.

I play the only chip we have left: Steven Soderbergh. He's editing *Solaris*, which is both a good time and a terrible time to contact a filmmaker. He's done with the madness of the shoot, but he's in the middle of an enormous jigsaw puzzle. I call the editing room and get his assistant. "How urgent is this?" she asks. Very. Steven, I know, always calls back. When he does, I spell out the situation, and he makes a call to Scott Greenstein, with whom he has a great relationship—and *bing*, problem solved. Steven was going to offer his own money, but Scott (to show Steven support) bankrolls us. When you work with artists like Todd, they tend to get friends in high places. Steven doesn't want Todd to have to compromise. More important, he knows *Far from Heaven* is not an out-of-control movie in any way. Everything we needed was shot, people showed up on time, we were not a runaway train. Clear Blue Sky hears about Steven's calling on Todd's behalf, and they pony up too.

We wrap. Todd takes his movie and his editor out to Portland to cut the film. I reduce my coffee intake by about sixteen cups a day.

"Fixing" **Heaven**

In April 2002 we test-market *Far from Heaven* with focus groups. I have no choice in the matter; Scott Greenstein at USA demands it. At each screening, viewers get slips of paper with twenty questions, but only the top two matter: "What did you think of this film? Excellent, Very Good, Good, Fair, Poor," and "Would you recommend this film to your friends? Yes—Definitely, Yes—Probably, No—Probably Not, No—Definitely." These are the questions your backers are going to be looking at. The testing company Dubin tells us that as a rule of thumb, for an independent film, "the average"—whatever that means—is about 45 percent of the audience would "definitely recommend" it to a friend and 25 percent would rank it "excellent." (Of course, USA wants those numbers to be around 70 percent "definitely recommend" and above 25 percent "excellent.")

On the surface, these numbers may sound reasonable, if optimistic. But an audience's appreciation of a film has a lot to do with the context in which they're seeing it, and test audiences have no context. Take a film like *Boys Don't Cry*. It's the kind of film that you can't just walk into the movie theater cold and watch. In a way, you have to be told how to receive it. (Fox Searchlight knew this and never tested it.) *One Fine Day* with Michelle Pfeiffer and George Clooney was rumored to be the best-testing movie in history. No surprise. It's a romantic comedy that is pretty much a brochure about falling in love.

At the testing, *Far from Heaven* performs terribly: 8 percent rank it "excellent" and 13 percent "definitely recommend" it. Scott Greenstein at USA gets nervous. Audiences couldn't tell if it was a comedy or not. They asked, "Is this supposed to be funny?" *Far from Heaven* is exactly the kind of movie that an audience will enjoy more when they go into the theater with certain expectations.

This whole process is anathema to my kind of filmmaking. One of the biggest lies I've ever heard is from studio executives justifying testing with a straight face: "This is not about the numbers. This is about getting a sense of whether we should market this movie to younger or older audiences, male or female." As soon as the first numbers come in terrible, which they often do on our movies, suddenly it is all about the numbers.

These testing numbers paralyze directors. If you're making a by-the-numbers action movie, it *should be* by the numbers. But why are you bothering to make a movie with Todd Haynes if you need to focus-group it? At Killer, we often set up screenings where we recruit people ourselves. What we negotiated with USA was to take off the top two boxes—"What do you think of this film?" and "Would you recommend it?"—and leave the others: "Which actors did you like the best? Did you feel the movie moved too fast, too slow, or just right?" etc. We did that with *One Hour Photo*—a movie that got tested *five* separate times—and it was a positive experience. Mark Romanek really got a sense of how it was playing to the audience. He wanted people to be *really* into his film. He liked the feedback. Rose Troche's ensemble drama *The Safety of Objects* had great numbers. (The box office proved otherwise. One of the few vitriolic answers to the questionnaire gave us a hint of what was to come: "Did anything throw you out of the movie?" "I wish!") But even after negotiating with USA for *Far from Heaven*, we get browbeat by the marketing department to put the two questions back on. You can never win against a marketing department.

Todd's first cut of the film is beautiful but long. We're seeing all the bells and whistles, and we're thinking, Wow. The second cut is a lot shorter but not nearly as emotionally involving. I know that if everybody would just back off and leave Todd alone and let him cut his movie—instead of sticking preview dates in front of him, telling him, "You've got to have it cut by this day 'cause it takes eighteen weeks to prepare for the preview"—he can get there.

Scott Greenstein at USA starts making noises. Twenty percent of our audience said the film is "too slow," so Scott starts trying to persuade Todd to trim it down significantly. Since Steven Soderbergh actually has "final cut" on the picture—an agreement we made to help broker USA's investment—Steven flies up to Portland to "consult" with Todd.

Steven arrives on a Saturday. For two days, he goes through the film meticulously with Todd in the editing room, trying to determine what the "problem" of the film is, based on the low testing numbers. These testing numbers are something Steven can't put out of his mind, and maybe no one can. The problem is, of course, the entire system of testing audiences who have no idea what they are going to see and expecting their comments to have any relevance in a world where films are so highly marketed. *Far from Heaven* is a movie made in a context, with sensitivity to film history and aesthetics. It's not *One Fine Day*.

With Todd, Steven acts the provocateur. "I'm going to be tough with you," Steven tells him. "This is the time when you challenge every single attachment you have to your cut." He speaks very directly. Steven's main point is that he feels the audience is ahead of Cathy's story. Todd needs to get rid of duplicate information or foretelling; the film needs to keep "some level of the unknown in the plot," Steven tells him. The whole scene with the black gardener and Cathy walking the woods? Cut it, says Steven. But that's the moment when Cathy ends up at the black bar, Todd argues. The tables are turned on Cathy; she's the only white woman in the room. "Not important enough to keep," Steven says.

Ultimately, Todd sees *Far from Heaven* as a melodrama, not a straightforward drama, and it's a distinction that matters. He argues that melodrama is an extremely unsubtle genre—that the pathos lies in the fact that the audience *does* know more than the main character. It's a different kind of suspense from "we're in the dark and the story is going to surprise us." But it's still suspense. It's the suspense of foreknowledge that keeps you hovering over Cathy, wondering what she will do. Todd loves Steven's films, but they are very different from his own work. *Far from Heaven* is a romantic film about tearful emotions, and that's not something that Steven has explored. It may not be something he's interested in, but Todd is. And the craft of engineering those feelings for audiences is what *Far from Heaven* is about.

Todd sticks to his gut. It's a healthy back-and-forth. By Monday, Todd has taken some of Steven's recommendations for trims and rejected others. More important, Steven completely respects Todd's final decisions and he leaves to go back to work on *Solaris*. But when Scott at USA hears that Todd didn't take every single one of Steven's ideas, he hints to me that he may not "support" the film in its release. This feels like a flashback to Miramax's treatment of *Velvet Goldmine*. We're at an impasse.

Now it's May 2002. I run into Julianne at a party for Robert Altman's company Sandcastle, with whom we're making *The Company.* She asks me how *Far from Heaven* is faring. I don't know what to tell her.

"What's the matter?" she asks. She can see the problems written on my face.

"Nothing," I tell her. "Steven and Todd worked together. It's fine." She doesn't buy it. "USA is going to fuck it up, aren't they?"

I can't lie to her, so I leave. On my way home, I get a call from Ted Hope and James Schamus, the heads of Good Machine along with David Linde. They're ecstatic. Scott has been fired. James and David—some of Todd's oldest and biggest fans—are taking over USA Films. They are now in charge of *Far from Heaven.*

I can't believe it. Home free.

Getting In

There comes a point when you are finishing a movie where even though you know it's great, even though you're sure it will be a hit with the public, you start to crave some "objective" affirmation that the movie is, in fact, terrific. It's usually around this point that I get a little jumpy when the phone rings, wondering if I'm about to hear whether my movie has made it into its first film festival. And even though I blithely tell anyone who wants to listen that "Cannes isn't what it used to be" and "Berlin doesn't matter," of course I am desperate to get my film in.

By July, we are confident that *Far from Heaven* will make the Venice Film Festival, held in September. It only takes one phone call to kick us off our pedestal. The call comes from our point man in Venice, David Linde, the indefatigable co-president of USA Films. David had submitted the film to the festival's director.

"He liked it . . . ," David says in an uncharacteristically tentative tone of voice. Uh-oh.

"He didn't love it. He thought it should have been well, either more gay or more black."

What do you say to that?

"Do we still have a chance at getting in?" I ask.

"No way I'm giving up now," David says. "I'm working on it!" David knows building an audience for *Far from Heaven* means winning some international kudos. A couple of days later David calls to say our film is going to make it into the festival, but it won't get a spot in the Competition. Films in Competition go before the international jury for a chance to win prizes; other films are there to entertain/annoy the festival crowds in hopes of picking up some press. Since until now the rallying cry has been "Competition or *bust!*" I can't hide the fact that I'm upset.

"Well," says David, "look at it this way: if we are not in Competition, Julianne can't win a prize—but she also can't *not* win a prize!"

True enough. Now we have a screening date: September 5.

I call Todd. I can't bear to disappoint him, so I try to give him a story with a happy ending. Even though we desperately wanted to be in Competition before, I tell him, *now* we have decided it is much better not to be. The following week, Venice announces its Competition lineup. *The Hours*—a movie whose all-star cast happens to include our very own Julianne Moore—is scheduled to play on September 3—two days before *Far from Heaven*.

Everyone on our side freaks out.

"If *The Hours* goes before us, they'll get all the press!"

"And we'll end up with the tab!"

"We are not flying Julianne to Venice so she can do press for *another movie!*"

I'm mentally toting up the cost of first-class plane tickets, a suite at the Gritti Palace, the outrageously priced drinks at Harry's Bar . . . Our film *must* show first. David negotiates with the festival and comes back with a date of September 1. Take it or leave it. We will be playing at the same time as *Road to Perdition*, but at least we'll get in there well before *The Hours*. OK, we all change our airline tickets.

Meanwhile, our Italian distributor has just woken up to the fact that *Far from Heaven* has not made it into Competition. Now the Italians say that they will *not* share any of the Venice costs because the movie is not in Competition. *Capisce?*

Jean-Charles from TF1 calls David and me, foaming at the mouth. With the Italians out, TF1 now thinks this festival is getting way too expensive and wants to cut our losses and pull the movie out altogether. Obviously they've been thinking about the Bellinis too. David pleads with them to wait. They ignore him and send a letter to the head of the festival withdrawing the film. So now that we've just made all our flight and hotel arrangements, we have no festival to go to.

But David has not yet begun to fight. He fires off letters to TF1 telling them how terrible this will make the movie look, as though it were damaged goods. I don't even tell Todd what's going on. I'm hoping he doesn't call. Maybe everything will take care of itself, and he'll never have to know.

A day goes by, and then David calls again, elated this time. *The Hours* has been withdrawn from Competition. David's theory is that Harvey Weinstein never wanted *The Hours* to screen in Venice in the first place and strong-armed Scott Rudin, the film's producer, into withdrawing it. With *The Hours* out of the picture, we have been offered its slot in Competition. David has already accepted.

Now we are screening September 3. I call Todd once again to convince him that when I argued that we did not want to be in Competition, I was completely wrong, and now we absolutely *do* want to be in Competition. David Rooney's *Variety* review comes out the day before (they caught a screening) and it's a rave. "The film is a jewel-like operation on every technical level," he writes. "Its visual sumptuousness seduces from the opening frame to the last." It's enough to make me magically forget the hell of production.

The next day, we're in the Competition.

And Julianne wins the Grand Prize.

Letter from L.A. II

MARCH 23, 2003, HOLLYWOOD, CALIFORNIA

The Governor's Ball—How to (Not) Win an Oscar—
Learning to Lose—Jerry Bruckheimer Knows Me!

I don't know what to say.

The lights in the Kodak Theater come up. All the stars in tuxes, ballgowns, and strapless whatnot meander to the elevators. What you can't see is that the floor has fallen out beneath us in the orchestra, eight rows from the front. Todd sits on the aisle to my right. He's dressed in the same elegant 1950s tuxedo Dennis Quaid wore for *Far from Heaven's* holiday party scene. Our cinematographer, the eminently dapper Ed Lachman, sits to my left, still clutching the pages of the acceptance speech he didn't get to read. I turn to Todd, but I can't find the words. Usually I'm good at this. As a producer, you're paid to have the words; you don't have time to go looking for them. When Nicole Kidman nabbed the Golden Globe for playing Virginia Wolfe in *The Hours,* I told Julianne Moore that Nicole "won by a nose." OK, not the most original line, but I had to say *something.*

But right now, I don't know what to say. After months of Oscar campaigning, upheaval, and bicoastal red-eyes, I can't help but feel crushed. *Far from Heaven* was nominated in four categories: Best Actress (Julianne), Score (Elmer Bernstein), Cinematography (Ed), and Original Screenplay (Todd). For months, it had the feel of a movie that could go all the way. A critical darling, *Far from Heaven* swept the New York Film Critics Circle Awards in December. Julianne won best actress at the Venice Film Festival. We even nabbed heaps of bronze at the Independent Spirit Awards two days before in Santa Monica. How did this rout happen?

Fortunately for me, Pedro Almodóvar fills up the silence. The brilliant, flamboyant, incredibly sweet Spanish director sat two rows in front of us for the entire ceremony—except when he won his Oscar for Best Original Screenplay. Now he runs up to us, gives Todd a big hug, and says in his great Castilian accent, "I hate to be competing against chu!"

Honestly, Todd doesn't need me—or anybody else—to say any-thing. Somehow he's able to float over these dramas. He's more relieved that he didn't have to give an acceptance speech than disap-pointed that he didn't win. I'll just have to be disappointed for him.

"Well," I say, "time to head upstairs?"

Translation: Vodka martini, anyone?

This year, the Governor's Ball is above us, on the rooftop of the Kodak on Hollywood Boulevard. It's the biggest bash of all the Oscar madness: a dinner party for 1,650 people. It's the official post-Oscar party. Anyone will tell you that on Oscar night, there are really only two parties in Hollywood: the Governor's Ball and the *Vanity Fair* party. Every other party, in the words of agent Norby Walters, is "filled-with-civilians crappo." We've got invites to both. At the Governor's Ball, the nominees and winners end up sitting next to each other, so it makes for a uniquely schizophrenic experience: one-fifth ecstatic joy, four-fifths monster's ball. As we step out of the elevator, the rooftop looks like a prom floor, decked out with massive tables dressed in black and white, corresponding to the films in competition. Each table has a floral shop explosion of white orchids and carnations with a Wolfgang Puck confection plopped in the center. Since it's the sev-enty-fifth anniversary year, antique frames with memorabilia from ye olde Oscar nights litter the tabletops. Like anybody's looking at the souvenirs in *this* crowd.

At the *Far from Heaven* table sit Julianne Moore, in an emerald gown, with her husband, the director Bart Freundlich (*Trust the Man, Myth of Fingerprints, World Traveler*). Julianne and Bart are joined by Brad Simpson. He's dressed in the tux that Gucci *gave* him. (For the record, I'm in a Yamamoto suit that I had to pay for.)

There's just one missing person from the *Heaven* team: Elmer Bernstein, our composer, who lost to Elliot Goldenthal for *Frida*. He's too upset by his loss to socialize. People think that Elmer, who scored *The Man with the Golden Arm, The Magnificent Seven*, and *The Great Escape*, has a shelf of thirteen Oscars. He doesn't. Even though he's part of the Hollywood Hall of Fame, Elmer has won just one Oscar, for the musical *Thoroughly Modern Millie* in 1967, which he shared with *five* people. At one point during the *Heaven* postproduction, the eighty-two-year-old Elmer actually thanked Todd for giving him one of the few chances he'd had to write "emotionally honest music." (In a sad postscript, Elmer passed away in August 2004.) Todd is angriest that Elmer didn't win. Somehow, though, it doesn't take much for the mood to become celebratory. At least the months of insanity are over. *Far from Heaven* is what it is. We can bask in that.

Then James Schamus sidles up to our table. In his trademark bow tie and glasses, he's over the moon. As the head of Focus Features, the specialty division of Universal Studios that we partnered with to market and distribute *Far from Heaven,* he was the one responsible for getting our movie to audiences. James also had one other contender tonight: Polanksi's *The Pianist,* which had to be the happiest film of the night. It was the surprise winner of three awards: Director, Actor, and Adapted Screenplay. James adored the film, bid on at it Cannes, and turned it into an unlikely hit. Their table at the Governor's Ball was a crush of well-wishers, photographers, and three statuettes.

"Oh, I've been at the losers' table before," James says to us, trying to be nice. Back in 1997, he wrote and produced *The Ice Storm,* another shoulda-been-a-contender.

Julianne replies, "I never thought of us as losers."

Thirteen years ago, James, an ambitious Berkeley PhD with no practical production skills, walked into my office at 225 Lafayette Street in Manhattan looking to break into film. Todd, James, and I made *Poison* and got ourselves on the map. If you need any more proof of the ascendancy of independent film, this is it: three of us come so far together, all the way to the Kodak Theater.

Yet I couldn't help but feel that our long history with James hadn't made the difference for *Far from Heaven.* The day after the Oscar nominations were announced in February, we were showered in gifts. Why? Because Todd is one of the most genuinely liked film directors in the independent film world. He doesn't have a mean bone in his body. Even the most jaded person can't help but respond to that. But after the gifts and good feeling, people started calling to tell us, "You were *robbed.*" What they meant was that even though *Far from Heaven* had four nominations, it had been overlooked for the top slots, Best Picture and Best Director. Focus hadn't pushed the movie enough, people said, running negligible ad campaigns while *The Pianist* seemed to be everywhere. Harvey told me personally, "You were fucked."

Who cares about Oscars? I do. It's easy to be jaded or cynical about the actual ceremony, but winning an Oscar is the climax of a film's life. The Academy Awards are the highest-stakes game in town, and increasingly it's an open table. In 1996, the watershed year, the Best Picture category of the Oscars was barnstormed by the independently produced films *Fargo, Shine,* and *Secrets and Lies.* It's been that way ever since.

In 1998, the first time I went, I pretty much snuck in the back door. Todd's *Velvet Goldmine* had been nominated for Best Costume Design, and all I really wanted to do was to hang out in the amazing little bar at the bottom of the Dorothy Chandler Pavilion, where you get to drink in a dream of celebrities, Goldie Hawn running out of the ladies' room and putting her breasts back in her gown. That year, host Whoopi Goldberg decided that she would dress in the outfits for each of the Best Costume Design–nominated films. Now, *Velvet Goldmine* had made negative amounts of money by Hollywood standards but was, hilariously, made more visible by this stunt. From the balcony, Todd and I giggled as Whoopi came out in Jonathan Rhys Meyers's outrageous silver, winged rock outfit from the film (well, enlarged a bit) while the orchestra struck up a version of Brian Eno's obscure "Needle in the Camera's Eye" in schmaltzy Vegas style. It was absurd. It was the Oscars.

In 1999 Hilary Swank went from *Beverly Hills 90210* to *Boys Don't Cry* to the Best Actress envelope and never looked back. At the Governor's Ball that year, everybody wanted a photograph: Hilary and Oscar. We didn't need to work the room. We couldn't. Everybody was coming at us. Kim Peirce, Hilary's director, who'd never even watched the Academy Awards before, was invited to a small private party in the penthouse of the Argyle Hotel with Tom Cruise, Nicole Kidman, and Russell Crowe. It happens *that fast.* And thanks to *Boys Don't Cry,* Killer reached a new level of legitimacy; we had proved that a $2 million budget, a nonunion crew in Dallas, and actors working for scale didn't matter if you made a great movie.

Even that win took strategy. As we went into Oscar season in 1999, Lindsay Law, the head of Fox Searchlight, which released *Boys Don't Cry,* told Kim, "I'm not going to spend a dime trying to get you a Best Screenplay nomination because you're not going to get it. And if you do get it, you won't win it." This was the year of *American Beauty* and

Election. He went on, "I need to put all my money into getting Hilary the Oscar because that's what's going to make the difference." It freaked Kim out, but he was right. Every party and every ad in every newspaper pushed Hilary. She became the focus. When Peter Rice replaced Lindsay Law, right after the Golden Globes, he kept up the same strategy. Peter Rice has provocative taste, gets behind risky pictures with bold campaigns (think *Napoleon Dynamite*), and goes for directors with talent: Alexander Payne (*Sideways*), David O. Russell (*I ♥ Huckabees*), and Danny Boyle (*28 Days Later*).

In terms of the Oscar campaign for *Boys Don't Cry,* we were a team with Searchlight, doing weekly conference calls with the marketing people to decide where to spend money. As Miramax proved, year after year, the Academy Awards can be gamed; you drop enough ads, you build enough buzz, and you can create the sense of inevitability. I bet if you could look at the votes in each category, there'd be just two films in close competition: a winner and an underdog, because Academy voters like a Hollywood ending and they like a third-act twist.

Campaigning

With *Far from Heaven,* we got our rude awakening in January at the Golden Globes. The Golden Globes are judged by the foreign press, who'd already gone wild for Julianne. We knew Dennis Quaid probably wouldn't win for Best Supporting Actor, since he was up against dying artist Ed Harris (*The Hours*) and Chris Cooper (*Adaptation*) in some scary orthodontia. But Todd's script was close to flawless, Elmer Bernstein's score was great. And we thought—we *knew*—it was going to be "Julianne's year." We'd even heard rumors that CAA had told Nicole Kidman that.

We knew we'd achieved some visibility with the movie when Jack Lechner skewered it in his eighth annual Oscar card. Jack does brilliant song parodies for the IFC Independent Spirit Awards. The *Far from Heaven* romp was to be sung to the tune of "On the Street Where You Live":

You have often served canapés before
But you never saw so many eyebrows raise before

What a blot on life
For a fifties wife
Knowing you're indiscreet where you live

Does your husband stray when he's not with you?
Did you learn he had to keep a same-sex rendezvous?
Better see that he
Gets some therapy
Not to be indiscreet where you live

Somehow
Your friends are suspicious
That you've crossed
The tracks for romance
And now
The gossip is vicious
They think your gardener's tending more than just your plants

All the looks you get are the glacial kind
They'll forgive a fling, but not the interracial kind
That's the etiquette
In Connecticut
Now that you're indiscreet where you live

But the joke didn't last. When Julianne lost at the Golden Globes, when we lost in every category, we looked at each other and thought, Did we screw up? We were blindsided.

There were two months left between the Globes and the Oscars, and we did everything we could for *Far from Heaven*. We campaigned like crazy. There are 6,000 voting Academy members, and the largest subset of them (1,315) are the actors. We went after them with every famous person we could get. George Clooney, an executive producer on the film, hosted a party for voters at the Avalon Hotel in L.A. Stacey Sher, who produced *Erin Brockovich* and *Out of Sight,* hosted one at her house. Ellen Barkin hosted another at her house in Manhattan. Eighty people attended each. We stuffed faces with free food and drinks and said, "This reception is in honor of Julianne Moore." We reminded people, "She deserves it. She hasn't won an Oscar yet." As in Hilary's campaign, we put our weight behind Julianne because we believed she was our best shot.

It didn't work. But something did work for *The Pianist*. If you spoke to James Schamus, he'd tell you that Focus didn't make a choice which film to promote. The distributors never choose, he'd say. Audiences choose for them. *The Pianist* stayed in theaters longer, ultimately making twice ($32 million) what *Far from Heaven* made ($15 million). To our complaining, "Our movie should've gotten more advertising and more nominations," he'd answer, "The movie should've performed better." We'll have to agree to disagree. There's no way to know what might have happened with *Far from Heaven*. Todd got to make the movie he wanted to make. That's what I was there to do. If we dreamed bigger for it, it's not as though we went into production thinking his film would be Oscar bait. You can't work like that.

I'm not good at the past tense. In my experience, what makes a successful film producer is the ability to live, almost entirely, in both present and future: the excitement of *what's next* mixed with a responsibility for *right now*. My job is to discover talent and find a way for you to know about it. The central discipline for a producer is a constant, inexhaustible enthusiasm.

Life of the party

OK, but there are parties to go to. The invitations for the *Vanity Fair* party at Morton's are given out with half-hour windows of time for arrival: the more famous you are, the earlier the time you get. (Ours is for 10:30, right after the ceremony and the ball.) This year there's no red carpet because everybody is afraid that since we're invading Iraq, terrorists will bomb the place. As if Al Qaeda had been thinking, "Let's get America where it really hurts! The *Vanity Fair* party!" One of the silliest things is how righteous some people in L.A. can be: "Don't let the terrorists break our Hollywood spirit!" We're at war and millions of people are getting their news from Oscarwatch.com. I'm happy knowing I'll be home tomorrow in New York.

Every famous person you can think of, living and some you thought were dead, are at the *Vanity Fair* party. It's a supernova of celebrity.

I'm the least famous person in the room. I don't know where Morton's ends and this shimmering white tent, like some futuristic gala, begins. Thank God John Waters is here, in a banquette talking to Fran Lebowitz, so I know there's some irony in the room. Todd and I gravitate to Susan Sarandon, who is a mother of three but looks like she hasn't aged since *Cat People*. I go to get a drink at the bar, and this guy with a perfect tan and well-coiffed grizzle introduces himself.

"Hi, I'm Jerry Bruckheimer," he says.

"Uh, I'm Christine Vachon," I answer.

"I know who you are," he says. "I'm a big admirer of yours."

I'm like, "You *are*?"

Then someone a hundred times more important than me comes over—Meryl Streep—and he's gone. I want to jump up in the air: Jerry Bruckheimer, the man who makes gazillions of dollars for people, knows who I am!

One of the most entertaining parts of these parties for me is watching Todd, detached from all the deal making and headlines, struggle to play the name game. Once a famous L.A. director came up to Todd to compliment him, and Todd was very gracious, but as soon as the director walked away, he turned to me and asked, "Who was that again?" Same thing happened with Chris Weitz (*About a Boy*). Todd was insatiably curious about Chris's mom, Susan Kohner, who played one of the daughters in Sirk's *Imitation of Life*. And then Todd asked, "So Chris, you're a filmmaker too, I guess?"

We linger. Todd hangs with Jake Gyllenhaal and Kirsten Dunst in a corner. Henry Thomas, who shone in *Gangs of New York*, seems upset that Scorsese didn't win. Lots of people are still in the stewing-over-the-results moment. At about 2 a.m., we leave. Having smoked a few cigarettes with Harvey, Todd gets a ride home. I take the car to a party up in the Hollywood Hills, in a mansion rented for the night by one of the heads of a talent agency. It's a slick young Hollywood bacchanal; you need a password to get in, then on the list to get past that, and once you do, it feels like everyone's on cocaine, dancing madly and screaming at each other. With that kind of vibe, I feel tired and old. I see Killer's Brad in line for the bathroom. Twenty minutes later, the line has barely moved. It's clear a lot of the "business" happening in the bathroom involves groups of people. Brad, at emergency level, cuts up to the front of the line. "Look, I'm really sorry, but I swear I'm just going to the bathroom to pee and nothing else." They let him through just as I'm leaving. At 7 a.m., I'm picked up to fly back to New York. I want to get home to Marlene and Guthrie.

Weeks later, Todd is already at work on something new. I have to keep fielding studio offers for him, directing assignments and work for hire. When he takes these calls, they always have the same tone. "When you're ready to become a commercial filmmaker"—meaning, when he's ready to give up everything that makes him interesting—"come talk to us." But Todd isn't swayed that easily. He's working on something tricky and impossible to categorize. Something to get excited about.

Spotlight: Todd Haynes

WRITER/DIRECTOR (*POISON, SAFE, VELVET GOLDMINE, FAR FROM HEAVEN*)

I'm Not There: Developing Dylan

I had become unhappy in New York. I'd just finished *Velvet Goldmine*, a film that had drained me entirely. Even though it was the film I had envisioned, it had just been a bitch to get made. It was becoming clear that unlike most directors, I didn't like being in production. Not since *Poison* had I really enjoyed myself. And yet, that's where all my energy had been going—into my work. Somehow my life had gotten a little lost along the way. I guess it was sort of an early midlife crisis I was going through. I took a break to rejuvenate myself. I read Proust and traveled. I changed apartments. But nothing I did really changed the situation.

I knew that eventually I'd get back to work, and that I would probably focus on this Sirkian melodrama I had in the back of my head—nothing very exciting (to me) but something I felt I understood and believed in. And while I hadn't solved all my problems during my brief sojourn from film, the process of making a film might help fulfill what therapy and Proust couldn't completely. But I didn't want to stay in New York to do it. My sister, who lives in Portland, told me that a friend of hers had an empty Victorian house that I could come and write in. I said, "What? That sounds amazing!"

So at the very beginning of 2000, I got in my car and I drove across country. For some reason, at this precise moment, I had started craving Bob Dylan.

I hadn't listened to Dylan since high school, when I listened to him a lot. But I hadn't really followed him much since. Suddenly, I was rushing to make all these Dylan tapes for my drive to Portland. It was as if I was tapping into that old adolescent energy that says anything is possible, there's a surprise around every corner, you don't know what life is going to bring to you. This music got me to the West Coast, into an amazing house and a beautiful city that was uncustomarily dry that spring with flowers blooming all over the place. I met smart, creative people who didn't ask me, "What do you do?" first—who liked my work and were happy I was there and who really seemed to dig me. It was such a nice change. And I wrote *Far from Heaven* in ten days. It poured out.

But the whole time, the Dylan music was my real fuel. I drew some energy from it that I couldn't even identify, a counter interest to the melodrama that had become my job. I started reading biographies of Dylan and amazing interviews with him from '65 and '66 that were so funny and absurdist, speaking on so many levels at once. I bought the official three-CD bootleg series. Then I started buying *all* the unofficial bootleg stuff available, the complete five-CD Basement Tapes, for instance. And if someone cracks open that door, they soon find that it leads to endless rooms of amazing music and lost art.

I loved the way that Dylan kept reinventing himself at a time that was very different from the self-consciousness of the Bowie era (reflected in *Velvet Goldmine*). This was a period giddy with authenticity and "truth"—the Civil Rights era (my God, it doesn't get any realer than that). But the more Dylan changed, the more authentic he appeared. And the more he tried to shuck off all the prescriptive politics and pressure and expectation, the more pivotal were the realizations he engendered.

I started to get this feeling: Uh-oh, I'm getting this itch to do something with this. I began to think of a Dylan film where a mixture of his life, ideas, and songs are portrayed as a cluster of characters, each with their individual stories interacting with one another. It was a way of *embracing* as opposed to dumbing down (like most biopics) his complexity. In D. A. Pennebaker's gorgeous documentary *Don't Look Back*—which focuses on one specific Dylan in early 1965—we get a very complex portrait. All his famous snottiness aside, Dylan comes off as an incredibly hard-working professional. And at the same time, he's so young, thinks he has all the answers, and is continually picking at the labels and assumptions of the time. I will never forget that scene where he and Robbie Robertson, I think, are sitting backstage while a swingin' jazz band plays, and they're just snapping their fingers, like "Hey, daddy-o . . ." Here was Bob Dylan at one of the most astonishing periods of his career—between "It's Alright, Ma (I'm Only Bleeding)" and "Like a Rolling Stone"—and he's a child! He really is just twenty-three years old.

So I called up Christine and said, "Oh shit." Because the one consistent problem I've had in my relatively short career has been getting music rights when the film I'm doing has anything even vaguely to do with a musician. I'm referring to the Carpenters with *Superstar* and David Bowie on *Velvet Goldmine*. We've had doors continually shut in our face regarding music rights when the artists felt they needed to exert control over what I was doing. In many ways, this conflict has defined me as a filmmaker who can't get the music rights to his films and is, therefore, a guerrilla. And here I was thinking about the music rights of the most difficult, scary-seeming musical artist of them all. Dylan can sound tough—at times, scary-mean.

"Christine," I said, "I have this idea about a Dylan-related project. But I know there is probably no way in hell we would ever get the rights. What do you think? Should I just, really, just stifle this now?" And she said, "Look, let's just take it a step at a time. Don't write it all out now, but write down what you need to, and let's just take a temperature reading. If it becomes immediately clear that we won't get them, then we'll stop. But we have nothing to lose."

Christine thought about Jesse Dylan, Bob's oldest son. At that point, Jesse Dylan was making music videos. He's since gone on to direct films (*How High, American Wedding*), and she had met him in the independent film world. She contacted Jesse, and we had a meeting in Jesse's office in L.A. Now, growing up in L.A., I knew a lot of stars' kids, so I know how hard it can be to be a famous person's child. But I felt it said a great deal about Bob Dylan to hear how secure and lucid Jesse was talking about his famous dad. Everything I've read about Dylan has backed that up: he has always been an attentive and devoted father.

While we were there, Jesse got Jeff Rosen, Dylan's manager for the past twenty years, on the phone. I described my idea to the two of them: the movie would be a set of stories derived from Dylan's life and mythmaking, and each story would have a very specific place, setting, moment, history. Somewhere in me, I believed, this idea might, in fact, be the only one Dylan *would* ever allow for telling his life story because it left it so open. His essence would be depicted as many individuals, with clashing views and different perspectives, which I think is the way any of us would prefer seeing ourselves, rather than as some single person with a perfect arc.

Jeff said it reminded him of something Allen Ginsberg had said about Dylan in some late interviews Jeff had collected, where Ginsberg had described Dylan as a series of "archetypes," a "cluster of finite entities" or distinctly American symbols that his life and career evoked. Both he and Jesse seemed intrigued, and Jeff said, "Write your idea down on one sheet of paper and we'll show it to Bob."

Then I got from each of them a litany of Don't's: Don't use the word "legend." Don't say "the voice of a generation." Don't just talk about the sixties. Don't don't don't. I thought, How do I do this? How do I literally write down my presumptuous little concept for Dylan's own ears? But I went ahead anyway and wrote out one sheet, which I titled "I'm Not There" (the title of a beautiful, famously obscure Basement Tapes–era song), "Suppositions on Film concerning Dylan."

The whole thing was somewhat esoteric—understandable, I suppose, considering where I was at that point with the concept. But I may have emphasized the obscurity factor in order to quell any suspicions on the part of my subject regarding rampant exploitation. This one-page proposal was what Dylan eventually read after looking at some of my films on his never-ending tour that summer. By fall of that year, I gave up my apartment in New York and put a down payment on a dream house and garden in Portland. I was in the middle of preproduction on *Far from Heaven* when we got word—to our complete surprise—that Dylan said, "Why don't we just give the guy the rights." First time ever. For me and Bob Dylan.

The same one-page proposal later went to Paramount as the only real description of what this project was about. Which is how Reuters picked it up, and suddenly, everywhere you turned in the trades and the glossiest magazines, this Dylan film showed up with my sophomoric subheading as its title: *I'm Not There: Suppositions on a Film concerning Dylan.* I was pulling my hair out, saying, "Guys, that was just the decoy version!"

Chapter 7
Dylan in Turnaround

Pitching Paramount's Sherry Lansing —Dylan goes
to Romania—Who is running this company?—
"Did not spark to"

LESSON: ACT LIKE IT'S HAPPENING UNTIL
SOMEBODY TELLS YOU OTHERWISE.

Ankling Posts

Todd might disagree, but I think Bob Dylan understands something about film financing. "He not busy being born is busy dying," he sings in "It's Alright, Ma (I'm Only Bleeding)." In other words, there's development and then there's turnaround.

Great scripts with great directors attached go into film-industry purgatory all the time. It's where 98 percent of projects live. Usually this is because the costs of making a film outweigh the perceived potential profits. Studios will buy a script, throw screenwriters at it hoping to perfect it, and then shove it in a drawer. Why? The director isn't happy with the revision. The linchpin star has moved on. The studio executives aren't "connecting" to the material, or maybe they're not even executives anymore. They're "pursuing other projects." All this assumes, of course, you can even get people on the phone to explain what the hell is happening.

When we first started developing Todd Haynes's Bob Dylan project, we were working with the British film company called FilmFour. They had helped finance Todd's *Safe* and *Velvet Goldmine*, but they were really known for the insane success of Danny Boyle's *Trainspotting*. Then a few years of not-so-terrific decisions—including investing big in the 2002 flop *Death to Smoochy*—put what was an essentially government-subsidized film company at risk. Just as we were finishing up our long negotiations for Dylan's music and his life rights, they folded.

Where to next? We wanted to move the whole damn package to one place instead of building the financing with bits and pieces. Todd's agent suggested Paramount, which had been run for a decade by the duo Sherry Lansing and Jonathan Dolgen, who was supposedly a big Dylan freak. Paramount's head of production, John Goldwyn, was a big Todd freak. They both eagerly welcomed the movie and agreed to throw some money at Todd to write the script. The project sat there nicely while Todd finished *Far from Heaven's* Oscar race in 2003. When the *Far from Heaven* dust cleared, Todd began to work on the script in earnest.

Meanwhile, in June 2004, Jonathan Dolgen ankled his post (*Variety*speak for "quit" or "was fired"). Then John Goldwyn ankled *his* post (though he's still at Paramount with a producing deal). Sherry Lansing stayed and became the sole head of the studio. She's had a lot of experience: she was president of Twentieth Century-Fox in the early 1980s, went on to to produce *Fatal Attraction* and *The Accused*, and finally ran Paramount and made such films as *Forrest Gump*, *Braveheart*, *The Manchurian Candidate*, and *School of Rock*.

When Donald De Line was hired to replace John Goldwyn, I called John Goldwyn and asked him if he would become an executive producer on Dylan and help me navigate the new waters at Paramount. I could tell I was going to need help!

Todd finished his script. It was an extraordinarily complex and exhilarating read: seven interweaving stories about multiple characters representing Dylan's life and songs at different ages and eras.

How the heck was a studio head like Sherry Lansing going to make heads or tails out of this? Goldwyn cautioned us not to underestimate her. However, he thought it was probably a good idea for Todd to sit down with her *before* she read it, to "contextualize" it for her. She was coming to New York for an awards dinner for Lorne Michaels. So Todd and I arranged to meet with her the morning after at the Carlyle Hotel with Goldwyn and Jeff Rosen, Dylan's business manager and my co-producer.

We got to the Carlyle and called up to her room, and she told us to come on up. We sat in a semicircle in her suite. It was a giant hotel room with no indication that somebody was staying there. We were excited rather than nervous. Todd talked about his script, which is always invigorating. Sherry Lansing is an extremely poised woman in a beautifully tailored business suit. Her manners are impeccable. She looks you right in the eye. And she is no dummy. Nobody of a certain age (Lansing was in her late fifties at the time) could have come through the 1960s without being affected by Bob Dylan. She had actually spent some time with him; she'd financed *Wonder Boys* and convinced him to write an original song for the soundtrack ("Things Have Changed," which, incidentally, won an Oscar).

We all drank mineral water and Todd told her his idea. She seemed genuinely intrigued. She wanted a copy of the script before she left for L.A., which was an hour from then. No problem.

When she got back to L.A., she was enthusiastic enough about the script to pay for a casting director to come on and start attaching actors and also for a line producer to budget the movie, so we would have some idea of what it cost. Up until this point I had said (with more confidence than I felt) that the budget was in the "mid twenties." Now it was time to see if my instinct was correct.

Killerspeak

Laura Rosenthal, our casting director (*Chicago, Far from Heaven, The Manchurian Candidate*), had an overwhelming response right away. Dense as the script might be, actors were dying to work with Todd. Colin Farrell quickly attached himself to play Robbie, the rock-and-roll, thirtysomething version of Bob. Julianne Moore came on as Alice, a singer in the folk revival and one of Bob's early collaborators. Adrien Brody met with Todd and then became Jack, the working-class, twentysomething folk singer Bob. (At the same time, we were trying desperately to find an actor to play Perry in *Infamous*, following Mark Ruffalo's unfortunate departure. Perry was a terrific part in a fantastic script, but for some reason we could not get the damn part arrested! The contrast between the constant yes for Dylan and the equally constant no for *Infamous* was at times comical and at other times heartbreaking.)

Then, in November 2004, we woke up to a *Variety* headline: Sherry Lansing had ankled *her* post. *What?* I called John Goldwyn: "Did you know about this?" "No," he said tersely, "I didn't." There was a flurry of speculation about who was now in charge. It appeared to be Donald De Line, who had replaced John Goldwyn. I had met him briefly and had spoken to him on the phone about *I'm Not There*. He was a hip, smart guy with designer glasses, a fan of *Far from Heaven*. We arranged to fly Todd to L.A. to sit down with him, as he had with Sherry.

Meanwhile our budget had come in: $32 million. So much for the mid twenties (and so much for my instincts). Colin Farrell or not, $32 million was waaay high for this movie; I didn't even know how I could say the number to Paramount with a straight face. We took a collective deep breath and started the long process of bringing it down.

We decided that the only way to really bring down the budget was to "reconceive" it—Killerspeak for "come up with a cheaper way to do it by thinking outside the box." To that end, we hired a line producer named Guy Louthan. Even though his most illustrious credit was *Seed of Chucky*, he seemed to have the right kind of mind-set to attack *I'm Not There*. His vision for the meaner, leaner version was to shoot a large part of it in Eastern Europe. Many movies have been shooting in Eastern Europe because labor is much cheaper and the dollar goes a lot farther there. Also, a variety of landscapes can stand in for other, more expensive landscapes. Miramax for example, shot *Cold Mountain* in Romania instead of the American South.

While we were wrestling with the budget, Todd sat down with

Donald De Line. They had a great meeting. He assigned us a production executive, Marc Evans, who would eventually go through
our budget with us and make an assessment of whether he thought
we could pull it off. For the first time, I felt like the movie was going
to happen at Paramount. Instead of worrying about how the hell we
were going to get this movie paid for, I worried about how the hell
we were actually going to make it. It was a nice feeling.

Welcome, Brad

And *then*. January 5, the frantic e-mails started to circulate, from
agents and other producers: "I hear Donald De Line is *out* at Paramount," said one. "Brad Grey—that *Sopranos* guy—is the new head
of the studio!" said another. And sure enough, the next day's *Variety*
headline screamed it to the world. (Well, to our little world anyway.
The rest of the world was probably a little more concerned about
things like Iraq.) So what did this mean for *I'm Not There*? I called
John Goldwyn. "Did you know about *this*?" I asked.

"No. No one here did. We found out when we saw *Variety*!"

Now what? Brad Grey was a completely unknown quantity to me,
although he has a great reputation and was clearly hired to breathe
some new life into Paramount. A few weeks after he was hired, Paramount Classics made the biggest purchase of the Sundance Film
Festival, *Hustle and Flow* for $9 million. The movie is a very stylish
crowd pleaser, and all the indie distributors were fighting for it. The
purchase signaled to me that Paramount *did* want to become a
cooler, edgier place. Which was good for us . . . right? What are
Killer Films and Todd Haynes if not the epitome of edgy and cool?

Armed with a new, reconceived budget of $25 million, we
pressed for Brad Grey to sit down with Todd. All the actors' agents
started to call: "Is the movie staying at Paramount?" "Is it still going
in the fall?" I was getting increasingly worried that without a clear
decision from Paramount soon, we were going to lose our cast.
When a movie starts to smell of "it's not happening," the actors
(understandably) panic and go after movies that look like they *are*
happening. We pressed harder for a meeting. Brad Grey's office was

apologetic, but "He's swamped, he just got there, and, oh, he's leaving for two weeks to take his son on a college tour."

Well, then. We decided to act as though this movie was happening at Paramount until somebody told us it wasn't. Guy Louthan sat down with Marc Evans, the Paramount production executive, and other physical production people and went through the budget line by line, explaining each financial choice. We had no idea if any of the people Guy was talking to were keeping their jobs; neither did they! Once the budget was vetted, Paramount ran numbers to see if the film could be profitable if it were made for this amount of money. All of these are the steps to the green light. But how do we get the light to actually change? Everyone that we had a creative relationship with at Paramount was basically gone, and we couldn't get to Brad Grey.

Another Dylan Freak

Somehow, casting continued. Richard Gere joined the cast to play Billy, the fiftysomething version of Bob. Todd became completely enamored of Cate Blanchett after seeing her in *The Aviator.* He decided she was perfect to play Jude, an eerily delicate figure of "radical ambivalence" that—in Todd's mind—only an androgynous woman playing it as a man could approximate. I sent the script to Cate's agent, Hylda Queally. Hylda called me and announced that Cate was "intrigued" and wanted to meet with Todd. The only time she could do it was February 27—Oscar Sunday! If it were possible, would Todd have breakfast with her? I asked Hylda if Cate *really, really* wanted to have a meeting with Todd on the morning of what could be the biggest night of her life. Hylda assured me that she absolutely did. They met, Cate won—and she signed on to play Jude. Our cast was now essentially complete. How could Paramount let this cast go?

March 29. Another round of e-mails and phone calls. Apparently Brad Grey has hired a president for Paramount Motion Pictures. It is Gail Berman, currently running Fox Television. Television? What gives? This means Donald De Line is definitely history. But what does this mean for us?

Jeff Rosen decided to call Viacom chairman Tom Freston on *I'm*

Not There's behalf. Freston was the guy who hired Brad Grey. He is also a Dylan freak, which is why Jeff knows him. Jeff called him up and said, "Hey, I know you're not sweating the small stuff, but we have a cool Dylan project at your studio. Can you see if you can get someone to focus on it?"

He barely had time to hang up the phone when *bang*, we got a call from Rob Friedman, vice chair, Paramount Pictures, COO Paramount Motion Picture Group. (What does that title actually *mean*? No clue.) He and Ruth Vitale wanted to meet with Todd because *I'm Not There* had been kicked over to them. Ruth ran Paramount Classics and was widely rumored to be on the way out. Since this rumor had been circulating for, oh, four years or so, I figured she might actually be sticking around. We told Todd that he had to fly to Los Angeles for yet another meeting. Off he went. This was meeting number three with a Paramount green-lighter. Maybe this would do the trick.

How Do We Get a Decision Around Here?

Todd's meetings are almost always good because he is so personable, so articulate, and so passionate about his vision for the film. This one, however, he didn't feel so good about; he had a bad cold, and he didn't feel that he was really reaching Ruth and Rob. But they agreed to read the script over the weekend and promised a quick answer.

So we waited. When I stepped back, it seemed inconceivable that Paramount would let this go—Richard Gere, Colin Farrell, Adrien Brody, Cate Blanchett. I braced myself, expecting they would get back to us with an impossibly low-budget figure.

Ruth called Todd's agent at CAA, Craig Gering, on Monday and told him she'd like to develop the script more. *What?* Paramount had had the script for months. If we descended into development hell, we would absolutely lose the cast. Ruth wailed, "But I just saw this for the first time! I can't make this decision!" So *who can*? Somehow the decision got made to give the script to . . . Gail Berman. This seemed finally to be the end of the line. I was worried. Craig assured me that she was a Todd fan—loved *Far from Heaven*, has enormous respect for Killer Films, etc.

She got the script on a Friday. We waited.

Monday morning, Craig got a call. "Gail 'did not spark to.'" That is Hollywoodspeak for "didn't like."

It was over. *I'm Not There* went into turnaround.

Postscript: *I'm Not There* is no longer at Paramount; neither is Ruth Vitale. As of this writing, we've financed the movie with a combination of foreign sales and equity. And we decided not to shoot in Romania and moved to Montreal.

Spotlight: Rowena Arguelles

AGENT, CREATIVE ARTISTS AGENCY

CAA and the Indie Producer

After the release of *Boys Don't Cry* in October 1999, Christine made it known that Killer was seeking agency representation for the first time. All the major agencies jumped into a highly competitive pursuit. CAA won in the end, but what was it that we all saw in this small independent production company based in New York? Why did we want to sign them? Why now?

Boys Don't Cry was the turning point. Here was an amazing film that came out of nowhere, a $2 million movie with no stars and a tough story to tell. It succeeded artistically and commercially, culminating in an Oscar for Hilary Swank. The visibility of *Boys* and its impact on mainstream culture are what raised Killer's profile in Hollywood. We were impressed by the passion and skill it took to get that movie made, and we wanted them as clients because we knew it wasn't a fluke. *Boys* was precisely the kind of movie Killer was known for making—a challenging, compelling, filmmaker-driven project. If Killer's success had come off a movie not reflective of their personality as a company, we probably wouldn't have pursued them. Instead, we saw *Boys* as a culmination of decades of producing led by Christine, an organic result of years of building a slate that reflected a specific sensibility and bravery.

Furthermore, it was apparent from looking at the current film landscape that the business was expanding and that "independently spirited" films were becoming much more significant. Remember, 1999 was the year that also brought us *Being John Malkovich*, *Three Kings*, and *American Beauty*. To represent a producer like Killer, clearly a leader in this space, seemed like a smart move all around. Our writer, director, and actor clients would benefit from exposure to Killer projects and their expertise, and Killer would benefit from direct access to the agency's clients and resources.

Our representation of Killer has encompassed everything from securing financing for their overhead to servicing their development to helping cast their movies. Oftentimes, our job as agents is simply to make introductions, to forge connections. In 2000 our client Mark Romanek wrote a spec script, and as a first-time director he wanted to be careful about the producer he chose. Through CAA, he brought the script to Killer, and together they made *One Hour Photo* at Fox Searchlight. In 2002, when Todd Haynes's *Far from Heaven* needed a boost to get over the final hump to a green light, CAA approached Section Eight, Steven Soderbergh and George Clooney's company, to come on board as executive producers. That partnership resulted in a movie at Focus released to critical acclaim and multiple Oscar nominations. In 2004, after a lengthy process to find an actor to play Truman Capote in Doug McGrath's film *Infamous*, a British actor named Toby Jones was cast. Though perfect for the role, his name was not enough to finance the picture at Warner Independent. CAA had shown the script to several A-list clients, and Sandra Bullock emerged wanting to play the supporting role of Harper Lee. Her attachment made the difference in getting the movie made.

The marketplace has changed tremendously since we signed Killer in 1999. There are fewer major studios, and studio specialty divisions and independent financiers have grown in number and importance. One only has to look at four of the five 2006 Best Picture Oscar nominations—*Brokeback Mountain*, *Capote*, *Crash*, and *Good Night, and Good Luck*—to register the impact of films made outside the boundaries of mainstream studio fare. This is good news for Killer, a company motivated by passion to make films of singular vision. It's tough going, but I know they're up for the challenge. They don't know how to do it any other way.

Letter from L.A. III

Pitching The Extra Man — Director meetings at Chateau Marmont — Julianne Moore ducks out of Savage Grace, again — A New Hollywood party — A New Ending for A Dirty Shame

Wednesday

We're driving all over L.A. to pitch *The Extra Man,* a script adapted by Keith Bunin (*A Home at the End of the World*) from Jonathan Ames's hilarious novel about a friendship between a young roué and a much older "professional escort" for rich widows on the Upper East Side. We've got Jason Biggs, from *American Pie,* attached to play the young man and Christopher Plummer as his mentor. Triple-threat Isaac Mizrahi, the fashion designer/TV show host/actor, is directing.

First stop: a corporate tower in Century City to pitch Media 8 Productions. Media 8 is having a good year: they did *Monster,* a huge gamble that paid off enormously for them. We all troop into a giant conference room with Brian O'Shea, the head executive, Isaac, Marisa (his producing partner), me, Jocelyn, and Charles, my assistant.

Brian tells us how much he enjoyed reading the script and explains exactly how Media 8 works: it taps into foreign funds but also functions as a producer. The ideal situation for him would be to partner with a domestic distributor to put in portions of the money. He goes on to talk to Isaac very intelligently about the script and his vision for the movie. Brian's very perceptive about the tone for the picture. It has to be funny but not too broad. Isaac, who is a rock star at meetings (he could sell you the clothes you're wearing), gets very animated and shows off his scrapbook/director's vision notebook for the film. Brian and Isaac hit it off, but he doesn't promise anything. This was just an exploratory first encounter. A smart, worthwhile meeting.

Then we trek out to Santa Monica to meet with Waste O Time Productions.* Santa Monica, from Beverly Hills, is a long way. And this is the second meeting we've scheduled. They canceled the first time. Waste O Time is the money part of the triangle: they're looking for projects to invest in.

We enter their small offices. The stoner receptionist offers us drinks and tells us it will be a moment. Tracy,* our contact here and one of the executives of Waste O Time, looks out from her office door (it's open) and says "Hi" but then looks down and keeps working. We wait another fifteen minutes, watching all the executives working away in their offices, ignoring us. No apologies come from the stoner who sits blankly at his desk five feet away.

Eventually, Tracy comes out, introduces herself, and tells me she took a producing class from me years ago. She ushers us into a conference room. There, Tracy is joined by a blond woman and a vaguely European man. Isaac and I start the whole dog and pony show, but it's clear that except for Tracy, nobody's really read the script. Tracy tells us that she thought it was "totally cute."

The blond woman is weirdly antagonistic in her questions: "Where else have you had meetings? Has anybody else shown interest?" Isaac says, jokingly but appropriately, "We're not going to tell you that." Then she announces that she has to leave the meeting. She does. Awkwardly, we chat with Tracy for a few more minutes before we leave. A meeting like that might be a waste of time, but it's helpful in one way: at least we know whom *not* to work with.

Thursday

More meetings, this time at the Chateau Marmont, where I'm staying. It's where I always stay. It's off the Sunset Strip but it's quiet and not too flamboyant, unlike the Standard across the street, where there's a

---

* Name changed.

model in a glass box behind reception and they pay models just to show up and swim at the pool. Most of the celebrity interviews you read happen in the courtyard of the Chateau because nobody bothers you.

First up is Agnieszka Holland, the fiftysomething Polish director of *Europa, Europa; Washington Square;* and *The Secret Garden.* She loved the *All of a Kind Family* script, Killer's first children's movie project, based on a series of books about the lives of young Jewish immigrants in the Lower East Side of Manhattan. Matthew Weiss, the writer of *Niagara, Niagara,* adapted it. We showed it to the agencies for their suggestions on directors; they got it to Mira Nair, whom Pam really wants to work with. They also sent it to Spielberg, whose agent (I loved this) talked about him like he was just a regular working director who needed material. Right. Agnieszka really likes the script, is interested. The conversations always work the same way:

Me: Hi, nice to meet you. We're such fans of *Washington Square . . .* (Whether you've actually seen the movie doesn't matter; you just need to know what it's about, whether it was received well, and whether it made money.)

Them: I love the movies Killer makes as well. (No specifics forthcoming, but that's OK. See above.) Who are you guys thinking about for the cast?

Me: We don't have a cast yet. Any ideas?

Them: I loved working with/I've always want to work with/I'll never work again with . . . Can we talk about the script? I love it, it's great, I want the third act to be beefier.

Me: It's something to talk about once you're on board. Would this be your next project?

For now, Agnieszka is committed to shoot something in Poland. Doesn't matter; we don't have a cast. Given the material, it's not like there's a huge part for Michelle Pfeiffer. We'll probably go with unknowns. But we don't even know which unknowns. This meeting was just to establish a relationship.

Postscript: Two weeks later, Agnieszka attaches herself to the project.

Friday

Timing is half the trouble of working with actors. No matter how good your script is, the good ones and the hot ones have schedules that book up solid for months, years even. At one point, Jude Law was locked up until the fall—of next year. As a producer, over time, you develop relationships with some actors and get preferential treatment; they can stay committed long after their celebrity has overshot your scale, keeping a project afloat when you have nothing else. They are also notorious for jumping ship.

This morning, I tape a segment for the A&E biography of Julianne Moore; *Safe* was her first lead role in a film, and *Far from Heaven* her third Oscar nomination. Right now she's attached to play the lead in our movie *Savage Grace,* shooting this summer in England. But the minute we finish taping, Killer's lawyer John Sloss calls to tell me that he sees on the front cover of *Variety* that Julianne's signed to play the lead in *The Prize Winner of Defiance, Ohio,* about a housewife who makes a fortune as a jingle writer, shooting this summer.

Our film is about the Bakelite plastics family murder plus a little pinch of incest. I optioned the book a million years ago when I had no money, so I partnered with a guy at the Really Useful Group, Andrew Lloyd Weber's publishing company. They decided not to make it, it languished, and a few years ago when the option was up, I decided to go back after it with Tom Kalin (*Swoon*) to direct. We paid a writer, Howard Rodman, the Guild minimum for a nonoriginal screenplay ($28,271), and he did a terrific job. Then we showed it to Julianne. She wanted to do it. Great, but we needed a strong male actor to play the husband, and once again, nobody was willing to play sideman to Julianne's lead. Clive Owen (*Derailed, Closer*) said he couldn't get the script out of his head. He attached.

But then Julianne begged us to wait a year. Set in England, Italy, and the Riviera, *Savage Grace* has to be shot in Europe. But Julianne has a rule: she only leaves New York once a year during the summer. (The rest of the time she wants to be with her kids.) That summer, in 2003, she wanted to do a screwball comedy, *Laws of Attraction,* shooting in Ireland. Tom was bitterly disappointed but agreed to wait a year, and she went.

Then, over the course of the year, Clive Owen *detached* himself. I'm sure he started thinking, Why am I playing second fiddle to Julianne Moore? At least in *Far from Heaven*, Dennis Quaid got to be gay . . . He also landed the lead in a trashy thriller, *Derailed,* so I'm sure he wasn't exactly itching to go back to a supporting part. We cast about for a replacement. Last month, summer coming up now, we decided to try for Guy Pearce or John Malkovich but we couldn't get hold of Julianne. (She didn't have actor approval. We just wanted her consent.) Her manager, Evelyn O'Neill, told us she was on vacation—at a theme park in San Diego—and unreachable. Oh yeah, San Diego, where you go when you want to get away from it all. That was the first bad sign.

So now, without telling us, Julianne herself has apparently detached herself. I get on the phone with Evelyn immediately.

"Julianne decided that she doesn't want Guy Pearce," says Evelyn. "She'd do it with Malkovich but . . . she has another offer for the summer."

As if I haven't heard about *The Prize Winner of Defiance, Ohio.* "I thought she was committed." I tell her. "What is she going to do?"

Without Julianne, we have no movie. No cast, no star. Evelyn hems and haws. She's not sure about the other film's dates. There might be a window. It actually takes another week for me to hear for sure, and the word comes from another agency. "I don't know what she told you, but she signed on to that movie," the agent tells me. "Now, how about Diane Lane?" When I end up seeing her a few weeks later at the GLAAD awards, Julianne comes up and says, "Oh my God, I feel so bad if I can't do the movie." I know that she's thinking, I hope Christine isn't mad. But the truth is I'm pissed. We waited for her, and now when it's set up to happen, she dumps us. It's not like I can sever the relationship; she knows we'll still go back to her with good roles. She even told Tom Kalin, "I hope everybody passes on the part so that you offer it to me again next year."

The only consolation is that most of the actors we're looking at are significantly younger than her, and maybe that broadens our options. Who knows? One year from now, Julianne may have won an Oscar for playing that housewife, and she'll say, "Thank God I wasn't in that loser incest movie."

Time to drink. Brad Simpson, the former Killer intern/producer/ head of development, has moved to L.A. to run Leonardo DiCaprio's production company, Appian Way. It's a great opportunity for him, though I suspect he's in for a shock about how much people in L.A. would rather talk about films than make them. Tonight Stacey Sher is hosting a party for him at her house in the Hollywood Hills. Stacey was formerly one of the partners in Danny DeVito's Jersey Films (*Erin Brockovich, Get Shorty*) and is now on her own, running her own production company Double Feature (*Garden State, Along Came Polly*) at Universal.

As much as I disdain the Los Angeles film industry, I know why people work there—for houses like Stacey Sher's place: the six-car garage, the personal screening room, the sushi in the courtyard, and the columns made up to look like palm trees. It's not what I want for myself, but I can understand that this is the payback. (The following night, we'd have our own party, albeit much humbler. Liz Karlsen, the co-producer on *Mrs. Harris,* hosted a pool party at the house she rented in the Hills for the length of the production. Mark Gill, the head of Warner Independent Pictures, showed, along with Kim Peirce, and Kevin Iwashina and Rowena Arguelles. Sir Ben Kingsley—you've got to use "Sir" with him (wouldn't you insist, if you'd been knighted?)— arrived with his assistant and his hair/makeup person. I guess I should just say makeup person. We all drank Coronas. It was a much smaller, quieter scene.)

At Stacey's, Leo, of course, shows up with his posse. Jake Gyllenhaal comes. It's the usual L.A. party conversation: "How *are* you? I haven't seen you in for*ever*!" An agent from the talent agency the Firm (which represents Leo) comes up to me. "So, Christine, is this bittersweet for you? Or do you feel like you've sucked everything you needed out of Brad?"

When we go, the valet has left a white rose on the front seat of the car. So classy, and so L.A.

Postscript: Julianne has since reattached herself to *Savage Grace,* to shoot summer 2006.

Monday

The Baltimore shoot of John Waters's *A Dirty Shame* went off without a hitch. When you have fifteen movies under your belt, it works like that.

Still, the original ending of *A Dirty Shame* wasn't quite working. John knew it; Bob Shaye at New Line, the distributor, knew it. Ironically, for a film about sex addicts, it still needed a climax. The characters have spent the entire movie looking for the "new" sex act, and in the final scenes, they find it: knocking heads. The film ended with a mob of suburbanites crashing into each other. Bob at New Line wanted John to come up with one more beat to push it over the top.

So John did a quick rewrite that we've begun calling the exploding-head cum shot. In it, all the characters finally learn how to take control of their sex drives, and they begin to levitate. Johnny Knoxville's character Ray Ray, who has instigated the whole sex revolution in this suburb, rises up into the sky and his head detonates and, well, ejaculates would be the word. It's not exactly subtle, but then the King of Bad Taste John Waters likes it that way. His most recent art exhibition featured a piece titled "12 Assholes and a Dirty Foot."

So today, on a soundstage at the L.A. Center Studios (incidentally, next to the *Mrs. Harris* shoot), we gathered Tracey Ullman, Johnny Knoxville, Chris Isaak, and the rest of the cast on a Baltimoresque street to reshoot the ending. The cast were on cables to lift them into the air and were shot against a blue screen. The shoot goes off without a hitch. The New Line marketing rep stops by the set to show us the potential posters. There must be twenty different iterations of "Here Comes the Neighborhood." John loves them.

Chapter 8

Locking Picture

A Home at the End of the World—*Giving/getting notes*—
"The first, best audience" questions a kiss—*Putting out fires*
with your hands—*John Wells, ambassador*—*Sissy Spacek*
unlocks the picture—*The release*

LESSON: THE BEST FILMS DON'T COME
FROM COMPROMISE. THEY COME FROM
COLLABORATION.

Execution Dependent, July 2003

"Locking picture" is the first definitive step toward a finalized film.
Before you settle the sound or music, you decide exactly what the
film will contain visually: what scenes, what shots, and in what
sequence. Once you settle on this edit, you "lock picture" and can't
make any changes. This is because the dialogue track and the
soundtrack must match exactly to the picture frames, and if you
change even a handful of them, you will throw the sync off. Everything hinges on fixing this visual template, and it can feel like you're
dealing with a thousand moving, troublesome parts: missing establishing shots, slow openings, tricky character introductions, conti-

nuity errors, pacing issues, on and on. It's also the moment in a film's life when aesthetics turn political. Every cut is a choice, and choices have to be defended, conceded, and made.

It's been almost a year since we signed the deal with Warner Independent Pictures (WIP) to distribute *A Home at the End of the World*, and we're locking picture. *Home* has been edited and reedited, and test-screened twice, and now we've come down to this: the filmmaker and the studio are stuck in a debate about two minutes of film that Mark Gill, the former marketing whiz at Miramax and current head of WIP, wants to cut. Two minutes, some with gay material, that Michael Mayer, the effusive director and theater veteran, is battling to keep. These two minutes can tell you a lot about the conflicted nature of "independent" filmmaking when studios, producers, and directors, all with competing visions for a film, become interdependent. These two minutes represent just two scenes. The movie is about two childhood friends, Jonathan and Bobby, trying to make sense of their love for each other when their best friend Claire comes between them. In the first controversial sequence, the arch twentysomething Jonathan (Dallas Roberts) leaves his office in New York, picks up a guy, and, well, gets a blow job. You see nothing, but it's clear what's happening. The scene is there to capture gay life in New York in the early 1980s.

In the other scene—which became the flash point for the entire edit—Jonathan and Bobby (Colin Farrell) kiss twice on a rooftop of Jonathan's apartment building. They've been friends since childhood and "experimented" with each other, but they've both grown up. To Bobby, the kiss is a spontaneous sign of affection. For Jonathan, it means much more. Neither of these scenes is a surprise to WIP. Both scenes are in the script. Colin Farrell didn't have a problem with them, and Warner Bros. signed off on them before we went into production. If anything, both of them are toned down from Michael Cunningham's book.

And the kiss was a beautifully executed scene. A Manhattan rooftop, a radiant sunset, a fleeting intimacy in a long, difficult friendship. It worked on a variety of levels. You got to see Bobby and Jonathan passionate about each other as adults. Narratively, the kiss drives the next portion of the story, since the kiss spooks Jonathan, who is confused and stunned by the physical affection he just got from his oldest friend. He leaves town. Without the kiss, audiences would wonder why Jonathan leaves so abruptly.

As you get closer and closer to locking picture, what is "necessary" becomes increasingly hard to identify and to agree on. Inevitably, certain scenes turn into sticking points, as if they carry the weight of the film's ambitions and reveal its failures. These scenes feel as though they send the film in a direction, for better or worse; whether they actually do or not is another question. Film is a subjective business, and what is vital to one person is utterly indulgent to someone else. Can two minutes really determine the reception of a film?

Warner, somewhat understandably, has a bit of resistance to *Home*'s explicitly gay scenes. It's less a question of homophobia—I don't think big Warner Bros. chief Alan Horn or WIP head Mark Gill are homophobic—than of economic potential. Ira Deutchman, the former president of New Line's specialty division Fine Line and an independent producer (who made *54* and *Straight Out of Brooklyn*), told me once that a movie with a passionate, same-sex kiss between men has a ceiling of $3 million at the box office. (Two years later *Brokeback Mountain* proved him dead wrong.)

WIP head Mark genuinely sees this as a film about friendship, not same-sex yearning. What Mark means when he talks about the kiss is, I think, that he's afraid that it narrows the film. And what I mean when I say "narrows" is that the film will reach fewer people. He has bigger hopes for it. *The Hours* made $41 million in the United States, nearly $70 million worldwide, with similarly touchy material. If we keep the kiss in the picture, Mark thinks, *Home* becomes a little picture, dooms itself to being a niche (read queer) film. Ten years ago, that would have been an asset, its whole reason for being.

This afternoon, the director Michael is on the phone with Mark. He's nervous but willing to negotiate. As many theatrical hits as he's responsible for (*Side Man, Thoroughly Modern Millie*), he'd never made a movie before, and he doesn't want to threaten his relationship with the studio. He's also, I suspect, more accustomed to theater's live collaborative environment than to the remote influence of film "executives." Mark's skill, on the other hand, comes from his previous career in marketing at Miramax. He operates on a marketer's instinct: you understand how something will play to audiences and work backward.

There's a fundamental disagreement. Michael considers cutting the blow job, but he doesn't want to give up the rooftop kiss. Mark doesn't want to budge; he and Alan insist the cuts be made.

Giving / Getting Notes, August 2003

If production is a spray of bread crumbs, the edit makes the trail through the woods. In locking picture, you lay down the asphalt. Sometimes you need to dig up the road and start over. One of my favorite film books is editor Ralph Rosenblum's *When the Shooting Stops . . . the Cutting Begins*, because it shows you just how late most directors find their movie. Or as Rosenblum would say, how late some editors find their director's movie.

Rosenblum cut the Woody Allen classics *Annie Hall* and *Interiors*, along with *A Thousand Clowns*. The first chapter of his book is about trying to rescue a flop, *The Night They Raided Minsky's*, from abject failure by editing it creatively. *Minsky's* was the second picture by then-thirty-one-year-old wunderkind William Friedkin, and it was an improbable movie no matter how you look at it. Here's the logline: an Amish girl named Rachel comes to New York City in the 1920s to become a dancer. She ends up on the Lower East Side at Minsky's Burlesque, doing lame Bible-inspired dances, until she inadvertently invents the striptease.

The first cut was a disaster, writes Rosenblum, tedious and uninvolving: Amish girl goes to the big city and bores you to tears. In desperation, Norman Lear, one of *Minsky's* co-writers and producers, asked Rosenblum to "fix it." But there was nothing to fix it with; the shoot was over, the actors long gone, the director gone off to Europe. So, to get inspired, Rosenblum went to the Museum of Television and Radio and requested archival footage about life on the Lower East Side in the 1920s. He was hunting new ideas.

In looking at the wild bustle of immigrant life, Rosenblum

noticed that the gray-bearded New York immigrants he was watching looked a lot like the Amish elders (read: actors) from Rachel's community whom Friedkin had already shot. Visually, here was a missing bridge from Rachel's horse-and-buggy background to the burlesque. So he licensed this archival footage and cut it into the opening moments of *Minsky's*, crosscutting Friedkin's images of Rachel in New York with the scratchy, sepia-toned archival footage from the museum. To stitch them together, he made black-and-white versions of the *Minsky's* scenes they already had and transformed them into color on screen, a segue from past to present. The opening now jumped with energy. Suddenly, the picture had a sense of journey, the feeling of an Amish girl's entrance into a foreign world, saturated with history, clashing against contemporary city life. Rosenblum made countless other changes to *Minsky's*, a film that could be saved but never exactly celebrated, and his book is laced with a real bitterness about how overlooked editors are. His experience comes to mind when I think about how much time, patience, and willingness to make mistakes directors (teamed with their editors) need to find their movie.

With *Home*, we initially paired Michael with the editor Lee Percy, who cut *Boys Don't Cry*. Over the summer of 2003—before Mark and Alan saw the film—Michael and Lee assembled a good first cut. Colin's Irish accent would definitely need to be ADR'd in a few scenes. (ADR stands for "additional dialogue recording"—going back and rerecording dialogue.) And as Brad Simpson first guessed, the first act, set in Bobby's childhood, dragged. It was time for Killer to submit to Michael some specific feedback. Katie Roumel, the no-nonsense, indefatigable Killer producer who had been on set in Toronto and was Michael's closest ally on the film, drafted an e-mail that assembled Killer's comments.

Michael found Katie's notes a little harsh. He'd already had some thoughtful, smart feedback from Tom Hulce, Killer's co-producer on the project, and the financiers John Hart and Jeff Sharp (*You Can Count on Me*, *Proof*). But this was Michael's first thorough critique of his first movie, and it was inevitable that he'd feel hurt. Michael is not a thick-skinned Oliver Stone. He's sensitive. He wanted people to love the film unconditionally. The irony is that I've found that directors say they don't want any interference while they edit. But then, every opportunity they get, they ask me, "What did you think?" Soft-pedaling at this moment doesn't help anyone. It's best to lay out all your issues early so that, as a producer, you can get out of the way and let directors feel their way to the movie they can believe in.

As it stood, Killer, not Michael, had the "final cut" on *Home*. This meant that ultimately we would have control over what was in the locked picture. But as a director-friendly company, we'd never steamroll Michael. Many directors fight for final cut, but as far as I'm concerned, it's a sham. It's something that filmmakers are taught to believe they have to have, that it's some mark of prestige. For a mature filmmaker (like Bob Altman, who had final cut on *The Company*), final cut is usually a gesture given by the studio when they believe the filmmaker understands that film is a commercial art form and won't screw them with a three-hour snooze-fest that they won't know how to market. Studios can dangle final cut in front of most filmmakers and then go screw them in a million other ways. A director has to consider that it might be more important to have final say over your cast or your crew than final cut.

With all the producers' comments in mind, Michael went back to *Home*. We brought on Andy Marcus (*Hedwig and the Angry Inch, The Remains of the Day, Jefferson in Paris*) as the new editor. Lee Percy and Michael had a perfectly good partnership, but it's not uncommon to replace editors during the process simply because of creative attenuation. The edit can be a long, slow haul; we'd told Lee we'd only need him for four more weeks, and that turned into four months. Editors in demand, like Lee, can't stay twiddling their thumbs.

Other times, the editor and director don't see eye to eye, and as their relationship erodes, so does the film. Editors get so little credit it's not uncommon for an editor to develop some form of I-Wish-I-Were-the-Director-itis. This kind of breakdown happened to us on *Mrs. Harris* when the director, Phyllis Nagy, found out the editor was cutting his own stealth version of the film. The editor was a great catch for our film, having cut some terrific pictures and a couple of Academy contenders. The first sign of a problem was that he wasn't terribly interested in what Phyllis thought about how the assembly should look. He argued that she was a first-time director and he knew better. He eventually sent the producers an e-mail about the "selects"—the certain takes for scenes that he'd cut together—but they didn't match with Phyllis's own choices. It became increasingly clear he was making his own *Mrs. Harris.* With two weeks of shooting left, we had to fire him.

Testing, November 2003

We now had an edited version of *Home,* and Mark and WIP wanted to test it. Usually, I hate test-marketing films, but given the debate about the rooftop kiss and the blow job—the latter, Michael and Andy had decided to cut—it made sense to see what audiences thought.

Studios test their films in New Jersey or San Fernando Valley malls, to sample mainstream audience reactions. Killer fights for the "first, best audience." For a film like *Home,* that meant in New York City, definitely downtown, preferably the Village. In a theater crowded with strangers (and one spy from Aintitcoolnews.com), we screened *Home* in the East Village, on a weeknight. All the film's interested parties—Michael, Mark Gill, Tom Hulce, John Wells, Michael Cunningham, Katie, Pam, and I—sat anxiously in the back row when the film started to screen.

The film skipped right into the action: young Bobby sees his older brother, Carlton, having sex with his girlfriend. It was funny and unexpected. I liked it. Later, the audience laughed uproariously at the early scene of Jonathan's mother, Mrs. Glover (Sissy Spacek), smoking pot, and we knew we had at least one unqualified winner. But they also laughed at the moment when Colin Farrell walks into the frame, buck naked, and comes and lies down tenderly next to Jonathan (Dallas Roberts). It's supposed to be a holy, quiet moment, and people giggled. (As we'll see, this scene would end up becoming one of the bigger headaches of the whole film.) When Colin finally gets a haircut and ditches his shaggy mane to reveal his chiseled, leading-man face, the audience exploded with applause. Stardom does that. After the film, they filled out the questionnaire and a number cruncher parsed the figure: *Home* ranked in the forties out of a hundred. Not great, not terrible. Typical Killer numbers.

The testing reps selected two dozen people out of that screening for a focus group to sit in the first two rows and rank the film's over-all quality. Their response was resoundingly more positive. Six said excellent, eight said very good, three said good, and one said fair. Surprisingly, they all fell for Bobby's ambiguous character and said that his ambiguity "felt authentic." "It's so awesome to see kindness between two boys," one person said.

If the raw numbers weren't stellar, this group proved that people responded to the film's complexity, to the idea that love is compli-cated. When one focus group member said he "felt like the movie was too short," Michael could barely contain himself. "That's what I keep saying!" he whispered to Michael Cunningham, sitting next to him. (The following day, one of these focus group folks leaked a review to the website Ain't It Cool News, and we couldn't have paid anyone to write a better review. "What I saw was excellent. This was Colin Farrell as I've never dared to imagine him, sweet, confused, sexually open, crying poignantly when first making love to a woman, dancing playfully with a close male friend and kissing him on the mouth," the person wrote. "I hope the film sees the light of commercial day in as good a shape or better than I saw it.")

Then the interviewer asked one final, critical question, the kind of question that sends filmmakers spinning: "What keeps you from rating this film higher?" This question is the Pandora's box of testing because it gives the studio specific ammunition about what to change to improve a film's prospects. At the same time, for us, a scene that sticks out also makes the movie memorable. I remember that in *Series 7*, the Killer film that is a parody of reality shows, when one character mentions his bout with testicular cancer, direc-tor Dan Minahan cut to a quick, documentary clip of an actual tes-ticular cancer surgery. Audiences, no matter who they were, hated it. In that case, Dan decided to take it out because it was distract-ing—and replaced it with an anatomical drawing of male genitals. The image was less graphic but far funnier and very memorable.

In the focus group, one member raised his hand. "The kiss on the rooftop. That felt like it went too far."

"Who agrees with that?" the interviewer asked.

Other hands popped up.

Headaches, December 2003

As you inch closer to a locked picture, primarily what you are doing (as the producer) is putting out tiny wildfires. With your hands. You've got your notes, the studio's notes, the director's ambitions, and annoying loose cannons.

People come out of the woodwork with issues. For example, in one scene in *Home*, there's an unremarkable landscape photograph—about a foot tall and about ten feet long—as set dressing in the background. We got it on loan from a local museum in Woodstock, New York. Michael liked the generic Americana feel and, since we were shooting in Toronto, he wanted it to create the impression of Woodstockness. For the rights to use it, we offered the photographer, a local artist/banjo player, $150, a figure equal to what the other licensees were getting. But the photographer wanted more money. He said people could recognize the photo and that we could afford more since we were a rich movie company. Then he promptly disappeared.

During production, we shot the scenes with it in there—Dallas Roberts's head obscuring it most of the time—not realizing that the paperwork wasn't done. Now it's December, we're two weeks from finishing the edit of *A Home at the End of the World*, and there's no way we're cutting the scene. But as the producers, we're responsible for securing all the rights to what is contained in the movie and delivering the paperwork. This banjo-artist guy needs to sign his release just like Colin Farrell does. If we don't get the right, he could sue and he'd have a case.

The art department should have dealt with this, but they didn't. They couldn't find him. This is one of those lingering problems that Killer has to deal with. We get to the point where we are willing to pay anything to make the problem go away. Michael calls the banjo player himself. He isn't in, but Michael leaves a message: "Listen, my producers are asking me to cut this scene out of the movie, but I don't want to do that. So let me pay you out of my own pocket. How much do you want?" Not quite a lie, but a definite play for sympathy.

The banjo player doesn't call back. Finally we hear from him with a price. He isn't interested in the $150. He wants $1,000 and won't budge.

We pay it and move on.

Next up: how do you fill a gap in narrative long after the shoot? You steal footage from another movie. Bobby's arrival in New York wasn't working. The story jumped from Bobby in Cleveland to Bobby meeting Jonathan on the street in New York without a transition. We needed a shot of Bobby landing in New York, something to cue his arrival. Movies are packed full of these pieces of dramatic cartilage, establishing shots to guide the audience. So we tracked down a shot from *Desperately Seeking Susan* of a Greyhound arriving, with "New York City" in the little window at the top. It could have worked except, as a 35mm shot, it didn't look technically right in our Super 35 film, which has more detail and a wider frame. Plus, the *Susan* shot was at night and Bobby meets Jonathan during the day, so we had a continuity problem. Andy slipped the shot into the edit as a placeholder while Katie continued to look. It turned out, for all the thousands of people arriving by bus in the city every day, a "bus arriving in New York" stock shot is not easy to come by. Katie eventually found another, this time an aerial shot, from the film *Joe's Apartment*. Since *Joe's Apartment* was a Warner Bros. film, it would be enormously easier to license, to the tune of $750. Michael liked it, Katie liked it, Andy liked it, but Mark at WIP didn't. The *Susan* shot, at $4,000, was so much more "concise and elegant," Mark said. Concise, fine, but elegant? Who was going to pay for that? Mark made the decision: we would use the *Susan* shot, and Warner Independent Pictures would pay for it.

However, we still hadn't resolved the controversial scenes. Michael's current edit still included the rooftop kiss and the blow job. He and Mark were at a standstill. E-mails were exchanged and tensions began to escalate.

Negotiating Upward, Late December 2003

I've been through dicey negotiations, and I'm used to cleaning up after defensive directors. During the postproduction of *One Hour Photo*, Mark Romanek would send high-stakes e-mails to Peter Rice at Fox Searchlight saying things like, "Peter: The cuts you're proposing will ruin my movie! Mark." I would call up Peter and tell him not to worry. What I respected about Peter was his equanimity. He would say, "Just tell me: what's the best way to approach Mark? I mean, I'm here, I've done this before. Tell him to use me." The lesson there is that, as a producer, the most important service you can provide is not to protect the film or the director but to protect the relationships. You need to keep everybody on speaking terms.

Michael turned to his closest colleague, my co-producer Tom Hulce. Tom called Killer and urged us to "stand up" for Michael's vision for the film, to yank it away from the studio if we had to (à la *Happiness.*) From Tom's perspective, the integrity of *Home* was in the balance over these edits. To me, the cuts Mark and Michael were arguing over had little to do with the essence of the movie. It would have been great if Mark conceded some ground, but Michael needed to as well. Someone was going to have to give. Our strategy was to go to the top. Katie advised Michael to keep working and said we'd ask to show his version to Alan Horn, head of Warners Bros. Putting the blow job in. Keeping the kiss. See what he says.

We FedExed the film to Alan. On December 23, we heard back. Alan, it seemed, had some concerns about the way drug use was represented in the film. The start of the film has decent amounts of pot smoking and some pivotal acid trips, and Alan was concerned that the film might glorify drug use. He wanted "Cleveland 1967" on screen at the beginning of the film to time-stamp it. With "1967" up there, Alan felt you could dismiss the drug use as an "artifact of the period." Two other scenes needed transition work.

Finally, two "strongly-felt notes":

Cut the blow-job scene.

Trim the kisses out of the rooftop scene.

Warner wanted the edits complete by January 11.

Michael had no problem with most of Alan's notes, but these last two he bristled at. My personal feeling was that the blow job was not worth fighting for but that the kiss was. At the same time, we're here to defend and represent the director. And Michael, stewed in anger, dug in his heels. Now what?

Killer had an emergency ambassador we could summon into service: John Wells. Wells, the writer/producer behind *E.R.*, *Third Watch*, and *The West Wing* (and producer on *Home*), has the Midas touch at Warner Bros. I was convinced he'd have Alan Horn's ear and could guide us through this before people drew too many lines in the sand. You want everybody to agree or agree to disagree on the final version of a film because a movie that nobody agrees on is a movie that will get slighted by the studio. From my perspective, Killer has to protect Michael's movie and Michael's relationship with Warner Bros.

It was a delicate conversation, but John listened intently. I needed to get John to see Michael's position. I started by accentuating how much Michael had already absorbed Mark's and Alan's notes. My fundamental argument was this: It's not like a critic would see Mark's version and Michael's version and write different reviews. Usually, I'm wresting over whole characters and the arcs and the ending. Here we were talking about two minutes, nothing that would make you walk out of the movie feeling any different. It seemed clear to me that everything that Mark was pushing would not radically affect *Home*. Cutting the kiss wouldn't make it much more of a "straight" film or more palatable to the mainstream. It was a quirky, complicated film, with a sexually confused main character, whose value comes from its idiosyncracy.

"Why not let Michael walk around town and say, 'I just had to make this film'?" I asked John. John agreed. He offered to talk to Alan on Michael's behalf. Score.

Concession, January 2004

On January 8, three weeks later, Alan told John, "I watched the film with my twenty-nine-year-old nephew. And during the kiss on the roof, my nephew turned to me and said, 'This is a gay director, isn't he?' If you keep the kiss in, it becomes a niche movie. I thought we all wanted it broader than that."

But John Wells is an expert negotiator. Isn't Warner Independent Pictures in the business of making riskier films? he asked. By the end of the conversation, Alan Horn had had a change of heart. Alan had decided that he wanted to put out a message. He called Michael and told him, "I want the word on the street to be that WIP supports directors." Michael practically cheered. WIP would resolve the edits from their end. Alan didn't back down. He didn't insist. He just found a way to let Michael have his movie.

However, on January 13, Mark called Killer with a firm ultimatum for *Home*, regardless of what Alan had told Michael: Michael must remove the rooftop kiss. It was time to bring this to an end; this cold war was torturing Michael and ruining Mark's attitude toward the movie and distracting us all. I put together a conference call. With Mark, Michael, and me on the phone, Mark couched his position as Alan's position: "Alan has laid down the law. Take out the rooftop scene." Didn't this contradict what Alan told Michael? No time for questions. It was a short conversation. We gathered all the producers on our side to decide how to respond. The question was, should John call Alan Horn directly? Were there other options?

Contractually Killer had final cut, but that doesn't mean anything if we're in a war with the distributor. And sure, the film had a contract to be released in at least a hundred theaters, but the distributor could still choose to kill it. They could release it in a hundred theaters one by one or take it out in a hundred random theaters (think Iowa or Ohio, not the art-theater circuit in New York, L.A., and San Francisco).

When Universal wanted to dump *Happiness*, Ted Hope and I tried to talk to Todd Solondz about possible cuts. Not only was he unwilling, but if we had cut all the potentially offensive material, *Happiness* would have been the length of a commercial. The entire film was unsettling. *A Home at the End of the World*, on the other hand, was a melodrama about rich, knotty relationships. But it had isolated edges—acid trips, gay intimacy—that could be sanded down by a skittish studio. I don't know what went through Michael's head in that conversation, but I can guess that he'd stopped thinking about the kiss or the blow job. As a director you start thinking, Which is the bigger grief? Cutting elements that you love or watching the movie's release turn into nonevent from the lack of support of a hostile distributor?

Michael budged.

He cut the kiss.

He cut the blow job.

Michael found a way to come around, and we locked picture. He gave in to Mark so that his studio would rally behind the film.

Should Killer have stood up for Michael more? Is there something we could have done? Michael thought that during the first round of feedback, we could have stood firm and rejected Mark's notes. But that would have been a huge mistake for his film, since a positive relationship with the distributor is the most essential condition for a successful indie release. In the end, the standoff happened because of what Mark thought was best for the movie. He didn't bend on any of his notes. We would have gone to the mat for Michael, but Michael didn't want us to. Smartly, he didn't want us to screw up the movie's "love" at Warner Bros., because then the studio would have had to take a fighting position. Michael told me, "I will go to my grave thinking that the kiss made it a better movie. I also think it's a wonderful movie without it."

Unlocking Picture, April 2004

Then Sissy Spacek saw the movie. We'd made a DVD of the final cut for her to watch at home. (In retrospect, a screening would have been better, since actors typically have better reactions to a large, projected film than a small-scale, TV version of the same performance.) We knew going into it that Sissy might be disappointed. The final cut was missing some big Sissy scenes—her intense breakdown when her husband dies, some colorful material with Colin, and one short scene of her at the end of the film. Her performance was undeniably strong in all of them, but those scenes had been cut for pacing reasons. This was the story of Bobby, Claire, and Jonathan. Not

Bobby and Claire and Jonathan and Jonathan's mother. To prepare her, Tom Hulce wrote Sissy a note with the DVD to let her know her performance was amazing but some material had had to be cut.

Sissy watched the film, called Michael, and asked, "Where is my performance? Why are so many of *my* scenes missing?" Not only were some of her big emotional moments not there, but she felt slighted by the edit. In one example she pointed out, when Mrs. Glover (Sissy) meets Claire (Robin Wright Penn) for the first time, Michael played the scene off Claire's face, so that you only saw the back of Sissy's head. There was no close-up of Sissy's face, no way to register how Mrs. Glover reacts to Claire. A minuscule decision to Michael, but a major snub to Sissy.

Her reaction created an opportunity. If Sissy wasn't happy, that might allow us enough leverage to *unlock* the film, to put all the missing scenes back in. Usually, you want to avoid this at all costs, because unlocking a picture is a massive headache—and expensive, right at the moment when you're down to the last pennies of the budget. At Killer, it's very rare that we'll unlock a picture. To do it, you've got to book more editing time (and pay an editor), redo the sound and the score, hire your postproduction supervisor for another few weeks, and get a whole new round of approvals. It's a decision that means hundreds of thousands of dollars. A distributor, in most cases, is the one demanding you unlock a picture to make changes, so typically they pay for them. In our case, WIP had already demanded the edits they wanted and Michael had made them. They were happy.

But when John Wells found out about Sissy's complaint, he had an idea. Reinserting Sissy's scenes would give Michael his opportunity to reinsert the scenes he wanted as well. With CAA involved—Sissy, Colin, and Robin are all clients—maybe we could use their leverage to unlock the picture. The plan became go with Sissy.

Meanwhile, in the final weeks of April, our press agent Jeff Hill coordinated screenings for magazines with long lead times (*Rolling Stone, Elle*, etc.) and sussed out their response. Would they do stories? Reviews? How did the film play? It's a valuable way to forecast a movie's reception. Caryn James at the *New York Times* liked it and admitted she wanted to do a Colin interview for the Arts and

Leisure section. Our first bit of good news. The *Advocate* wanted to offer a cover story on gay parenting to Colin. More good news. Peter Travers at *Rolling Stone* liked it too but thought the film was "too short." (When does anyone ever say that?) To Michael, Travers's comment confirmed his fears that the film had been edited too much. *Elle*'s Karen Durbin, a well-known film critic, said that the film was "OK but not great, an endearing but flawed flick. Loved the guys, loved the mom, loved the whole sensibility of it. But I thought Penn's character was way underdeveloped . . . Coverage TBD but does not look likely."

Now we had ammunition: even the critics thought there should be more movie. I went out to L.A. to meet with Tom, John Wells, and Mark Gill to talk about unlocking the picture. Meanwhile, I'd begun to believe that without the kiss, the film lacked a certain confidence in its own convictions. (The blow job, at this point, was a lost cause.) All the producers agreed. We had a list of seven discrete changes, including restoring the Sissy scenes and the kiss on the rooftop. The reedit would take two weeks. Total cost to restore the scenes, score new music, and relock the film: between $100,000 and $200,000. Would WIP pay?

The pressure—from CAA, Sissy, and us—worked. Mark agreed to let us make the restorations: the Sissy scenes (especially the reverse shot of Sissy when she meets Robin for the first time) and the kiss only if John Wells could convince Alan Horn. Sissy was happier, we were happy, and once John made the call to Alan, Michael was over the moon. "This is so exciting!" Michael said. He was thrilled. "When do we start?"

But then Colin Farrell's penis got in the way. In his early press interviews about *Alexander*, Colin was getting frequently asked about the gay material in his upcoming movies: "You kiss a boy in *Alexander* and you show your dick in *A Home at the End of the World*. What's the deal?" For Colin, these were two important movies for him, both lead performances, and he wasn't happy with the fact that this was all the press was asking about.

Colin's lawyer called: Colin didn't want his full frontal in the picture anymore. We dropped it. But suddenly, a month before our release, the *New York Post*, the New York *Daily News*, even *The*

View ran with a story that Colin's full frontal was getting excised from *Home*—because his penis was too big. This lie was everywhere. "The producers cut it because it was too large and distracting," one tabloid wrote. How many months did we spend struggling over the kiss and the blow job? It turned out the most notorious shot was the one we never thought twice about.

The Release, July 2004

A Home at the End of the World opened the weekend of July 23 in five theaters, mostly in New York and San Francisco. It didn't open extraordinarily well, earning just $20,000 on average per screen. So-so. When WIP expanded to twenty-six theaters the next week, that figure dropped to $7,000. I remember having a conference call with Tom Hulce and Mark Gill to discuss strategy for San Francisco. San Francisco is a city that you'd think would like Killer films but doesn't. Tom asked, "Is there anything we can do?" Mark answered, "Yeah, buy tickets."

By the end of its run, *A Home at the End of the World* made just over $1 million. I ask myself why. The reviews were mixed, and that didn't help. Positive reviews are critical for a movie this size, with this subject matter. It could be that there was not enough public awareness. A lot of people asked me, "Is *Home* out?" I answered, "Hello, it's come and gone already!" *Home* wasn't the only film on WIP's first slate of movies that struggled to click. WIP's success that summer, *Before Sunset*, pulled in $6 million. Other dark and offbeat pictures like *We Don't Live Here Anymore* and *Criminal*, both WIP films, fared about as well as *Home*. (A year later, the success of *March of the Penguins* changed everything for WIP.)

It's hard, if not impossible, for a first-time director to know where the perimeter line of a studio's influence lies. It's my job, as a producer, to guard that line, but I believe it's the director's job to draw it. Even an inexperienced director can have the confidence and clarity of vision to do that. Some directors will say to their distributors, "I'll play ball," and some will say, "Fuck you, I won't listen to a thing you say." There's always a negotiation, as there should be.

I'm used to the situation where the filmmaker is given studio notes, there's back-and-forth, but at a certain point—particularly with a "classics division"—the filmmaker has to feel it's his or her movie. Isn't that why these divisions exist in the first place?

With *Home*, it felt like we were getting big-picture studio scrutiny on our offbeat little picture. For me, this gets at the conflict inherent in the studio "specialty" divisions themselves. They exist, in part, to preempt the acquisition dependency of most small distributors. Instead of buying a completed movie at film festivals, specialty divisions have undertaken film development. (By the time of this writing, we have actually ended up producing our Truman Capote project with WIP.) Development helps them regularize their output: they control what they produce. It also allows them to bring big-studio-style concerns to the movies they're making: How can this film recoup the most money? How can it appeal to the broadest audience? This approach can work great, especially for genre movies. I think of the *Scream* series, released by Miramax's Dimension division. But for *Home*, that pressure from on high turned the film into a mix of interests and issues: Michael Mayer's, Killer's, Mark Gill's, and Alan Horn's.

Would *Home* have fared better if we'd been able to produce it independently from WIP and then sold it to them? If we'd been able to make it the old way, in the style of *Go Fish* or *Poison* or *Swoon*, and then taken it to the marketplace? Of course, in hindsight, this kind of speculation doesn't go very far. It's doubtful we would have been able to draw such stars or cobble together a budget if we'd made it independently. It would have been a much smaller, much less notable film. But one thing's for sure: it would have been Michael's movie and nobody else's.

Spotlight: Mark Romanek

WRITER/DIRECTOR *(ONE HOUR PHOTO)*

Photo Finishing: Editing *One Hour Photo*

The very first thing I wrote when I sat down to write the script for *One Hour Photo* was a narration about the causes of the "red-eye effect" in snapshots. It came out of the blue. I typed it up in a weird, sort of automatic-writing mode, like I was taking dictation from somewhere. It was an odd, disturbing, and oblique way to open the film. We cut together a rather successful version of this idea—a sort of Errol Morris meets *National Geographic* montage. And I liked it very much. It was in keeping with the tone of the film I was keen to make, which was something dark, cerebral, yet emotionally engaging.

When I screened the film for the first time—even though the test scores were abysmally low (which I'll get to in a minute)— there was a palpable sense that the audience had connected with the film on a very deep, almost visceral emotional level. They either related to Sy's loneliness very intensely or they were worried for the family's safety—very intensely. And during the course of the film, their allegiances switched and evolved in interesting ways. As a first-time filmmaker, I became very excited by this, and started to feel that this montage (and other aspects of the film's voice-over narration) were *too* cerebral. I was concerned that these more academic aspects of the film's tone might somehow lessen or short-circuit this visceral emotional connection. In retrospeet, this was a naïve assessment. Perhaps I was chasing something, some lower common denominator. Perhaps I became afraid of seeming pretentious or overly arty. In any event, I convinced myself that the film might connect more deeply without these elements. Looking back now, I think losing those bits made the film a little less eccentric, a little less singular, less interesting and I regret having omitted them. But these are the subtler effects of the first-time filmmaking experience.

In the edit, the structure of the film continued to change on a fundamental level. I edited *One Hour Photo* for more than ten months. Because we were using a nonlinear editing system, I felt that we could try every conceivable variation of every conceivable good take, or structural concept, and so we did. Originally, the story was told in a linear fashion. We meet the Yorkins. They take birthday pictures. They bring the film in to the mall. We meet Sy Parrish (Robin Williams) at the photo counter of the Sav-Mart, etc. What I didn't anticipate was that the studio's marketing would fill the audience in on the basic premise of the film (as it should). This rendered the first act a bit draggy, because the audience knows that something bad is going to happen, so all this setup seemed a little belabored to them. At the test screening, the audience knew they were going to see a dark "thriller" (a term I was loath to have the studio use in the recruiting of an audience), so they were a step ahead of the story, which causes unrest (of the bad kind). So now I had a first act that seemed interesting and necessary but somehow useless at the same time. A conundrum.

Since the film was heavily influenced by my admiration for Francis Coppola's *The Conversation*, and since I had some fleeting access to him, I was able to show the rough cut of the film to Francis. I told him that the film was "kind of a thriller and kind of a character study," and I asked him his opinion about why the first act seemed a bit enervated. His very astute response was that you can't make a "kind of a thriller." It's either a thriller or it's not. He suggested something that would get the thriller aspect of the film going from the very start, so the audience would know immediately where things stand, but his specific suggestion didn't really work. It did, however, lead to a variation on his idea. We bookended the film with Sy already having been arrested for having done something awful and criminal. The audience doesn't know what he's done exactly. This one change suddenly rendered the first act more compelling. The first act played out almost exactly as before, but now the audience is paying closer attention. They're now put in the position of trying to discover clues as to what Sy might've done. They've gone from passive viewers to detectives of a sort. And the first act came alive again.

This brings to mind another interesting feature of the preview process: the necessity to create a temp score for the film. At that stage of the editing, I didn't really have the film figured out, so to speak. I was still making a "sad character study" (as opposed to an "unusual genre exercise"), and most of my choices for temp music were very character-based, meaning more sad and draggy. Later I realized that the score had to propel the narrative and maintain the genre tension to a far greater degree. I realize now that a lot of what made the film slow for the first preview audiences was the temp music and not the actual cut of the picture. I was still too much in love with the loneliness of my main character, and the temp music was in a way redundant. We were already clearly showing the character's loneliness. I didn't have to underscore it with an odd waltz in a minor key. I see now that many of the picture changes we made may not have been necessary. The music was the real issue. We just didn't know it then.

As for Peter Rice and Fox Searchlight, the dynamic between us was very complex and not at all antagonistic. *One Hour Photo* was Peter's first green-lit film after becoming the head of Searchlight, and the main question was how to sell a film that didn't fall squarely into a genre niche. That's not to say that Searchlight was looking for *Fatal Attraction* or *The Hand That Rocks the Cradle*. They are sincere in their desire to make original, filmmaker-driven movies. But the test scores at the initial screenings were abysmal. They were in the thirties, which is just murder. At the same time, the studio liked the movie and saw that even though the scores were low, the audience was riveted by the story. The focus group discussions fully contradicted the scores. In the focus groups, nineteen out of twenty people said they'd recommend the film to a friend. So, to their credit, I think the studio people realized that the scores were somehow erroneous and may have had something to do with the fact that the film was sad and disturbing and didn't play by the normal genre rules.

Searchlight is trying to set itself up—genuinely, I think—as the anti-Miramax. They don't pay people a lot of money, so what the filmmakers get out of the deal is that they get to make their films the way they want. It's still the studio's money, and they have strong opinions, but they can't say to the filmmaker, "Cut that scene out or I'll shelve your fuckin' movie." What they do say is "Try it again. Keep working. Try something different. Keep cutting. It's not there yet." And they hope you will eventually stumble upon an incarnation of the film that they can endorse and support. So, in retrospect, I realize that I lost a very benign war of attrition with the studio. There were two instances during the process when I said to Peter Rice, "No. This is it. This is my version of the film. I'm sorry it's not what you wanted it to be, but it's what I want it to be, and I don't really want to keep trying a million variations, chasing a better score at a preview." My instinct told me that the film had found its intended form. But Peter would say, "Keep cutting. Maybe you'll discover something." And since I love editing so much, and since—contrary to what I claimed—I *am* actually the type who does want to keep trying a million variations, I was seduced. In the end, I think the film lost some of its uniqueness.

On another point, I regret retaining Sy's outburst of backstory at the end where he reveals that he was molested by his father as a child. I felt that critics would hate this. But Peter felt that the audience wanted to see Sy become emotional. I thought that this poor man (Robin's character) needed his own catharsis, and that the scene was less about the *fact* of his backstory than about his finally having some sort of emotional release. Perhaps Peter felt that these narrative histrionics might increase Robin's chances for an Oscar nomination. I don't know. Many critics praised the film but highlighted this scene as a distinct flaw. And I can't say I disagree with them.

I will say that the thing that saved the film was its premiere out of competition at Sundance. When we screened the film for an audience of thirteen hundred people, there was none of the equivocation we saw at the previews. The audience started hooting and applauding the film even before the final shot had fully faded out, and they gave Robin a standing ovation. It was at this screening that Searchlight forgot the horrible previews and saw that the film could be embraced by a big audience. After Sundance, Searchlight decided to go out and sell the film with enthusiasm. Up until that point, *One Hour Photo* was a film that they themselves really liked but weren't sure the rest of the world would like. The Sundance premiere reaction let them know that everything was OK.

Still, marketing the film to wider audiences posed a real challenge. I think Fox Searchlight may have tricked audiences a bit into making them think the film was scarier than it actually was. They used a quote from Peter Travers from *Rolling Stone*—"truly, deeply scary"—which I understand is a tempting sound bite but one that may have heightened people's expectations of the film's thriller aspects unreasonably. A move like this gets butts in seats initially, but you risk creating a disappointed word of mouth. I think since the release of *One Hour Photo*, Searchlight has grown far more confident in marketing tricky-to-sell films, like *Napoleon Dynamite* or *I ♥ Huckabees*. I wish they had had the confidence and sense of inventiveness then that they seem to have now. All that said, at the time, *One Hour Photo* became the most successful Searchlight film after the freak phenomenon of *The Full Monty*. And it made an astounding amount on home video, so they were very happy with their investment.

MAY 2004

Producer's Diary III

10 A.M. First up, Brendan Fraser. Honestly, I kind of hate meeting with actors. Unless we have something to talk about, we just end up staring at each other. I'll do it as a favor to certain agents, and George Freeman at William Morris (who reps Russell Crowe and Dennis Quaid) has been very good to us.

Brendan has taken a year off from acting, become a father, and lost some of that twentysomething bluster. "I've done too many *George of the Jungles*," he tells me, sitting in the chair across from my desk. "I paid my dues. I don't want to be a concept. I want to be a character."

Suddenly, it occurs to me that Brendan would be perfect for the husband in *The Good Life*, a great new script that's come our way about a down-on-their-luck couple (a former prom king and queen) who kidnap an Exxon executive for the ransom. They bungle it and the executive dies. I've been pitching it as something like *Dog Day Afternoon*. Sarah Jessica Parker is attached to play the wife. We're out to Tim Robbins right now, a fact I don't tell Brendan. Officially I'm not supposed to be talking to anybody else. But the more I think about it, Brendan would be perfect.

You've got to stay open to these serendipities. When we were developing *One Hour Photo*, Mark Romanek had written the lead for Philip Seymour Hoffman, who turned it down. And we thought we were doing him a huge favor. Out of the blue, Robin Williams's agent called. Robin was looking to branch out in more interesting parts. So Mark and I had a three-hour lunch with him, and I was sold. He wasn't a manic Patch Adams; he proved to be utterly sincere and driven, ready for *One Hour Photo's* hyperrestrained Sy Parrish, though in production he never could quite kick the antics. One day Mark shot a scene where Robin runs though a convention hall. Robin said he wasn't happy with his performance and asked for another take. When Mark called "Action," Robin burst through the door and ran across the room. Naked.

10:20 A.M. With Brendan gone, I call Scott Elliott, the director and writer of *The Good Life*. He's a theater director who also did the film *A Map of the World*. I tell him that I have an idea; what does he think about Brendan Fraser? "I was actually just about to try to reach him!" he says. "I want him to play the Redford part for a *Barefoot in the Park* revival I'm doing this summer." The fact is, at thirty-five years old, Brendan is a far more believable husband to Sarah Jessica Parker than Tim Robbins. You need to see the movie and think they actually went to school together. This is definitely not a movie that needs to wait for Tim Robbins. With Scott's OK, I "unofficially" slip a copy of the script over to George at William Morris for Brendan to read, letting him know that we're already out to Tim Robbins. Now we just have to hope that Tim passes.

I consider myself lucky for the projects that just waltz through our door, but there have been some that I'm still kicking myself over. I loved the script for the Christian high school comedy *Saved!*, but I couldn't get support for it internally at Killer. Ditto for *Secretary*. It kills me that Killer is not producing for Kenny Lonergan, the writer/director of *You Can Count on Me* and the play *Lobby Hero*. The script for *You Can Count on Me* came our way, and I just didn't see it then, but the film he directed of it was terrific. Sometimes you just have to trust the talent no matter what. With a project as good as *The Good Life*, I'm never going to let go. I push as hard as I can.

Postscript: Brendan Fraser never attaches himself to the project. Instead, Matt Dillon does. As of this writing, we're still looking for financing. But Brendan does attach himself to play Halston in *Simply Halston*. After ten years, we're still looking for financing on that too.

11 A.M. We're having a small tiff with Warner Independent Pictures over the casting of *Infamous*. For the past year, the casting director Ellen Lewis (*The Interpreter, Gangs of New York, The Aviator*) has been consulting on it *for free*. She loves Doug McGrath and she wanted to see a great project get off the ground. Ellen is a huge asset. She has such a good reputation that actors are willing to do auditions for her when they won't do them for anyone else. So she's scheduling a round of test shoots in L.A. and London with eight potential Truman Capotes. But now it's time to get her paid.

Ellen doesn't want much, but she certainly shouldn't have to pay for her flight or the taping. Right now we're stuck in the middle of a semantic debate with the studio. We sold Warner Bros. the rights to the book and the script for *Infamous*. Our Warner Bros. contacts are telling us that these test shoots are preproduction expenses, and therefore we should be paying for them out of what the studio is going to give us to make the film. (Of course, we haven't seen that money yet.) From our perspective, they're a development expense, since if we were in preproduction, we'd be paying Ellen Lewis her full fee and not a much smaller "consulting fee."

I fire off a quick e-mail to Warner proposing to split the fee. We're hoping that if they turn our offer down, the studio will look bad in front of Doug, the filmmaker they're trying to impress.

11:45 A.M. ASAP: Someone's got to call the Chateau Marmont in L.A. We left Peter Sarsgaard's audition tape for the Truman Capote part in the VCR in my room. We've got to get that back before it ends up on the Internet.

12 NOON. *The Extra Man* just may be yanked out from underneath us. Ah, Hollywood. Last week we went to renew the option for Jonathan Ames's book, and we got a shock. The lawyers told us, "The author does not care to renew the option." Even though we've been paying the option costs every year since 1999, even though we've spent thousands to develop a script and Isaac has become deeply invested creatively, it's becoming clear that Jonathan Ames has his own ideas. We find out that Hart Sharp—right down the hall from us—are about to buy the rights to the book. (The option *is* open.) With Jonathan Ames himself attached to adapt the script.

We own the script that Keith Bunin wrote for us, but we can't produce the movie without the underlying rights. We don't know what to do. This screws Isaac over. Time for the lawyers to resolve this.

Postscript: Our rights expire. We lose *The Extra Man.*

1 P.M. Poor Todd Graff. It's always painful to have your passion project pulled out from underneath you. Ten years ago, long before he wrote and directed *Camp,* Todd was both an actor (*The Abyss*) and a screenwriter. He got hired by New Regency to write a script about a mental patient with twenty-four multiple personalities called *The Crowded Room.* Todd met an actual disturbed man, built up a lot of trust with him, and wrote a script with a huge, challenging role for an actor that was a clear Oscar contender. Everybody in town wanted to bid for it. John Cusack was set to play the lead with James Cameron directing until Cameron backed out. Brad Pitt almost did it with David Fincher, Sean Penn with Steven Soderbergh, and Leo DiCaprio with Danny DeVito. But as good as it was, the project could never get itself together. Over time, it just faded into turnaround.

After Cannes in 2003, with *Camp* under his belt, Todd came to us and said he wanted it back to direct. New Regency still had the rights, but they had pretty much forgotten about it. So we went back with a budget of $12 million—lower than had ever been proposed—and began trying to bring *The Crowded Room* back to life. But that only seemed to prompt New Regency to remember just how much they liked it in the first place. So today the news is on the front page of *Variety: In the Bedroom* director Todd Field has committed to direct *The Crowded Room,* based on Graff's script, for Fox Searchlight and New Regency. Poor Todd Graff.

2:30 P.M. Well, the MPAA started watching *A Dirty Shame* in L.A. 10 a.m. PST, so they should be nearing the end of the rating-appeal hearing. Right now it's NC-17, which is absurd. You can watch eyeballs getting squished in *Kill Bill,* but you can't make a joke about felching. John Waters is out there with Carolyn Blackwood, the legal and business affairs rep from New Line. John wrote us a nervous e-mail yesterday outlining their strategy. When they announce their verdict, he wrote, "I'll find out their home addresses and ritualistically slaughter the entire board. That's my morning tomorrow. How's yours?"

John calls: the appeal got rejected. "The hardest thing to fight," he says, "was when the MPAA lady said, 'Seventeen-year-olds, seniors in high school, and all college students will be certainly allowed to see this movie with an NC-17 rating.' What do you say to that?" I call Ted Hope, my producing partner on the film, to strategize. It'll be New Line's choice whether to fight, but soon *Variety* will get the story and it'll be out of our hands. "If we're going to come out swinging," I tell Ted, "we need to do it on our own terms."

3:30 P.M. Tom Kalin, the director on *Savage Grace,* just can't get excited by Annette Bening or Diane Lane or Catherine Zeta-Jones to replace Julianne Moore, even though each of these women would significantly alleviate any financing problems. None of them feels right to him. Cate Blanchett would be perfect, but she's pregnant and unavailable. We've got John Malkovich attached to play the husband, and he's our ace in the hole. So the question becomes, do we wait a year for Julianne Moore (and risk losing Malkovich), or do we find someone else and shoot now? How do we know that Julianne won't pull the same trick again and take another offer?

"On the phone, when she called to apologize, Julianne seemed remarkably sincere," Tom tells me. "I think she legitimately wants the part. She gave her *home phone number.* That means something."

What about Kate Winslet? "It'd be too insane to rewrite the script now," Tom says. "The age gap between her and Malkovich is too big." Since Tom clearly is set on Julianne, we have to cast her now. If we're going to wait a year for her, he's got to convince her that there's no backing out.

The next issue is that our option on the *Savage Grace* book is about to run out. The book's literary agent is making noises that he'd like to see the price go up or get the chance to shop it around. "Who the hell else is going to option this material?" I tell him. "This movie is this book's best shot!"

4 P.M. What do you think about a happy ending? We've got screenwriter John Ridley (*Three Kings, Undercover Brother*) and fellow producer Fisher Stevens on the phone. John just delivered his second draft of his adaptation of *Positively Fifth Street,* the poker epic he's going to direct. With this second draft, he addressed all our concerns; it took him about a month. It's so nice to work with professionals. (We end up doing a lot of training here at Killer.) The script is totally ready to start attaching talent. But I'm wondering if James McManus, the author of the book and the true-life poker player, should win the $247,000 he actually does in the book. We know John doesn't want to show it, but Fisher and I think it might be the ending note that the script needs.

For the moment we decide to let it hang. There will more script notes down the line once we get a distributor involved, especially a studio. John knows this well enough, since his all-black version of *Three Kings* was rewritten by David O. Russell. We're here to prevent that from happening.

"Should we trigger going after Tom Hanks?" I ask. Hanks is repped by Richard Lovett at CAA, and the last time we submitted to Tom, for Capote, we were taken seriously. There's some debate about whether we should first fill in the colorful minor characters, but in the past when we have tried to do that, casting always comes down to who is playing the lead, which can change the entire scale of your cast. We hang up, and Killer FedExes a copy of the script to CAA. I've got a good feeling about this.

Postscript: A week later, Tom Hanks passes.

Letter from Sundance, 2005

*Where is my gift bag?—Secret deliberations—Condo
parties—The new dealmakers—What will it take to get
Mark Ruffalo into our movie?—Award ceremonies*

Wednesday, January 19

Leaving for Sundance. Today is the day that most people take to the air, so the phones are quiet. For the past few days, there has been a mad flurry of mass e-mails sending out the details of where everyone in show business will be staying. All the places have names like Canyon Lodge or the Silver King. All these people staying in ski lodges who have never skied. I am just staying in a condo, and even though I'm on the jury, I am allowed to be with everyone else.

Right now everyone is comparing party notes to make sure that there aren't any parties they were excluded from. Pretty much every big agency has a party (CAA, UTA, WMA, etc.). Some of the movies that have a distributor already will have a bash (if the distributor wants to pony up), and sometimes even production companies like Killer will have one. We gave a homemade chili party several years in a row at our three-bedroom condo. It was great the first two years, but by year three, we had to hire security to keep the desperate hordes out of our bedrooms.

The thing is, most of the parties are awful. They are supercrowded. Everyone is looking over everyone else's shoulder to see if this year's Sundance celebrity is there (one year Ben Affleck and J-Lo infamously stopped all traffic on Main Street) or even regulars like Steve Buscemi. The stars are there because they have a movie to promote or their significant other has a movie to promote. (Ben was there with the Project Greenlight movie, *The Battle of Shaker Heights*.)

The bars and restaurants that host these events are completely overwhelmed, and it is damn tough to get a drink. Even worse, there are often gift bags. These bags (usually) contain a mundane assortment of baseball hat with a logo; some cologne; maybe a small bottle of a weird liquor like, say, melon tequila; a free *Entertainment Weekly;* a

CD of music from a movie; a T-shirt that is too small or too big. You get the idea. But people get rabid at the notion that they may leave empty-handed and tend to collect around the table anxiously, and when, as inevitably happens, there are not enough bags, they pitch a full-fledged tantrum. Even the stars want to get their mitts on an infamous Sundance Channel gift bag.

Thursday, January 20

My first day here, but my second time as a juror in the dramatic competition. Ten years ago, there were four of us and we deadlocked. This year, we're five. It's me; critic B. Ruby Rich; actor John C. Reilly; actress Vera Farmiga (*Iron Jawed Angels*, *The Manchurian Candidate*), who won a special acting award last year for *Down to the Bone*; and film director Chris Eyre (*Skinwalkers*, *Smoke Signals*). Our deliberations are secret, so I can't go into detail, but most of the action is outside that room anyhow.

It is hard not to make the ten-year comparisons. Of course, the overwhelming one is just that there were not so many people ten years ago; we chose between two or three parties every night, not ten or fifteen, but we still complained about the crowds, even then. Supposedly there are 45,000 people here now for the week, for a festival that can comfortably accommodate 10,000.

As a juror, I may not be able to rave about specific movies, but I can write about the feeling in the screening of *Brick* tonight. It was a heavily "buzzed" film, a film noir set in high school, and all the distributors turned out in force. This created a feeling of electricity and anticipation in the room that was intoxicating. The filmmaker, Rian Johnson, clearly had a lot of buddies in the room, and when he took the stage, there was a surge of applause. He thanked a ton of people, and I thought how every road to Sundance is almost the same: "It was so so hard . . . Somehow we got the film made. *Omigod* I can't believe we are actually here." (A week later, Focus Features acquired the rights to distribute *Brick* for $2 million.)

Saturday, January 22

Last night I went to a party at the This is that condo, the company run by my friend and producer Ted Hope. The party seemed like a throwback: the hosts had prepared food; guests brought bottles of wine and (at Ted's request) single-malt scotch. There was an ebb and flow of maybe fifty people, most of them people who were here ten years ago and are now running the companies that they once just worked for.

Parties now seem to be very organized affairs, in restaurants or bars. Invitations are printed and sent out in advance, and there is a very strict person with a clipboard at the door. In the old days almost all the parties were at condos, usually far from Main Street, with addresses like the Nordic Village at Deer Valley. We would get hopelessly lost, the car would get stuck in a snow drift, and then finally we'd hear the music and find the party and trudge through snow into a two- or three-bedroom condo filled with filmmakers, their buddies, agents, distributors, you name it. Everyone would be drinking bottles of beer or wine out of plastic cups. The condo would already look like a trashed college dorm room. There would be a huddle smoking and freezing outside. Why were those parties so fun? Partly because you really never knew who would be there, and because there were always films to discuss, so there was always something to say. And the condo living room did lend a (false, but still) sense of intimacy.

So that was Ted's party. Tonight I will be going to the other kind, the more prevalent kind: an agency party at a well-known Sundance venue called the Riverhorse. (See what I mean about the names?) I just hope I am on the list . . .

Monday, January 24

One of the cool and confounding things about Sundance is how different each film in competition *feels*. Obviously, some are dramas, some are comedies, but what I mean is that some feel like they were a tiny intimate enterprise, with a handful of unknown actors and a location I can only describe as "regional"—in other words, *not* New York or L.A. but somewhere in between. Usually the filmmaker attends the screening with a handful of crewmembers and well-wishers who are all probably sleeping on the floor of the condo Sundance provided him or her.

Other films are dotted with Big Names (a few this year: Keanu Reeves, Campbell Scott, James Woods, Evan Rachel Wood) who attend the screenings with a phalanx of agents and managers and publicists. The director of that kind of movie probably also has an agent and a manager and a publicist at this point. When he or she hits the stage to intro the movie, it feels as if the whole place is cheering them on. It doesn't seem fair.

I attended a screening like that yesterday for *Thumbsucker,* a first film by Mike Mills, about a teenager who still sucks his thumb, produced by Ted Hope's This is that. It's got Vince Vaughn, Tilda Swinton, and Keanu Reeves. But even they were upstaged by a movie sale. UTA, which represents *Thumbsucker* (and Ted) had just made the first Really Big Deal of the festival, the $9 million sale of *Hustle and Flow* to Paramount. It's the story of a middle-aged pimp in Memphis who tries to become a rap star. The UTA agents were beaming.

Wednesday, January 26

Guthrie is here now, so it's getting harder to be a juror, mom, and diarist and *still* go to parties. But here goes: one of the things that is making me oddly cynical as a juror is seeing Geoff Gilmore or John Cooper, the guys who run the festival, go up to the stage sixteen times for the films in competition, and sixteen times introduce the movie as "one of the *truly* special titles we have the privilege to show this year," and I sit there thinking, Yeah yeah yeah, let's start the film already, even though I have choked back tears many a time when it has been my film and director up there.

Yesterday, the *New York Times* ran a front-page article about John Sloss, our lawyer, as the major deal maker for the independent film world. The star sales agent at this exact point in time is not Sloss but the boys of UTA, Rich Klubeck and Jeremy Barber. Their sale of *Hustle and Flow* is the talk of the festival. When people are not talking about the movies they've seen, they are talking about the deals they've heard about. Often, folks swear up and down that the sum reported is completely inaccurate. Or they relish the idea that a competing company lost out on the movie. (It's widely reported that James Schamus and David Linde of Focus are absolutely furious that they didn't get *Hustle and Flow.* I have no clue if that's true or not.) It's nice being a juror because you're not expected to know the gossip.

Thursday, January 27

The real drama in my life right now is not the Sundance movies and the jury deliberations. My fellow jurors are all pretty affable, and the movies (with a few exceptions) are consistently interesting and strong. What has been consuming me (and making me struggle during competition films to *not* check my BlackBerry) has been yet another casting disaster on *Infamous.*

When the script first circulated, Mark Wahlberg's agents heavily pursued us; they thought he was perfect for the role of Perry, the murderer whom Truman Capote befriends and falls in love with, and they were pretty sure he would agree. He responded to the material. ("Responded to the material" or the newer "sparked to the material" are Hollywoodspeak for *he liked it*). Mark and Doug met, and they hit it off. The only thing not sealed at that point was that we didn't yet know who was playing Truman. Still, Mark was happy to attach himself while we continued the Truman search.

Well, that search took quite a bit longer than anticipated. A lot of name actors turned the role down because they were scared they wouldn't be able to embody the Tiny Terror with his caustic intellect and falsetto voice. We started screen-testing unknowns. During this process, we had no contact with Mark Wahlberg except for the occasional check-in with his agent. (Us: "He's still playing Perry, right?" Them: "Yes! *Absolutely!* He *loves* this project!") Finally we discovered the terrific British stage actor Toby Jones, who is unmistakably Capote's doppelgänger. *Phew!* We have a Truman!

So we call Mark's agents, who don't call back. Uh-oh. Warner Independent decides to run a piece in the trades announcing some casting—including Mark Wahlberg. It hits *Variety,* and the next day we get hit with the news that Mark is no longer interested. But *why*? Them: "He just isn't." Us: "Will he talk to the director?" Them: "He doesn't want to waste the director's time." Back to the drawing board.

Even before Doug had been approached so aggressively by the Wahlberg camp, he had been drawn to the idea of Mark Ruffalo. Mark had apparently been offered the role in the *other* Capote film circulating around but had turned it down. When we approached him for ours, his manager was put out that we had gone to Wahlberg first. Much apologizing ensued. Ruffalo read our script and (here we go again) "sparked to it." He and Doug met, it was a lovefest. We had our Perry!

But. Mark was in two movies back to back—a DreamWorks comedy and *All the King's Men*, a big movie for Sony. We had originally wanted to start shooting mid-January, right about now. If we really wanted Mark, we would have to push production back at least a month. We checked everyone's schedules, including Sandra Bullock, who was set to play Harper Lee, Truman's best friend. But as we went later, we were pushing Sandy Bullock to the edge because of her publicity commitments on *Miss Congeniality 2*. We configure and reconfigure, making a schedule that has Mark starting at the beginning of March.

Then right before Christmas, Mark's agent calls and says *All the King's Men* won't release him until mid-March. Uh-oh. We just can't push anymore, but Doug desperately wants him in the part—

Wait a second. I have to go see my last movie!

Later Thursday

Christmas comes and goes, and we hear from Mark's agent that his other movies are progressing well and it looks like he will be available for us when we need him. What a relief! But I am having a nagging worry. I know that Mark's wife is due with their second child at the beginning of April. Doesn't she want her husband around? Isn't Mark going to finish his DreamWorks movie and *All the King's Men* and want to just stop? No, no, insists his manager and his agent. But sure enough, right before Sundance, we get the call: Mark has changed his mind.

We go into high hysterical gear. He can't do this to us, he made a commitment, and most important, *We are shooting in three damn weeks! Who the hell is going to play Perry?*

I call Mark. Doug calls Mark. Doug e-mails Mark. As I suspected, the pressure of being away so much at such a difficult time has come home to roost. Mark is clearly very burnt out and wants to do the right thing professionally *and* personally. Finally, as I am leaving for Sundance, Mark reverses his decision. He will play Perry.

I land and there are no urgent e-mails. No 911 phone messages. I actually start to relax and enjoy the movies. And then, Tuesday evening I go to John Sloss's enormous condo in Deer Valley. It feels like a cross between a frat house and a corporate retreat. Meetings are going on in clusters everywhere, the Clash is blaring out of someone's closed door, beer cans and soda cans are sprinkled around liberally. I sit down for my meeting, and my phone starts to vibrate frantically. It is Mark Gill, head of Warner Independent Pictures.

I excuse myself and answer.

Two big problems. Number one: Sony, the studio producing *All the King's Men,* is refusing to give Warner Bros. a stop date on Mark, which means we have no way of knowing if they will actually release him when we need him. Number two: Mark wants it contractual that if his wife goes into labor early, we will release him immediately. It is *very* unlikely that Warner Bros. would put something like that in a contract, but Mark Gill and I call Mark's agent and swear up and down as parents, as human beings, that we will make sure Mark gets home to his wife. As I hang up the phone, a little worry starts again. What if she *does* go into labor early? What will we do, shut down? No insurance would cover that. How would we pay for it?

Is Mark Ruffalo really worth it?

The next day I am watching movies and trying very hard not to check my e-mail. I am getting a bad feeling. Sure enough, the phone starts to buzz. It is Mark Gill. "I think we've lost him," he says. What? After all that? Mark Gill explains that he went back to Sony to get them to give on the stop date. He had done the same for them recently and thought perhaps he could call in a favor. Their response was basically no. We heard later that one of the stars, Jude Law, had hurt himself, and as a result shooting was falling behind. So that's it. Mark Ruffalo is out. We shoot in three weeks.

Friday, January 28

By last Wednesday afternoon, Sundance had become strangely quiet. All the acquisitions people had swooped in for the first few days, seen absolutely everything that was available, and left. Which meant that suddenly there were no more parties. And seats were available in restaurants!

This also meant that the specter of the awards started to loom larger. In the tiny, insular Sundance world, they started to seem important, even though every year another magazine publishes a (shocking!) exposé that reveals that actually the Grand Jury winners are overwhelmingly—with a few exceptions—the most arty and least seen films.

Friday afternoon I went to see my last competition film, and it was the only technically bad screening of the whole festival. Ten minutes into the movie, the sound became indecipherable. The lights came on; everyone milled around for a while. Then the film started up again and stopped again. The filmmaker's distress was almost palpable. Finally the movie revved up and managed to continue with no more drama (except on screen).

At around 7 p.m., all us jurors are picked up and whisked to the Stein Erikson Lodge in Deer Valley. I had heard of this place for years, usually as "the place where the *really* big stars stay." We are sequestered in what seems like a corner of a large convention-center-style ballroom, so I don't see what all the glamorous fuss is about. We are given a choice between chicken and fish (no venison or wild boar for us!) and offered plenty of sponsor wine (Turning Leaf), and the deliberations begin.

What follows is a completely exhilarating five hours. We argue, and there is the occasional speaking out of turn or interruption, but for the most part I feel as if I have fallen into another time, a time when talking about movies means you argue plot points and try to dissect the director's point of view. I cannot remember the last time I talked about movies without discussing their worth in the marketplace.

Saturday, January 29

Saturday morning my phone starts to ring: people who have left Sundance already think I might tip them off to the big winners that night. Marcus Hu, from Strand Releasing, calls me from Rotterdam:

"Come on, I'm thousands of miles away!" Marcus says.

"No," I answer.

"It's *Thumbsucker*, isn't it?" he says. "Cough if it is!"

"I can't tell you!"

"Is it *Hustle and Flow*?"

And so on. The cool thing is that nobody, not one person, asks me if the winner is the movie that will actually win: a moody, character-driven film called *Forty Shades of Blue*. When I get to the Racquet Club, where the awards are given out, I am very nervous. This evening is going to be a big deal for a lot of filmmakers, maybe change their lives. It did for me, starting out with *Poison* and *Swoon* and *Go Fish*. I am anxious to say the right thing. I huddle in the staircase with the other jurors. We all read each other the comments we've written. Ruby corrects some grammar. John intends to read out the name of every filmmaker in the Dramatic Competition, which I think is a pretty generous, clever idea.

Of course, when I finally get up there, I realize that I and my little remarks are *so* beside the point, that all anyone cares about is the last part, "And the award goes to . . ." I give out the Special Jury Awards for Originality of Vision to two stunning first films: *Brick* and *Me and You and Everyone We Know*. The drama in the room is intensely satisfying: all the winners gasp, tear up, stumble to the podium, talk for too long. I find myself tearing up at every speech. All the energy in the room seems to swell into one giant desire to make great movies, and it is intoxicating.

Spotlight: Jocelyn Hayes

**PRODUCER AND HEAD OF DEVELOPMENT,
KILLER FILMS**

Twenty-four Hours in Sundance

I arrive in Park City late Thursday night to a strange-looking condo with windows between every room but few to the outside. I'm staying with Brad Simpson, who used to be a producer at Killer and now runs a production company called Appian Way (and more important, is engaged to me). Brad has brought his creative executive Franklin and the talent manager Jennifer Davisson from the management company The Firm to Sundance, the first time for both of them. It turns out the director Richard Kelly (whose movie *Donnie Darko* was the talk of Sundance when he debuted it here as a precocious twenty-five-year-old a few years ago) has shown up at the last minute and is crashing on the sofa. He is supposed to be finishing a script in L.A. but has flown to Utah to procrastinate. It's a little tight, and there is some argument about whether smoking is allowed in the condo, but otherwise it's pretty jolly.

When I arrived, the condo was already packed with the usual Sundance necessities: lots of water, Emergen-C (that vitamin powder you mix with water), and plenty of snacks, so I don't need to do anything. You have to remember to drink lots of water because the altitude really affects you for the first couple of days.

The thing about Sundance that nobody tells you before you go is that you get to either see movies or eat. It's not really set up for both, so you end up carrying around PowerBars and water, sneakily eating and drinking in the theaters. Our clock is an hour off, so despite expert planning, I have a mad rush in the morning to meet Christine at the festival headquarters, pick up my pass and tickets, and get to the screening on time. The pass shows that I am officially a member of the industry and lets me into certain areas where I can get *Variety* and free coffee. It's mostly good for holding my movie tickets and party passes. It hangs on a lanyard around my neck, announcing to the world that I work for Killer Films. I tend to turn it around in crowded situations because the aspiring filmmakers who come to Sundance are savvy and aggressive: they can read those little words from three blocks away, and I don't want to carry around ten scripts and a bag full of DVDs all day.

It's always exciting to go to headquarters the first day. The place is buzzing with anticipation. The producers and directors are nervous, the reporters are prowling, and the publicists are *on*. John Sloss has a sales company called Cinetic, which represents movies and makes the deals with distributors. His crew is already on the prowl, spotting all the possible buyers and making sure they have tickets to all of their screenings. Everyone is running around, comparing movie schedules and gossip. I see a lot of people I haven't seen since the last festival. We exchange hellos and vague talking-on-the-phone gestures—festivalspeak for "I'll call you or we'll just run into each other at one of the parties."

I find Christine holding court in the corner. She is a juror this year, so the Queen of Sundance is even more sought-after than usual. The festival has provided her with a driver, so we make it to the screening in time and then get whisked inside, ahead of the line. This is the life. The agents and acquisitions people buy special passes that allow them to get into all the screenings ahead of the line, but I have always been a regular old ticket holder. Our first movie is at the Racquet Club, the new theater by a group of tennis courts, far away from Main Street. If you have a few movies there in a row, you just have to stay there, freezing in the parking lot and trying to avoid using the porta-potties. The theater's seats and sound are pretty good, but the only food there is a small Mexican cart, which is rumored to be very good, but a theater full of people who ate tacos and beans for lunch sounds dubious.

Christine discovers the one real place to eat on the first day. It is a small, grubby sports bar, hidden away up an anonymous-looking staircase, overlooking the tennis courts. The hamburgers are pretty good, and within twenty-four hours it becomes *the* power spot. The heads of all the major companies are huddled around the little bar tables with their executives and lawyers, busily making deals. The bar does not know what hit them; they run out of hamburgers halfway through the second day.

The first movie is a total cliché of what people think independ-ent films are. The whole thing seems to happen in slow motion, full of meaningful glances and painful revelations. I'm happy to leave and run across town to my next movie, a French film set in a low-income suburb of Paris where racial tensions run high.

Well, I don't actually run. There is a free shuttle that runs a con-stant loop between all of the movie theaters. Of course, I don't take that very often either. My goal at the end of each movie is to spot an executive with a car who is going my way.

I hop a ride to the Egyptian, which is right on Main Street, and end up sitting in the Paramount SUV next to two guys I know: an executive from Paramount and an executive from Scott Rudin's company. Our reactions to the French movie are comically consis-tent. The Paramount guy hated it and is grumbling, "I'm not buying the ridiculous movie. I mean, it's in French, that girl was a slut, and it didn't make any sense. Do you think I even have to write it up for my report?" The guy from Scott Rudin's company is hedging, say-ing, "Well, I understand what he was going for, mostly, and I thought it was pretty interesting and beautifully shot. Not commer-cial, though." I am all swept up in it, arguing passionately for plot-lines and character development that I have made much clearer in my retelling than they really were on the screen, rooting for the filmmaker who has made this sympathetic and ambitious movie that, to be honest, does not fully work.

It's on to the next movie. Another very Sundancey first movie, but this time in a good way. Needs to lose twenty minutes, hire an editor who isn't the director's brother and a composer who isn't his cousin, but totally fresh and original. It's the kind of exciting debut that makes it worthwhile to come to Sundance. The film has a good chance of getting bought and released, but it will probably be the last time anyone will ever see the movie this way—in all its raw, unpolished, ambitious glory.

I am dying to get Christine to talk about it, but she's a juror, so she has to keep her thoughts to herself. I wonder how she is going to make it through the week. I can tell it is hard, especially after the really bad ones. I try to get her to crack, but she manages a pretty good poker face. Movies and deals are the only two things people talk about here, and who wants to talk about deals all week?

Dinner is with a group of writers and directors and producers, which is always interesting, especially at a festival. There is some snarkiness—who can help feeling a little competitive as the next big things parade up and down Main Street?—but for the most part people are supportive and admiring of each other's work. There aren't that many restaurants with decent food in Sundance, so everyone seems to know at least one person at every other table. There is lots of running around and table-hopping. I get to catch up with some people I only see at festivals and meet some other people I have been interested in getting to know. Then there is the high school aspect of things, where people who ignored me in the past are suddenly nice to me because of the people sitting at my table, or because they left their high-powered studio exec positions to become independent producers and have suddenly found themselves at the bottom of people's phone sheets.

After dinner, I run to a crowded party in a tent and fight my way through the crowd to catch an actress friend win an award for being a woman filled with the spirit of independence or something. The music is good for a while, but then it gets all crowded with fake boobs, and we escape to a party for a hot documentary about a new type of dancing called "krumping," where the performers paint their faces like clowns.

The party is packed into what appears to be the hallway of a mall. There is going to be a performance. We find a great spot to watch, but then the publicists spot our actress friend and go into a frenzy, shoving through the crowd and pulling us all into the "VIP lounge," a smoky, crowded room filled with Paris Hilton and lots of other celebrities who would not even think to go to the film. You can't even see the stage from in here. What has happened to parties in the last few years? It is such a crush that people get in fights just on the lines to get in. Did it used to be more fun once you got inside, or was I just younger?

Condo parties are starting to look very attractive.

We leave and call it a night. Suddenly feeling very old, we tell each other that it's only the first night and we all have 8:30 a.m. screenings that we really don't want to miss. When I get home, it is later than I thought, and there is a strange man asleep on the floor. Richard found an old fraternity brother on Main Street who I guess forgot to plan for a place to stay. Maybe things haven't changed so much, after all.

Chapter 9
A Tale of Two Trumans

The look that says, "This must be so so hard but <u>damn</u> am
I happy!"—Thank <u>The New Yorker</u>—Stalking horse
productions—Best/worst case scenarios

Second in Line

It's March 2006 and for the past several weeks, ever since the Oscar nominations came out, I've been feeling this dull ache. I keep having to stop and think to put a name to it: *Capote*. When I saw Philip Seymour Hoffman win the Golden Globe for his portrayal of Truman Capote, it almost killed me. Killer's own Truman Capote story, *Infamous*, is due out in October 2006. Is there room enough in the culture for two movies on almost the same subject?

I spent Oscar night at *Infamous* director Doug McGrath's place on the Upper West Side, drinking a considerable amount of wine. We just wanted it all to be over, for better or for worse. For us *not* to be the bitter second film. About a week before, we'd sent flowers to Philip Seymour Hoffman. I wanted to let Phil know that despite everything, we were rooting for him. We'd sent along a note that read, "Good luck—and we really mean it."

And we really *did* mean it. When I stand back, I'm proud of Phil and how far he's come; he was in *Happiness*, in a big role, and his success makes me happy. I don't ever wish another film ill. And

Capote's story is as much a Cinderella story as anything I've done in my life. But it's been hard to get excited about *Infamous* without *Capote* in the way. So, as soon as the Oscars were over—and Phil had won Best Actor—Doug and I let out this enormous sigh of relief. The best and worst thing had happened: *Capote* was the toast of the town. But the dull ache stopped immediately. Finally, we could go back to focusing on our film.

Some days I am reassuring ("*Capote* merely sets the stage for our film! It shows that people are indeed interested in that story!"), sometimes defensive ("Ours is funnier!"), sometimes hopeful ("Great work rises to the top in the end! Right?"). But way too much of the time I'm stuck in a state of what-if despondency. ("*Why* didn't we just go out at the same time! *We are so screwed!* Who wants to see the same damn movie about the same damn story *a year later*?") *Capote* has managed to spark a number of magazine features not just about the film and its stars, but about the man himself and the facts behind *In Cold Blood*. Those are exactly the features we would be looking for, to promote our film.

I went to lunch the other day and saw that Phil was several tables away from me. I figured I would simply pretend I didn't see him in order to spare us both an awkward chat, except I knew the journalist he was with, and *he* pulled me over. The look of pity Phil gave me was *exactly* the same one I got from James Schamus when *Far from Heaven* bombed at the Oscars and *The Pianist* won everything—a look that said, "This must be so hard for you, but *damn*, am I happy!!" (He *did* eventually send us candy, in response to our flowers, with a note that said, "Thank you so much for your message—I really can't tell you how much it meant to me." So no hard feelings.)

Today, Warner Independent Pictures has sent Killer a bunch of one-sheets, the potential posters for *Infamous*. I look at them and think, Do they look different enough from *Capote*'s campaign? Do these images distinguish us? We get on the phone with WIP's head of marketing, Laura Kim, and we hash out all the things that *do* make our movie different and that, therefore, we should try to highlight. We quickly agree that one of the strongest elements that we have and the other movie doesn't is a sense of glamorous society life in New York City. We talk about images that embody that: martini glasses? The New York skyline? We agree we need a strong, iconic image. We just don't know what it is yet.

Obviously, watching *Capote* would help, and it took me a long time to do that. I got a screener early on (when Sony Pictures Classics sent them out to Academy members) and stared at the box for a few weeks. I was torn about watching it because in my heart of hearts, I knew that I would never be able to talk about it in any other way than through the prism of my own anxiety.

So yes, I watched the damn movie.

It was an odd experience. There were certain scenes that were virtually identical, facts that were interpreted slightly differently, some quite a bit differently. I honestly don't have a clue whether it's a good movie or not; the circumstances never allowed me to fall under its spell. I think about what happened on *Boys Don't Cry*, when we went into production and effectively scuttled Fox's competing project (although I don't think it was officially dropped until we showed some footage from the film and Hilary's astonishing performance). We were definitely the David to Fox's Goliath, the little movie that could. And in all honesty, I never gave much thought to how the other filmmakers must feel. Maybe it was also *their* dream to tell this story. So is the shoe really on the other foot now? Killer as Goliath—now *that's* funny!

We've got to find a way to differentiate *Infamous*. But how?

Why is there so much Truman Capote in the air?

The most obvious answer—but an incomplete one—has to do with George Plimpton's biography, *Truman Capote, In Which Various Friends, Enemies, Acquaintances, and Detractors Recall His Turbulent Career.* The book was published in the fall of 1998, and *The New Yorker* excerpted a particularly fascinating chapter about the writing of *In Cold Blood*, which speculated that Truman Capote and Perry Smith, the killer, had had a physically intimate relationship.

A few years later, when Doug McGrath pitched Killer a story that would not only delve into the (sometimes hilarious) trials and tribulations during Truman's writing of *In Cold Blood* but would also examine Truman's personal relationship with Perry and its profound effect on the work *and* on Truman himself, we optioned the book and then sat back to wait for Doug to finish *Nicholas Nickleby* and his script. (Coincidentally—or not—we received another Truman-inspired pitch that year—based on Capote's legendary black-and-white ball, which defined high society.)

After a few tweaks and polishes to Doug's first draft, we had a magnificent script. The first order of business was to get an actor who could tackle Truman. A physical resemblance was very important to Doug, as was the ability to mimic Truman's extraordinary voice. Initially, I thought Doug was making too much of both things—my argument was "Who the hell remembers what he sounded/looked like?"—but Doug's point was that both things had an extraordinary effect on how he faced the world—and how it faced him. As it turned out, his insistence on both could not have been more right for our movie.

Then the unthinkable happened. In 2003 Katie and Jocelyn had a general meeting with a talent agent from Paradigm named Sarah Fargo. These meetings tend to be general discussions about what Killer is doing that Paradigm's clients might be able to get in on. I was in L.A. at the time. Suddenly I started getting a rapid series of calls from the Killer office. I stepped out of my meeting and called back. What could be so important? Katie and Jocelyn both got on the phone. "Sarah kept talking about the Truman Capote script, and we thought she meant ours," they say. "*But she didn't*. There's another one!! And it's also about writing *In Cold Blood!*"

We found out that the script was written by Dan Futterman, the actor who played the son in *The Birdcage* and had a recurring role on *Judging Amy*. A high school classmate of his and documentary director, Bennett Miller (who made *The Cruise*) was attached to direct. They had optioned another Capote biography, this one by Gerald Clarke. I didn't know what to say. Then they told me what was really the worst news of all: the "other movie" (as *Capote* came to be known at Killer) had something we did not have—a Truman. Namely, Philip Seymour Hoffman. But their script just could *not* be as good as ours. Were we doomed?

It's no surprise that *In Cold Blood* would spark multiple projects, particularly in our era of fascination with true crime. (Think *CSI*, *Law and Order*, etc.) Capote's book is the standard by which all other true-crime books are measured. On top of that, we've got a brewing nostalgia for and fascination with the notion of "society"— the kind that you cannot buy your way into, no matter how rich you are. Truman Capote obviously chronicled that world and in some ways became its iconic image.

To spook our competition, I pushed for a story in *Variety*. On July 21, 2003, David Rooney's story hit the front page: "Killer Stalks a Literary Lion." It shored up our project, gave us momentum. Except that Rooney also called us "one of two indie projects" dealing with the same material and gave equal light to *Capote*.

We tried to not get distracted by *Capote*. After all, we had a seasoned director and they had a first-timer. And we had a studio behind us. Mark Gill had just come over to run Warner Independent. I liked him from his Miramax days, so we sent him the script before he had even officially taken the job. He fell in love with it and agreed to finance it, pending cast.

But as it increasingly became clear, a seasoned director, a terrific script, and studio backing couldn't solve the basic problem of finding a Capote. We needed an actor to fill those quirky shoes. And we absolutely did not have that.

Warner Bros. wanted a star. So we began the long, agonizing dance. The actors were universally enthusiastic about the quality of the script—and just as universally emphatic about their inability to see themselves in the lead. Pam said to me one day, "We just aren't going to get a star. There is too much baggage attached to playing a guy like that. We should go for an unknown who can *become* Truman."

And remarkably, Warner Bros. allowed us to do just that by casting Toby Jones as Truman. Daniel Craig, the next James Bond, plays Perry. Sandra Bullock, who believed in the project from early on, plays Harper Lee. Gwyneth Paltrow, Sigourney Weaver, Hope Davis, Jeff Daniels, and Isabella Rossellini round out the cast.

But looking back now, I wonder if the search for Truman might have cost us our advantage. If we had gone with an unknown from the beginning, we would have been in production at the same time as

Capote. Both movies would have gone into the market at nearly the same time. If that had happened, would audiences be raving about Toby Jones as much as they are about Philip Seymour Hoffman?

Typically, studios don't let this kind of competition ever get all the way to the marketplace. At one point, Baz Luhrmann, the director of *Moulin Rouge,* was developing a movie about Alexander the Great at Twentieth Century-Fox. That went south when Oliver Stone rushed into production with *Alexander.* Jennifer Lopez was working a biography of Frida Kahlo with United Artists when Miramax and Salma Hayek managed to muscle their way to the front of the line with *Frida* and UA abandoned the project.

The ones that do go head to head usually become cautionary tales. *Dangerous Liaisons* was released in December 1988 and made $34.7 million—a great cast and terrific script made it an art-house smash. *Valmont,* released a year later and based on the same French novel, made $1.1 million. One of *Valmont's* producers told the *Wall Street Journal,* "I'm glad I did it, but I feel sorry for my friends who helped finance it." The spring of 1997 saw two killer volcano movies in release—*Dante's Peak* and the predictably named *Volcano.* Guess which one made more money? *Dante's Peak,* with $67.2 million and a February release, compared to *Volcano's* $47.5 million and April release. Maybe the only example in recent memory of a second film that managed to outdo its predecessor is *Armageddon. Deep Impact,* the other comet-hitting-the-earth movie, came out in May 1998 and earned $140.5 million. (We'd be happy with a fraction of that!) Still, the audience's taste for the apocalypse evidently wasn't sated; *Armageddon* pulled in over $200 million when it was released two months later.

At this point, I'm not thinking numbers. I'm thinking: How do we get people to notice our film? I pay attention to the whispers and the word of mouth. A few well-placed nods in our favor can change everything. For example, Graydon Carter, the editor of *Vanity Fair,* wrote in his April editor's letter about impersonating Truman Capote for Philip Seymour Hoffman at his magazine's party the night before the Golden Globes. It hadn't gone over too well. Philip Seymour Hoffman "shot me a pissed-off look and walked away," Carter wrote. A few weeks after this "Hollywood faux pas," Carter happened to see *Infamous*, "the other Capote movie." He called the film "superb." "In McGrath's hands, Toby Jones, the young British stage actor who has the lead, doesn't just play Capote," he wrote. "He becomes Capote. The film opens in October, and I'm looking forward to going head-to-head with young Mr. Jones, Capote-impersonation-wise."

Since the film's Oscar win, the reactions to *Capote* have only become more complex, opening larger questions about *In Cold Blood* and the liberties the film took with history. In April, Wallace Shawn and Allen Shawn, the sons of *The New Yorker* editor William Shawn (who edited Truman's dispatches), wrote a sharply worded letter to *The New Yorker* about the film's misrepresentation of their father, a minor but critical character in the film (played by Bob Balaban). "The William Shawn depicted in *Capote* is invented out of whole cloth," they wrote; Shawn disliked the subject's bloody details, never accompanied Truman on his journalistic excursions, and never organized a reading for Truman in New York. "The real Shawn never went to Kansas," they wrote, "and never had the experience of flying on an airplane." (For what it's worth, Shawn barely figures in *Infamous*, Capote's book editor is far more central.)

All films that deal with historical subjects have to compress characters, alter the facts, invent dialogue. There's no way around it. Many of the films I've made have done this. But these kinds of letters prove that there's much more to the making of *In Cold Blood* than *Capote*'s version of events. The swirl of debate can only be good for us and for *Infamous*.

I've got two scenarios in my head: a worst-case scenario and a best-case (and probable) scenario. In the worst case, *Infamous* is ignored. We'll have spent three years putting together a movie that I'm incredibly proud of, and nobody will see it. *Infamous* will be well regarded, maybe even better reviewed, but a smaller movie. This is always a possibility.

In the best-case scenario, we're the *Armageddon* to *Deep Impact*—the second movie in line that ends up being an even bigger success. *Infamous* captures a broader audience that *Capote* only began to tap into. Often, a later movie's success depends on the cast: how much do audiences want to see those people in these roles? (Think about *Dangerous Liaisons* and *Valmont*, though I haven't seen either.) I think we're in luck. *Infamous* has a cast with enormous name recognition. I believe in Doug McGrath's light touch and a script that made me laugh out loud. These are huge assets—if we can get audiences into the theater. Even more, Warner Independent Pictures has reduced their risk. The studio expects to cover about 70 percent of *Infamous*'s $13 million budget through the sale of foreign distribution rights.

I can't speculate with any authority about whether *Infamous* will do well or barely register. But I can say the experience has taught me a kind of empathy for other producers that I don't think I've ever felt before. When you are making your movie, everybody involved has a take-no-prisoners attitude. You barrel ahead and don't look up. You don't stop to think about what other films or other producers are going through. With *Boys Don't Cry*, I never spent a second thinking about what Fox Searchlight and Drew Barrymore were feeling when we scooped them, rendering their project irrelevant. We had the upper hand. Now I *know* what they were feeling: That sense that your passion and dedication isn't always enough. That the world is chaotic and you can't control everything. It's a lesson I have to keep relearning.

But the hard work of a producer is to remain optimistic in the face of enormous potential tragedy. I do this every day. I talk with Doug and we do some mutual cheerleading. Already, we're sending him potential books to option; he's looking for a new project. He's proud of *Infamous* but he's also preparing for what comes next. And we made our movie. This isn't a tragedy. No matter how you look at it, the story of a movie that gets made is a success story.

Spotlight: Pam Koffler

PARTNER, KILLER FILMS

When Screening Movies for Your Source Material

Some weeks in this business are definitely more interesting than others. Weeks can go by when the slow, painstaking process of developing and financing movies seems to be a never-ending morass of entropy. Will anything ever happen? Then, you have a week like I did, which brings back into focus what an interesting and strange business we are in. That was the week when, in the space of ten days, I screened our film *Mrs. Harris* for Jean Harris, and I screened *The Notorious Bettie Page* for Bettie Page. Not your typical day in the office.

We had been in touch with Jean Harris during the production of our film about the scandalous murder of Hy Tarnower, the "Scarsdale Diet" doctor, and subsequent trial in 1981 in which Jean Harris, a classy and erudite headmistress of a girls' school, was sent to prison for life for his murder. We had optioned a book about the story—*Very Much a Lady* by Shana Alexander—so strictly speaking, we did not need Jean Harris to make the film. But Annette Bening, who was playing her, had wanted to talk to her, so we made contact and they spoke. Jean Harris was not unfriendly to our production but deeply skeptical that anyone would be interested in as sad and distressing a story as hers. She preferred to leave it all in the past and did not want to be bothered with a movie about her darkest hour. Almost two years later, with a finished film and an air date on HBO, we needed to know how Jean Harris would react to the movie. She had also expressed a desire to see the film. As she said, "All the ladies in my home will be talking about it. I should at least know what they're talking about."

I was very nervous. I had faith that the film was well made and entertaining. I knew our source material, the book, was an intelligent, honest, and sympathetic look at the tragedy. And I knew that our perspective as filmmakers was to find truth and compassion in a situation that was ugly and messy. That didn't change the fact that I was going to be sitting in a small hotel room watching a film about the murder of a loved one, the ruin of a life, with the very person who experienced it all firsthand. Would she be overcome emotionally? Would she be angry and defensive? Would she cry? How would I react if she absolutely hated the film and was offended by it? I went through scenarios in my mind, came up with talking points so I would feel less nervous, and soldiered into the New Haven Marriott, where Mrs. Harris was waiting.

She came with a friend from her nursing home, a sweet old lady wearing a Christmas wreath pin on her sweater. Jean Harris looked terrific. Wearing a seasonal red sweater and plaid pants, and a matching headband in her crisp blond hair, she had all the grace and poise she was famous for. She sat on the couch, polite and charming, and asked me to fetch her a cup of tea while I was helping myself to the spread HBO had provided. (I was pregnant and hungry after the long car ride from the city.)

We talked a little bit about the provenance of the project and how she had spoken to Elizabeth Karlsen, the producer in the UK who had had the idea to make the film, option the book, and hire Phyllis Nagy, the writer-director. She talked about the book, which she says she never read because Shana was a dear friend and she didn't want to be angry with her. She talked fondly about Shana, who had passed away recently, and said how much she missed her, what a fascinating person she was. Without too much more chatter, we started the film.

The experience of watching the film with her was surreal. Right off the bat, she started humming the opening credit song along with the soundtrack: "Put the Blame on Mame" was mentioned in the book as one of Jean's favorite songs. That really threw me off. Wow, this is really her life! And it went from there. As she settled into watching the film and began to see that it did not have an agenda, I felt her palpably relax. She'd often talk at the screen, making comments like "Yes, that's how it was" or "The prosecution got the jury to believe that that's what happened." Sometimes she said, "I never used that kind of language!" or "Hy would never have done that." I remained tense until we got through the final scene of the film—the one depicting the prosecution's version of the murder, in which Jean comes to Hy's home and shoots four times, in cold blood, right into his heart. When the scene played, all she said, softly to herself, was "That's what they made everyone believe."

When it was over, she turned to me and said, "Well, that didn't bother me as much as I thought." She said it was fair, it was not untrue, it was what happened. Given that under no circumstances did I expect her to dance a jig, I could not have hoped for a more positive outcome. She was gracious, and very grateful that we enabled her to see the movie. She remained puzzled, though, about why anyone would want to see this story. "I think we both seem like jerks. I was downright pathetic, but that is how I was." What touched me most was how she said she still missed Hy Tarnower. If I ever had any doubt about what really happened that night, or whether Jean should have been punished for pulling that trigger, it was dispelled in that instant.

I rode home in the car that night calling my fellow producers and HBO to report the good news—that the film had not upset or offended Jean Harris and that, in fact, she had praised it. As I went over the events of the evening, making sure I remembered the details, what stayed with me most was this extraordinary woman.

Showing *The Notorious Bettie Page* to the real Bettie Page could not have been a more opposite experience, though equally fascinating. It happened not in a quiet hotel room with an understated, poised old lady but in the Playboy Mansion with a group of Hugh Hefner's friends, one of whom was dressed in a pink latex dress. The guest of honor, Bettie Page—reclusive, in poor health, and in her eighties—arrived just as the buffet dinner was ending. Right away it was clear to me: this would not be easy.

Again—despite my belief that Mary Harron, the writer-director, made a loving, sensitive, and fascinating film about a chapter in Bettie's life and, inextricable from that, a period in the history of American sexual politics—I was a nervous wreck at the prospect of Bettie's seeing the film. We had been developing this project for over eight years. We think it is the longest one in Killer's history. We made multiple efforts to make contact with Bettie over the years, but for a variety of reasons, including shady representatives, other filmmakers' buying her life rights, and her general reluctance to respond to us, we never were able to talk to Bettie directly.

It was actually Mary's idea to show the film to Bettie through Hugh Hefner. We knew that they had a friendship and Hef had taken care of Bettie in her advancing years. Bettie had posed for *Playboy* at the height of her modeling career, and everything about it seemed right. Hef, a known cinephile, has movie nights in which he gathers an assortment of friends, former Playmates and other folks, and screens films in his home. We arranged for our movie to be one of those nights and for Bettie to be there. Colin Callender, the head of HBO Films, and Dennis O'Connor, their head of domestic film releasing, joined me.

My mother worried before I left, "Is it safe there?" But the screening was actually very cozy and informal. It took place in a modest-sized library room, with chairs set out and bags of popcorn. Without going into the details of the screening, suffice it to say that when the lights came up, Bettie was not happy. Bettie had made a lot of comments while the film was running, most of them highlighting her poor memory and her generally deteriorated state of mind. Even so, until the last reel, I thought we were in good shape and she was actually enjoying herself.

Then it happened. One thing really set her off: the inclusion in the last fifteen minutes of the film of the Kefauver Senate hearings, in which the father of a boy who died by autoerotic asphyxiation testifies. It was suggested that the boy was influenced by pornography of a sort similar to what Bettie was posing for.

Bettie, sitting next to me, became deeply distressed, and my guess is that this is a very old open wound, that she was somehow implicated in that tragedy by association. Nothing could be farther from the truth, and the film in no way makes that suggestion. My belief is that there is no way Bettie could, or would ever have been able to, understand the tone of the film or its creative goals. Mary is a very sophisticated filmmaker, and in this movie she as much tackles the issues of sexuality in the fifties as she does the "facts" of Bettie's life. In many ways, the essence of Bettie as she is portrayed in the film was really dead on. She had a very naïve quality and lacked any kind of guile. The Bettie who watched that film seemed exactly that way—taking everything at face value, unable to see the nuance or irony of even the title of the film, which she spoke out against. "I'm not 'notorious'! Why did you call it that?"

When the lights came up, the group of forty or so people sat silently while Bettie railed against the film and court scenes Mary included (which, in fact, were lifted from court transcripts, so their validity is not in question). I slunk out of the room with Dennis O'Connor and Colin Callender to take a deep breath.

We took a risk and it backfired. At least everyone else in the room seemed to really love the film, and I was especially proud that the former Playmates thought it was terrific. Now our job was to manage Bettie's reaction and have confidence that our film, based on meticulous research and a deeply sensitive and intelligent film-maker's interpretation of history and of a life, would withstand the unfortunate reaction of a person whose own grasp on the facts of her life at this point was tenuous.

Flustered as I was to have been in that line of fire, I was grateful for the experience. Not only did I get to be inside the Playboy Mansion, I got to meet Bettie. Even if the details of her own story riled her, it was unforgettable to be next to such an icon.

Postscript: Left Field

Once, when I was about ten years old, my best friend and I played hooky from school and went to Times Square. In the 1970s, that's where all the cheap theaters were. Some of them were very porno, but most of them were one-dollar movie houses, and you could sit there all day long and skip from one theater to the next, watching movies.

We wanted to find a horror movie because, to us, that was the height of fun. So we walked down Forty-second Street until we saw a marquee with a movie title that sounded like a decent horror movie. We bought tickets. The film was set in the 1880s, with a pair of sisters watching over their other sister, who is lying in bed, dying. As she gets more sickly and pained, the sisters start to retreat from her. In flashback, you see just how awful they've all been to one another. And when the dying sister reaches out for their hands—for some kind of final, human contact—they avoid her. I sat there in stunned silence, because it had never occurred to me that you could make a movie like this. It was a horror movie, but it was a kind I'd never seen before. It was Bergman's *Cries and Whispers*.

When was the last time you went to see a movie you knew nothing about? The last time a film disoriented you, surprised you, and swept you off your feet?

I want you to try this: Go to your favorite movie theater and buy a ticket to one of the little pictures. Don't read the reviews or the weekend box office tallies. Don't ask your friends what they think. Buy a ticket to one of the films *without* a giant cardboard cutout in the lobby or a banner hanging from the ceiling or its name emblazoned on the soda cups. Another way to do this is to track down a college campus theater or local film festival. There are a lot of them these days, across the country. I'm not talking about Sundance or Telluride, though you're lucky if you live close enough to get tickets to those. Colleges usually have student film collectives, which will send representatives to festivals to scout movies; they'll take risks none of the commercial theaters can afford to.

Do this because you want something uncommon. Because you want a story where the actors look like people you know. Where there's not some symphonic score lacquering over every scene, telling you what to feel. Where things are complex and not just complicated. Where even if someone is dying, it doesn't mean she's a hero. Do this because you want to go where an interesting story can take you.

What I'm proposing here isn't supposed to be homework. This isn't like eating your vegetables. I know that when we go to the movies, often we want distraction and entertainment—an escape with some romance and a little spiritual uplift. But is that all people want?

Recently, I read about a researcher named Shirley Heath who studies audiences, specifically readers, the ones who can't live without books. She interviewed hundreds of people and looked at why they choose what they choose. These people aren't necessarily moviegoers, but I couldn't help but think Heath's insights were applicable to film. What Heath found was that these readers are drawn to *unpredictability.* They want stories that come to grips with subjects that, elsewhere in our culture, are dumbed down and oversimplified. (In America, what *isn't* treated that way?) Why do they want these stories, with a disjunction or change at their center? Why do they buy those books? Because they themselves have had to deal with unpredictability in their lives, Heath argues. The serious readers are usually people who have swerved off course in their own first acts—who have gone through major changes in their lives. (Many of them, not surprisingly, are women, whose lives have turned out to be pretty different from the lives of their mothers.) These avid readers are looking to see how unpredictable lives play out.

Now, movies have to appeal to mass audiences on an entirely different scale than books. A book that sells a hundred thousand copies is a hit; a movie that sells that many tickets barely makes a blip. But I believe the appeal of unpredictability is the same. There will always be tent-pole, franchise trilogies to plaster every available surface of our culture. Romantic comedies will continue to come out of a tube, every spring and fall. Right now, and for the foreseeable future, a car is exploding on screen somewhere, a drug deal is going bad, a couple are overcoming the obstacles between them and true love. The slate of every studio looks pretty much the same, year to year. But the hunger for a surprise, for a story with an unconventional structure or politics or ending, stays with us because moviegoers crave unpredictability. It looks like life.

In a time when movies are marketed to us more than ever, when art films are tested and analyzed, and profits predicted, when we've got all these forces trying to strip unpredictability away, I love the fact that a movie can still come out of left field. Movies like *Whale Rider, You Can Count on Me, Me and You and Everyone We Know,* and *Napoleon Dynamite*—movies that nobody could have anticipated. Singular movies. I try to work and make my life in left field. I'm convinced audiences will continue to meet me out there, along with bold, compelling directors and writers and actors. Left field is where most of us live.

Christine Vachon: Filmography

Produced

Infamous (2006), dir. Doug McGrath
While researching his book *In Cold Blood*, writer Truman Capote (Toby Jones) develops a close relationship with two convicted murderers.

The Notorious Bettie Page (2006), dir. Mary Harron
The story of the ubersuccessful 1950s pinup model (Gretchen Mol), one of the first sex icons in America and the target of a Senate investigation.

Mrs. Harris (2006) (executive producer), dir. Phyllis Nagy
Based on the sensational 1980s murder. Famed diet doctor Herman Tarnower (Ben Kingsley) meets a particularly brutal end at the hands of his jilted lover (Annette Bening).

A Dirty Shame (2004), dir. John Waters
A car accident sends an uptight suburban housewife (Tracey Ullman) into the world of sexual addiction.

A Home at the End of the World (2004), dir. Michael Mayer
A love triangle between two childhood friends (Colin Farrell, Dallas Roberts) and the bohemian woman (Robin Wright Penn)

who comes between them. Based on the novel by Michael Cunningham.

The Company (2003), dir. Robert Altman
An ensemble drama about a ballet group, focusing on one young standout (Neve Campbell) who's poised to become a principal performer.

Camp (2003), dir. Todd Graff
At a musical camp for young performers, a failed songwriter (Don Dixon) stages a comeback.

Party Monster (2003), dir. Fenton Bailey and Randy Barbato
The true story of club kids Michael Alig (Macaulay Culkin) and James St. James (Seth Green) and their downward spiral into drugs, deception, and murder.

Far from Heaven (2002), dir. Todd Haynes
A 1950s Connecticut housewife (Julianne Moore) faces a marital crisis with her gay husband (Dennis Quaid) and mounting racial tensions in the outside world.

One Hour Photo (2002), dir. Mark Romanek
An employee of a one-hour photo lab (Robin Williams) becomes obsessed with a suburban family.

Chelsea Walls (2001), dir. Ethan Hawke
A novelist, a dancer, a painter, a poet, an aged jazz singer, and a young troubadour sort out their personal and artistic lives in one day in New York's storied hotel.

The Grey Zone (2001), dir. Tim Blake Nelson
The true story of Dr. Miklos Nyiszli, a Hungarian Jew chosen by Josef Mengele to be the head pathologist at Auschwitz.

Storytelling (2001), dir. Todd Solondz
A college writing group and an awkward documentarian (Paul Giamatti) explore prejudice, taboos, and moral judgments.

The Safety of Objects (2001), dir. Rose Troche
The intertwining lives of four neighboring families as they struggle to understand each other. Based on short stories by A. M. Homes.

Women in Film (2001), dir. Bruce Wagner
Three Hollywood women—a casting director, a masseuse, and a producer—tell the stories of their crumbling lives.

Series 7: The Contenders (2001), dir. Dan Minahan
A reality TV parody in which contestants are selected at random to kill one another for a top cash prize.

Hedwig and the Angry Inch (2001), dir. John Cameron Mitchell
A transsexual punk musician (John Cameron Mitchell) from East Berlin tours the United States with her band as she tells her life story and follows the ex-boyfriend/bandmate who stole her songs.

Crime and Punishment in Suburbia (2000), dir. Rob Schmidt
A teenaged girl kills her abusive stepfather in a contemporary fable based on Dostoyevsky's *Crime and Punishment*.

Boys Don't Cry (1999), dir. Kimberly Peirce
The story of the murder of Teena Brandon (Hilary Swank), a young transsexual living in Nebraska.

I'm Losing You (1998), dir. Bruce Wagner
A wealthy movie producer (Frank Langella) discovers that he has less than a year to live and doesn't tell his family. Based on Bruce Wagner's best-selling 1997 novel.

Velvet Goldmine (1998), dir. Todd Haynes
A British newspaper reporter (Christian Bale) investigates the rise and fall of his 1970s glam-rock hero (Jonathan Rhys Meyers) and his American counterpart (Ewan McGregor).

Happiness (1998), dir. Todd Solondz
Three middle-class New Jersey sisters (Jane Adams, Lara Flynn Boyle, and Cynthia Stevenson) struggle with their families and sex lives.

Office Killer (1997), dir. Cindy Sherman
A downsized magazine proofreader (Carol Kane) goes on a killing spree.

Kiss Me, Guido (1997), dir. Tony Vitale
A gay man (Anthony Barille) and straight pizza cook (Nick Scotti) become roommates.

I Shot Andy Warhol (1996), dir. Mary Harron
The true story of radical feminist Valerie Solanas (Lili Taylor), the author of the *SCUM Manifesto* and the failed assassin of Andy Warhol (Jared Harris).

Stonewall (1995), dir. Nigel Finch
A history of the 1969 Stonewall Riot, the opening battle in the gay rights movement, narrated by a regular customer (Guillermo Díaz) of the popular village bar the Stonewall Inn.

Safe (1995), dir. Todd Haynes
When a California housewife (Julianne Moore) comes down with a mysterious environmental illness, she seeks out safety at a new-age retreat.

Kids (1995) (co-producer), dir. Larry Clark
An amoral young skater (Leo Fitzpatrick) sets out to deflower as many virgins as possible, but things go badly when one gets tested for HIV.

Postcards from America (1994), dir. Steve McLean
The biography of a young, gay artist, inspired by the poetry and visual art of David Wojnarowicz, who died of AIDS in 1992.

Go Fish (1994) (executive producer), dir. Rose Troche
A cheeky Chicago romance between Max (Guinevere Turner), a trendy, young lesbian, and her frumpy, older suitor Ely (V. S. Brodie).

Swoon (1992), dir. Tom Kalin
The true story of gay lovers Richard Loeb (Daniel Schlachet) and Nathan Leopold Jr. (Craig Chester), who kidnapped and murdered a child in the early 1920s for kicks.

Poison (1991), dir. Todd Haynes
Three intercut stories about outsiders, sex, and violence, inspired by the writings of Jean Genet.

Acknowledgments

Thank you to everyone who shared their experiences for this book. Killer is a team and I couldn't pull off the films I make *or* this book without the help of my colleagues: Pam Koffler, Katie Roumel, Jocelyn Hayes, Michael Wiggins, Yee Yeo Chang, and especially Charles Pugliese, whose attention to this book was invaluable. And thanks to former Killer Brad Simpson for his insights and contributions.

Also, thank you to Tom Kalin, Bob Berney, David Linde, John Cameron Mitchell, Todd Haynes, Rowena Arguelles, and Mark Romanek for talking so eloquently about what they do, and also for doing it so well.

Thank you to John Sloss for helping Killer do the impossible and Jeff Hill for supporting Killer for so long. Thanks also to Killer's CAA team—Kevin Huvane, Craig Gering, and Kevin Iwashina. And a big thanks to John Wells; without him there would be no Killer.

Finally, thanks to my agent, Suzanne Gluck, and editor, Terra Chalberg, for helping set up, guide, and shape this book along the way.

About the Author

Christine Vachon is one of the leading independent producers in the film industry. She has produced over thirty feature films, including *Infamous, Far From Heaven, One Hour Photo,* and *Boys Don't Cry.* She is a member of the Academy of Motion Picture Arts and Sciences and has received numerous awards, including Independent Spirit Awards, the producer award from the National Board of Review, the IFP Gotham Award for producer of the year, and special tributes from the Deauville, South by Southwest, and Provincetown film festivals. Her first book, *Shooting to Kill: How an Independent Producer Blasts Through the Barriers to Make Movies that Matter,* was a *Los Angeles Times* bestseller. Vachon lives in New York City, where she runs her company, Killer Films.